"Flowers again? Seriously Alexa, how many times does that man have to send you flowers and ask you to marry him before you finally cave," her longtime friend and coworker asked, with a look of exasperation clearly written all over her face.

"Maren," Lexi as she was known by her closest friends, replied with the same response that she'd been using for four months now.

"When it feels right, I'll know it, and I'll say yes to Bradford. Until then, we'll keep our relationship the way it's been for the past six years. It's worked just fine so far. I honestly don't see why a ring on my finger really is that important," she replied, trying to convince both herself and her closest friend.

"You're doing it again you know," Maren stated flatly.

"Doing what?" Alexa asked, somewhat defensively.

"You, my friend, are not only lying through your teeth, but also avoiding the real issue," Maren answered as she pushed her chair away from the cafeteria table, picking up her lunch tray as she stood.

Following Maren's lead, Alexa also stood but not before whispering "Bull shit" under her breath.

Alexa waited until they were walking back to their classrooms to ask what her friend really meant by her comment.

Laughing, Maren's quick response was dangerously accurate.

"Alexa, I have known you since we were kids in grade school. Back then, and still to this day, if you didn't want to deal with someone or something made you nervous, or if you were lying," she added with a wink, "You would start twirling your hair around your fingers. Right now, you're not only avoiding responding to Bradford's proposal, but you're also lying to yourself as to why you really won't give him an answer. He's gorgeous, financially stable, and completely infatuated with you. And if you don't want to marry him, then set him free and I'll snatch him up in a New York minute!"

"Aren't you just the witty one!" she snapped back, laughing as she did so. They made their way down the corridor to their respective classrooms in relative silence, both knowing that Maren was probably right in her depiction of her relationship.

Maren and Alexa had grown up in upstate New York, in the heart of the Adirondack Mountains in a town that was no bigger than a blip on a map, if you didn't count the tourists, who tripled their population during the short summer season. Their graduating class had been one of the largest in the Town of Webb's history. Typically averaging between 20 and 30 students in each graduating class, theirs was considered huge as the 42 kids in their class walked out of the red brick building for the last time. Even though it had been almost ten years ago, Alexa still remembered the day that she heard the old oak door slam behind her as she exited her Alma Mater for the last time.

Alexa's parents had packed their belongings and moved to Hilton Head as soon as they realized that their baby was never returning to the nest. With four older siblings, that all relocated far away from the snow belt that had been home for their formative years, her parents followed suit. Her parents had said that it was probably just wanderlust and definitely only temporary; so they kept their tiny bungalow on the outskirts of town. But now that they had it rented out to a young couple, it gave them an excuse to never return north. Even after almost ten years of calling Yonkers home, she still chuckled when born and breed New Yorkers such as Bradford Pendington and his family, referred to Poughkeepsie and the Catskills as upstate. Alexa truly knew what living in upstate meant!

Her parents, born and raised in Saranac Lake and Ray Brook respectively, couldn't believe it when their youngest, and their only daughter, had signed a letter of intent to play softball for NYU. Trying to soften the blow, Alexa explained to her parents that she wouldn't be moving from Old Forge to the city alone. She went on to explain that both Maren, and Molly Mullroy would also be accompanying her, and attending the University as well. The three girls had spent hours working out their arguments and rebuttals to every concern that they knew their parents would throw at them. Molly's parents were the first to give in, followed by Maren's, with Alexa's taking nearly a month to come to terms with her decision.

But in the end, she was not only given their blessing, but also given their ten-year-old Subaru, with the promise that she'd come home often.

Thinking about it now, she realized how hard it must have been for her parents to cut the cord and let her chase her dreams in the Big Apple. She truly loved the excitement of the city, the pulse that seemed to never slow, and the constant flurry of activity around her. Since dating Bradford, she'd eaten at nearly all of the finest restaurants in Manhattan, had seen far too many Broadway and off Broadway shows to count, and had vacationed on Long Island's Gold Coast, Nantucket and in the Hamptons every summer for the past six years. Alexa considered herself a transplanted New Yorker but unlike Bradford, it would probably never be home. Even with her parents no longer there, Old Forge, NY would always be her real home, the one true place where she could find solace when the world became too hectic and she needed a refuge.

In their first years together, Alexa had invited Bradford to join her whenever she and Maren had decided to take a road trip to the mountains for a long weekend or the holiday. When they headed to the Adirondacks over summer break, he'd also been invited. But each time, he always had a reason, an excuse really, as to why he couldn't venture out of his comfort zone and accompany her north. In their six years of dating, seventy-five months to be precise, he'd never once accompanied her to back to her home town.

As she walked back into her classroom with three minutes to spare before her fourth grade class of 24 returned from lunch, the first thing that she saw was the bouquet of red roses standing at attention in their porcelain vase on her desk. Never one for subtlety or the ordinary, Bradford must have handpicked the Wedgewood vase himself. The roses were very long stemmed, and perfect in appearance, as was everything that Bradford had a hand in. He would never allow anything less than perfection. Knowing how true her statement truly was, she couldn't help but scowl when she looked at the stunning bouquet. Suddenly their elegance and obvious expense was like an epiphany. It had finally dawned on her why she'd avoided saying yes to his numerous proposals.

It was like a swift kick, the realization that she'd postponed saying yes because quite simply, she didn't belong in his world, nor did she want to. He and the people in his inner circle valued their money and their net worth over a person's character. They judged others by the cars that they drove and where they lived, and not by their moral make up. Bradford and his family and everyone that they associated with were blue bloods and anyone who didn't fit into one of their preordained molds was considered beneath them. Alexa learned that realization quickly when she'd first visited his parents' home on the upper west side. Bradford had not only provided her with the proper outfit to wear, right down to the correct nail polish color, but also subtly groomed her the entire ride across the city. She'd been told what topics to discuss, what to avoid all together and what topics were neutral enough to comment on, should they come up in conversation. The evening had gone off without a hitch, and she'd been reluctantly accepted, but not before Mrs. Pendington had not so subtlety mentioned numerous times how Bradford's former girlfriend Katherine did this or did that. The final word of advice from Bradford's mother had come in the form of a threat when she conveniently let it be known that Katherine was no longer in a mismatched engagement with someone "beneath her class." She went on to drive the point home by flatly stating that there were people for "playing with" as she had put it, and "people like their own to settle down with and marry." Alexa started to detest the matriarch before the Earl Gray tea that she was sipping on had even had a chance to cool. And the feeling was mutual by the end of their first evening together.

Alexa picked up the bouquet and quickly tucked it into her closet just before the bell rang and twenty-four rambunctious nine and ten-year-old students with sugar highs filed into her classroom. She realized as she shut the door as the first ones entered, that she'd never read the card that Bradford had probably written in his precise penmanship. "Oh well" she thought now as she turned and smiled at the semi angelic looking faces. "It could wait a little longer." And with that, the afternoon session in classroom 101 began.

~Chapter 1~

The afternoon flew by and just before the children lined up to make their way to their buses, their parent's cars or start their walk home, Alexa had a brilliant idea. The thought of carting home yet another couple dozen flowers on the subway appealed to her about as much as having a filling at the dentist, so when the idea hit her, she smiled.

"Children, everyone please take your spot in line. Quickly now, I have a very important assignment for all of you. It's sort of like a secret mission okay?"

"What's a secret mission?" a freckled faced redhead asked.

"Well it's sort of like a surprise that only we know about" she smiled back. Walking to her closet, she lifted the rose laden vase and placed it on her desk. Knowing that it was only momentarily occupying a place of importance, she didn't wince as she heard the oohs and aahs from her entire 4th grade class.

"You see," she continued, while walking down the line of children, handing a long-stemmed rose to each one of them as she made her way from the front of the line to the back.

"Today is National I love my caregiver day. Now," she said as she handed the last of the flowers out, "I know that some of you have moms and dads, and some of you live with your nanas and papas, or maybe just one of your parents. It doesn't matter who you live with, it's a special day celebrating the people that love you and take care of you at home," she said reassuringly.

"I want each of you to go home with the rose that you were given. But remember, the rose isn't what's important, it's simply a reminder of your mission at home," she said, crouching down and whispering to gain the classes undivided attention and to add to their growing excitement. "When you get home, give your rose to someone in your home that you love. Give that person a huge hug and thank them for loving you. Can you do that?" she asked excitedly.

As expected, each of the children excitedly screamed "yes" in unison. When she was finished, she smiled knowing that with a little luck, majority of the roses might actually make it to their final destination and make a mother or father's day. Realizing that she was entrusting delicate flowers into the hands of nine and ten year olds, she added, "Remember guys, the flower isn't the gift so if you break it or lose it while riding home, it's okay. Your mission is to hug the people in your home that you love and make you happy. Alright you monsters," she said with a twinkle in her eye. "Get out of here and I'll see you tomorrow morning."

The dismissal bell rang and after she heard twenty-four "Goodbye Miss Greenwood," her room was empty and finally silent. Or at least until they did it all over again in the morning. It was only after she sat, changed from her practical work shoes into a pair of Sketchers, that she opened the note and started to read its' the neatly written message.

My Dearest Alexa:

I have loved you from the moment we met. And I have asked for your hand in marriage on more than one occasion. I could give you anything that you could ever dream of and so many more things that you don't even know about or have even heard of for that matter. I still love you dearly and still wish to marry you my dear Alexa, but I'm done asking you and quite frankly, I'm tired of waiting. When you come to your senses and are ready to say yes, get ahold of me. Until then, I think it's best if we start seeing other people. But Alexa, don't wait too long to make up your mind.   A man in my position won't stay unattached for long...

> Still love you.
>
> Bradford

She read and reread the perfectly formatted note. If not for the fact that the note had been in a monogrammed envelope and signed with his distinctive signature, she would have thought it was a practical joke, albeit an expensive one. She laughed at the absolute absurdness of it. The damn jerk must have shelled out well over $300 for the roses and dainty vase; only so that he could break up with her in style. As she sat at her desk reading the precise and to the point note for the 5th or 6th time, she found herself not upset, but furious.

"How dare he?" she thought to herself.

"He thinks so highly of himself and so little of me that he thinks I'll come sniveling back to him because he gave me an ultimatum? Screw him and the fancy Mercedes he rode in on," she said out loud and as she stood up, tore up the note and discarded it in the trash; much the way it appeared Bradford Pendington III had just discarded her. She straightened up her blouse, grabbed her jacket and walked out of her classroom, not only closing the door but the chapter of her life that had included what she thought had been her future.

~Chapter 2~

The month following their separation, was a cross between a blur, a sick joke and something akin to the stages of grieving. She found it easiest to avoid the topic when her well-meaning friends tried to talk about him or offer their opinions of how much of a scumbag they though he was. She ignored his phone calls and messages that initially were almost arrogant and cocky, then quickly turned to condescending, and lastly pleading when he finally realized that he'd lost her. The last message had been nearly a week ago and through what she surmised was a drunken stupor, he'd called her unforgiveable names and told her that she'd be alone the rest of her life while he moved on with Katherine, his longtime girlfriend from high school. Ironically, his tirade only made her realize once and for all, how silly she'd been to waste over six years on someone who was all about show and polish, and not about substance.

"Hope you and Katherine, fake tits and plastic surgery goddess extraordinaire are very happy together," she said aloud as she erased the message from her phone and blocked his number.

From that moment on, she felt liberated once and for all. She started sleeping better, and found herself waking rested. Gone were the mornings when her first waking thought was to reach over to Bradford's side of the bed, that now remained empty. She slowly found herself thinking less and less about the man that had been the center of her world for so long. The loneliness wasn't nearly as suffocating as it had been that first week. She politely declined her co-workers' insistence that she needed to "get back on the horse" so to speak, and flat out refused to even discuss signing up on one or more of the numerous dating websites that they suggested. Everyone seemed to think that she needed another man in her life in order to complete her. Alexa found that while her apartment's walls did feel constricting and as if they were closing in on her from time to time, she welcomed the silence and solitude. After she made it through the first two weeks as a once again, single woman; she found that she was slowly rediscovering the person she'd lost, while trying to be someone she wasn't. After the initial shock of the break up wore off, Alexa realized how much she'd changed over the course of her six-year relationship with Bradford. She'd never realized how he'd slowly transformed her into the person that he wanted her to be. He and his family had been incredibly discreet about it, giving her subtle tips here and there. His mother had offered on more than one occasion to "have a girls' day out" in order to influence her hair cut and style and had been forward enough to even dictate the shape in which her eyebrows should be waxed and her manicure should be shaped. Alexa had to admit now, that while frivolous things such as sipping champagne while being groomed had never mattered to her, she did in fact love being pampered. The truth was that she wanted so desperately to be accepted and please the man that was the light of her life, that she overlooked the way that her spirit was slowing disintegrating. They'd molded her into a Stepford style girlfriend and she hadn't even realized it, and that fact made her furious every time that she thought of it now. But as Maren had pointed out, they had tried but obviously hadn't succeeded, as evidenced by the fact that she'd turned her nose to what he was offering and walked away. Maren reminded her that she had in fact remained true to herself and hadn't allowed their money and influence to change who she was, and so ultimately, she'd won.

But sometimes sitting alone, in her studio apartment didn't feel like she was the victor. Alexa knew in her soul that she could never live her life the way Bradford had wanted. She wasn't willing to give up her teaching job to lead a socialite lifestyle. He'd politely informed her that she would never work another day in her life once she became Mrs. Pendington and that her responsibility would be to make the rounds at the various social gatherings that he and his mother needed to be seen at. That blanket statement had started the first of many huge arguments over what would be the downfall of their relationship.

It had taken two weeks for her to learn that while Bradford was still calling her and demanding that she "come to her senses" as he'd put it; that he was already out prowling for a new showpiece for his arm. It had inadvertently gotten back to Alexa that Bradford had been seen at the nightclub that they'd used to frequent with a voluptuous blue eyed blond. Seeing the quick flash of pain, in her eyes, her girlfriends quickly tried to interject that his date not only looked cheap but like a plastic Barbie Doll. No, she honestly didn't want Bradford in her life, but she didn't want him to be over her quite that quickly either.

Spring finally arrived and as the buds slowly started making their way out of their dormant sleep, so did her children's energy levels. Maren and Alexa frequently shared the playground so that their classrooms could play together and give the women time to take a break from the drama that only elementary school can provide. The sun felt refreshing as it warmed their faces as they stood off to the side watching their children play and burn off some of their endless energy.

"So what are you doing for Memorial Day weekend Lexi?" Maren asked tentatively. "Frank and I are heading up north for the long weekend and we were wondering if you'd like to join us?"

"That's very sweet of you Maren. But I don't want to encroach on your holiday and you don't need a third wheel tagging along."

"Oh stop it Lexi. You are no more a third wheel than I was all those times that I went on dates with you and Brad.

Oh shit Lexi," Maren exclaimed, with a look of remorse on her face. "I didn't mean to bring that dick heads name up. I'm so sorry."

Waving her off, Alexa smiled. "His name doesn't bother me anymore Maren. Oh, and dickhead is too forgiving; so how about we don't even discuss him anymore okay? And to be honest with you, if you really don't mind, maybe a trip home is just what I need! So yes, I'd love to head north with you for the long weekend."

Hugging her best friend quickly, she smiled. "This is awesome! We will have a great weekend and maybe if we have time, we can bag a few peaks!" Maren added excitedly.

"That sounds like a very strong possibility. Now I can't wait!" Alexa added, meaning it.

The rest of the afternoon flew by as Alexa found herself thinking about her hometown and the anticipation of returning, if only for a long weekend. Even though it had only been six months since she'd last headed up the highway and through the foothills of the Adirondacks, in her heart, it felt as if it were light years ago. She still found it disconcerting that she no longer had a home in which to stay and no family left there. Once she hooked up with old friends from grade school who had never let the area, or had since moved back sometime during the last ten years since they'd graduated, she knew that Old Forge would once again feel like home. She just hated having to invade her friend's home every time she returned to the nest.

Both Maren and Alexa tried to frequent the gym located across the street from their school at least three times per week. Since neither had pets nor children to rush home to, they found it easiest for them to walk over as soon as the buses had departed the school yard, get their one-hour workout in, and then go their separate ways. Many days they felt like just heading home after managing their classrooms for six hours; but they usually pushed through their fatigue and forced themselves to walk over anyway. Today was no exception.

When the final bell sounded, and the room was finally empty, Alexa grabbed her gym bag and headed outside her room to meet Maren. As she approached Maren's classroom, she heard her before she saw her.

"I don't care what the guys want to do Frank, you promised me that we'd go to Old Forge for the holiday weekend and that's what I expect you to do. I told my mother that you were coming and I'm going to look like a damn fool if you stand me up again."

Alexa didn't know whether to proceed into her room or pretend she hadn't heard her best friend's side of the conversation or if she should just go back to her office. Before she had an opportunity to decide, she heard Maren finish the conversation in one sentence.

"Frank, if you don't come with me to Old Forge for Memorial Day Weekend, don't bother looking for me when the weekend is over because your number will be blocked and I won't be waiting around for you anymore, got it?"

Hearing her swearing under her breath, Alexa looked up to find Maren standing next to her.

"Guess you heard all that?" Before Alexa could respond, Maren continued talking. "Don't say a word. He's a dickhead just like the one you threw to the curb. Let's go take out our frustrations on some gym equipment okay?"

And with that, the topic of men was dropped.

~Chapter 3~

"Kelsey, you know the rules. You cannot ride your bike over to Abby's house until your homework is done."

"I don't want to do homework. It's stupid and Mrs. Gleason is stupid, and I hate going to school."

Feeling himself being pulled into the same argument that had become a weekly battle, Luke took a deep breath before responding to the child standing in front of him with her arms crossed. Her look of steel and pure defiance reminded him of someone else he knew all too well. As he peered into her deep blue eyes that currently were as gray as night, he knew how mad, but more importantly, how frustrated she was. They'd tried tutors, Sylvan Learning Center, therapists and anyone else who had offered assistance, but could never find the origin of his daughter's learning disability. Kelsey was no different than any other of her classmates except that she couldn't read and process the words in a book or on the chalk board, much less a computer screen, the same way her classmates did. She excelled in Math, and Science and anything that didn't require reading; with her favorite subject being History. Thanks in part to her Grandpa Ben, Kelsey could cite statistics, dates and facts that she'd memorized over the years better than most college professors. It never ceased to amaze Luke, that his little girl could hardly write a sentence at a time, but could quote word for word the Declaration of Independence, and name the Presidents of the United States, in chronological order and name the years that they served.

He looked down at the cherubic face and it was as if he was looking into her mother's, and he caved. He'd love Anastasia from the moment he'd met her in sixth grade. They'd both had their crushes on others during Junior High but by ninth grade, Luke and Anastasia had become an item and stayed that way. There was never just Luke or just Ana, they were a pair, a couple and basically one unit. She was his reason for living, his soul mate, and she took half his heart with her the day that he received the call that she'd been in an accident. As he looked at the blue eyed little girl still standing defiantly in front of him, he smiled and simply took her into his arms. As she squeezed back, for just a moment, it took him back to the very moment, that her mother had held him in very much the same way and told him that they were going to have a baby. Even though they were barely eighteen and still had two months to go before graduating high school, they both wept not tears of sadness, but tears of joy. No Kelsey certainly hadn't been planned and they had used protection, but as Anastasia put it, "some things are just meant to be." And with that, they became a family and were a solid unit, until the day a deer crossed in front of her SUV.

He'd raced to St. Elizabeth's hospital when he'd gotten the call. Despite speeding over 100MPH to get to Utica, he'd arrived too late. She was pulseless in the ambulance and even though the paramedics worked on her with everything they had available, she'd been pronounced dead upon arrival in the ER. They'd found out afterward that the deer's antler had punctured her aorta when it crashed through her windshield and she'd died instantly. He was barely 23 years old when he lost the love of his life and became the sole caretaker of their rambunctious four-year-old. Now nearly seven years later, it was still just Luke and Kelsey and that was just fine with him. She'd been the only reason that he'd been able to continue breathing after he lost Ana. Their little girl was the one reason that Luke was still getting up each morning, still functioning, and still living. He'd lost nearly everything when he lost Anastasia; but she'd given him the most precious gift the day she delivered their daughter and through their little girl, his soul mate continued to live.

"Tell you what kiddo, I'll make you a deal. If it's okay with Mrs. Jones, you can ride over to Abby's and play until suppertime. But," he winked, the second supper is done, you and I are going to work on your homework. Deal?"

Reluctantly, she smiled and answered. "Deal," putting out her hand to shake her father's the way she saw grownups do it.

"But I think part of the deal should be that we discuss getting me one of Marisa's puppies. I know that having a puppy would help me study better daddy."

"You Miss Kelsey Rose are going to be the best Attorney there ever was," he laughed. "Nice try with the puppy argument. Kels, you know we've had this discussion how many times? Grandma is allergic to dogs and we can't expect her to take care of you after school when I'm working if there's a dog in the house. That's not fair of me to ask her, is it?"

Pouting, his daughter wanted desperately to argue. But after just a moment of thinking about her grandma and how much she loved spending time with her, she shrugged her shoulders as if in defeat.

"I could stay home alone if I had a puppy," she retorted, lip quivering at the thought of being in their house alone.

"You could Kels, but Grandma wouldn't know what to do with herself if she couldn't come over here to hang out with you like she does. She's told me on more than one occasion how much it means to her that you let her get away from her housework and gardening every now and again. You know how much Grandma loves spending time with you and playing games and coloring and beating you in video games."

Seeing her eyes light up, he saw the quick flash of fire in her expression.

"She does not beat me! Grandma stinks at Star Invader, and Treasure Island and I can almost beat you in Chasing Matty so don't tell me that you think Grandma is better than me at gaming!"

"You're right Kelsey Rose. I didn't mean to tease you. You have become really skilled at those games. And I won't pick on you again. But do me a favor; don't beat grandma every game okay? Let her win every once in a while, okay honey?"

"Okay dad. I love you."

"I love you too, Kels."

"Daddy. Once I'm old enough to stay home after school alone, can I get a puppy then?"

"We'll see pretty girl, we'll see."

~Chapter 4~

Maren and Alexa spent nearly two hours running, lifting, kicking and sweating their frustrations out. When they finally quit and retired to the locker room to change out of their now drenched workout clothes, both felt physically exhausted but cleansed mentally. Alexa had already severed all ties with the former man in her life, and Maren was very close to making the same decision regarding her on again, off again boyfriend of nearly a year.

"Thanks Lexi, I'll let you know what time we're heading north on Thursday okay?"

"Great, but I thought you said that we weren't heading up until Friday since Frank has to work late on Thursday?"

"I did initially tell you that. But since I uninvited Frank, do you mind getting on the road as soon as class is out?"

From the expression on her best friend's face, Alexa didn't want to ask why the sudden change in plans.

"Sure, Thursday is even better so we hopefully avoid the holiday traffic from the city," she smiled, searching Maren's face for answers.

Her poker face revealed nothing.

"Great. I hear a very large glass of wine calling my name. I'll see you in the morning Lexi. Oh," she said as she lifted her gym bag over her shoulder. "Something tells me that we're going to have a great holiday weekend back home."

"Home. Yes," Alexa thought, "Old Forge was and would always be, home."

~Chapter 5~

The two weeks had flown by and now they were not only packed but on the road heading north. The music in Maren's Forerunner was blaring as they rocked out, albeit not always on key, to Classic Rock. Neither had pets that required making housing arrangements for, and spontaneous trips like the one she was currently embarking on, proved all the more reason that having a pet while living in an apartment in a city just wasn't feasible. Yes, she sometimes got lonely and longed for company in her tiny abode, but knew it just wasn't practical at this stage of her life. As she sang one song after another with her best friend, she made a silent promise to herself, that one day when she had a home of her own, she'd invest in a puppy as soon as she moved in.

Two hours into the drive, Alexa finally asked what had been on her mind for days.

"Maren, what happened between you and Frank?"

Keeping her eyes on the road as she sped along the highway, Maren didn't sugarcoat her answer.

"I loved him, or at least I thought I did. But there was something missing and it didn't feel like forever you know," she answered, looking over at her best friend.

Reaching over and simply squeezing her hand, Alexa smiled warmly. "Yeah, I know."

They rode in silence for a few minutes before Maren spoke again.

"We deserve better Lexi. We deserve the kind of love that knocks our socks off, the kind that day in and day out doesn't seem like it could get any better, yet it does each day. A love that is born out of love and respect for one another and a love that grows as the relationship grows. I want that kind of love, Lexi. I really want that kind of love," she finished, with one lone tear trickling down her cheek.

"We all would like that kind of love Maren. But I think that kind of love might have ended with our parent's generation, or just be in fairytales, my friend. How many of our friends, coworkers or relatives our age, are in that kind of relationship?" Alexa asked, not angrily, but passionately.

"It was somehow different for our parent's generation and the generations before them. Somehow relationships have changed. And I just don't think that kind of love exists anymore."

Always the romantic, Maren smiled. "It does my friend. We just haven't found it yet. When we do, it'll knock our socks off and with a little luck, several other articles of clothing as well," she winked.

"You're incorrigible!" Alexa laughed.

"Nope. Just horny!"

Laughing, they continued making their way north and into the mountains.

~Chapter 6~

"But daddy, you p-r-o-m-i-s-e-d…. We used to go camping every year on Memorial Day, and now all you ever do is work, work, work. I hate work, I hate your job, and I hate you sometimes!" she screamed, as the tears flowed down her face as she ran from the kitchen.

"Luke, she doesn't mean it. She's just a child and doesn't really know what she's saying. She's just frustrated and sad, and still has so many fond memories of the way things used to be. It's not your fault and she'll get over it by tomorrow."

Running his fingers through his golden colored hair, Luke turned to face his mother.

"I know mom, I know. It's just not that easy making a ten-year-old understand that if I don't work, we don't eat and I don't pay the bills. Maybe she's right mom; maybe I should just say screw it and take her camping like we used to. But mom," he said, turning suddenly very serious. "She was four, my baby was only four when Ana died. How could she possibly have memories of the three of us going camping. She was just a baby when she died," he added, feeling the punch to his gut again. He certainly should have expected it since it was the same feeling that he got every time he spent more than a second or two thinking about his Anastasia. No time does not heal all wounds. He above all knew that it didn't.

"Oh honey, I don't think that she necessarily remembers the actual memories. I think that she just remembers the love that you and Anastasia shared. She feels the love that you shared for one another and the love that you both had for her. She looks at the pictures in my albums every time she comes over to my house you know. She has every picture memorized, along with every story that I've ever told her. She's so incredibly intelligent and sometimes I can just see the frustration simmering from her head when she's doing her homework. It's like she has a very small short circuit in her brain that makes reading so difficult for her. But your little girl is wise beyond her years." Changing topics, she smiled. "So what can I do to help you free up your time in order to join your daughter on a big adventure this weekend?"

Thinking out loud, he answered honestly. If you're really okay with it, let me work tonight and tomorrow night and I'll get everything organized and we'll head up to the cabin Saturday morning."

"I'll cover your weekend shifts, but I don't think Kelsey wants to go to some dark, creepy looking fishing camp in the woods Luke. She wants to go camping, really go camping; you know, tent, dirt, showers you put quarters in to run etcetera."

Seeing his look of disdain, Samantha laughed.

"Lucas Mathew, you used to love camping so it's only natural that your little girl does as well. Relax, I'll whip up some ready-made meals so that all you and Kels have to do is throw them in a pot on the stove and they'll be ready in no time. Okay?"

Knowing that it was futile to argue with his mother, he smiled just enough to allow his dimples to show.

"I don't suppose one of the meals can be your famous Beef Stew, could it?"

She looked at the son standing beside her and felt her heart not only burst with pride for the man that he'd become, but also with sadness for having to shoulder the responsibility of being both mother and father to her only grandchild. She never doubted his ability to be a good father, even when he and Anastasia had tearfully told her that they were bringing a child into the world. Seventeen, going on thirty she'd said to her husband of twenty-five years. That's what Luke, her oldest by four minutes, had been forced to become. But neither she nor her husband had any concern once they saw their son holding his infant daughter for the first time. Anastasia and Lucas became a family that cold rainy morning and remained a tight unit, even after her untimely demise. She and Matt, Lucas's father, had been there for love, support and a helping hand from the day that their granddaughter had arrived; but never because Lucas asked for help or admitted just how hard it was to raise a child, but because they wanted to be. Luke and Ana went without, to provide all the essentials for their little girl, and did so humbly. Now, all these years later, even though her first born was very financially stable, she still found him living well below his means in order to provide his only child with everything she needed to make life a little easier than it had been for him. But in no way did he spoil his child. Kelsey had her assigned chores around the house and the bistro, and knew that she was accountable to uphold her duties. Family was the backbone that held everything together and Samantha couldn't think of any more precious gift, than the gift of her amazing granddaughter.

"Camping mom, you really think she wants to go camping?" he asked, still not 100% sold on the idea.

"Yes I do. Now head on over to the Bistro and I'll take care of feeding Kelsey after she's done being mad at you.

And don't worry Luke, we'll have a grand time organizing for your big adventure this weekend," she winked, laughing at his expression of disdain as he walked toward the door.

Luke arrived nearly an hour before his usual start time. With the holiday weekend upon them, he knew how crucial it was to be organized and ready for the unexpected. He didn't anticipate being crowded since it was only Thursday and most out-of-towners would just be making the drive into town and most likely not be eating out. Even so, he wanted to make sure that everything was set for Friday night, and more importantly for Saturday and Sunday since he wouldn't be there to help. "Camping, in a tent, on the ground," he muttered to himself as he inventoried his wine supply. Satisfied that they had an ample supply, possibly an overabundance of beer, wine and seltzers, he made his way to the front of the Bistro.

He never would have imagined when he was playing football ten years ago, that in less than a decade, he'd be living in Old Forge, NY and running a feminine looking Bistro. It had been Anastasia's brain child. They hadn't been raised in the town of Webb, but after Kelsey came, both refused to leave the area to go on their honeymoon; instead choosing to spend two days in Old Forge in order to be less than twenty minutes for their newborn, should she need them. Anastasia had always envisioned one day taking Kelsey to Paris and showing her the city. They'd have their tea parties when Kelsey was merely a toddler and pretend that they were sipping fine tea or cider at a riverfront Bistro along the Seine. After high school, Lucas gave up his scholarship to play D1 football, refusing to leave his wife and daughter behind. At Ana's insistence, he'd attended Utica College and graduated with a Business Management degree. To help make ends meet, both he and Anastasia took jobs at a local mom and pop restaurant. Ana would leave their daughter for less than an hour with either her mom or Luke's, and then she would work the supper shift nightly except for Monday's when they were closed. Luke bused tables and bartended Friday through Sunday. The arrangement wasn't ideal for a young married couple but neither seemed to mind. Both had been working at the restaurant right up until the night that Anastasia died.

    He tried to block the night from his mind because thinking about her certainly wouldn't bring Ana back. He had mentioned to her on numerous occasions that they should maybe move closer to town and that he hated her driving home so late at night with all the deer that traveled as soon as the sun went down. She faithfully called him each night as she started her drive south toward their tiny apartment and each night he told her to "watch for deer." That was their routine, and now, seven years later he still refused to forgive himself for not saying those three words to her on that fateful night. They'd had a disagreement, and though they weren't fighting, he was frustrated with her stubborn streak, a streak that she had passed down to their daughter. He'd told her he loved her, and that they'd discuss the disagreement at home, and then he hung up.

But there would be no discussion, and no tomorrows for his bride. She never made it home.

~Chapter 7~

"Maren, your mom hasn't changed a bit," Alexa commented as they started unpacking their clothes in Maren's tiny bedroom. Alexa looked around, and other than a new comforter on her bed, it essentially looked unchanged from the room that she'd spent countless nights in during high school. It truly felt good to be home, back in a town where everything didn't move at the speed of light. Sure, Alexa remembered what summer was like living in a tourist destination, with Enchanted Forest Water Safari, Bald Mountain, and Nick's Lake in her back yard. She remembered the continuous stream of cars, trucks, and campers that snaked their way through town on the only road leading to their final destination. And she clearly remembered how irritating it was trying to make a left out of Keyes Pancake House after working the morning shift and having to cut someone off in order to leave the parking lot so she could finally go home. Home, yes, Old Forge was the one place that truly felt like "home." Maren's mother always welcomed her as one of their own, but it still didn't feel the same. She didn't know why, but this trip back made her realize that she was longing for something, something that she didn't have while living in the city. It hit her that what was missing was the sense of identity, the sense of belonging, the sense of home. As she neatly folded the last of her T-shirts into the dresser drawer that Maren had provided her, she asked her best friend if they could possibly drive by her parent's home sometime over the weekend.

"Sure Alexa, we can go anytime you'd like. What do you want to do for supper this evening? Want to go into town and grab a pizza and wings or cook some burgers here on the grill?"

"I don't want to put your mother out and since she's already eaten, why don't we head into town and grab a pizza. That is if you're game and not too tired from driving."

Laughing, Maren smiled, "Give me a break would you! If we stayed here, we'd have to watch Jeopardy with mom and then I'd realize just how wasted my education was. She can usually answer almost every question despite those crazy categories that they have on that show. I truly have no idea where she comes up with the answers, but it's humiliating watching it with her since I'm the teacher and she kicks my ass every time. So, in answer to your question, no, no I am absolutely NOT too tired to head into town and grab a pizza."

"Should we ask your mom if she'd like to come?"

"You're so sweet. Go ahead and ask her but Marsha wouldn't think of missing Alex and her Jeopardy. It's her nightly date she reminds me."

Smiling back at her best friend, Alexa felt just a quick tug on her heart. She'd missed her hometown, always missed her family, and realized now that maybe she missed having her nightly date as well. Being fiercely independent didn't mean that she didn't have a heart, and feelings, and the longing to be loved. Bradford just hadn't known the kind of love that she was after.

After settling in, talking with Maren's mother for nearly an hour, they quickly changed into something more suitable for going into town and said their goodnights. Marsha was already glued to her flat screen and barely waved as they headed out the door toward Maren's truck.

"Where to? I don't care where we get pizza as long as it's hot and the beer is cold."

"It doesn't matter to me Maren; anywhere is fine."

Turning toward her best friend, Maren saw the serious look on her face. "What's wrong Lexi?"

Silent for a few seconds, Alexa shrugged her shoulders. "I don't honestly know. I so looked forward to coming home with you this weekend and now that we're here; it's depressing me for some reason. I think it's made me realize just how much I've missed this place and how much I truly love it up here, but also made me realize that this is no longer home. I don't have any place to call home anymore with mom and dad renting out the house I grew up in and them now living down south. It just seems weird having strangers living in my childhood home now."

"Oh Alexa, New York is our home now," she said softly, reaching across the seat and gently squeezing her best friend's hand. You couldn't possibly ever want to move back to our little one-horse town would you? We've got everything we need in the city. We have tons of friends, nightlife, great jobs, excitement, the Jersey Shore close by and enough culture to satisfy any craving that we might have."

"Oh we've got culture where we live alright," Alexa laughed. You wouldn't see the colorful people that we saw last weekend at the club wandering around the Old Forge Hardware, now would you?" she laughed, suddenly feeling better, and ready to eat some pizza.

"No we would not," Maren agreed as she pulled into the parking lot and they walked into their favorite pizza shack.

After enjoying a double cheese and pepperoni pizza, 20 very hot wings and a pitcher of beer, neither Maren nor Alexa were feeling any pain. They'd run into a few friends from high school, flirted with a few single men and laughed endlessly. The atmosphere was relaxed and the summer crowd currently inhabiting the Clam Shack was a mix of young and old, singles and families alike; all there to enjoy a good meal in a relaxed atmosphere. Alexa and Maren were no different. They sat in their corner booth for a few more minutes after paying the bill, hesitant to leave. The night was still young and neither seemed anxious to head back to Marsha and her reality TV that most likely was blaring from the living room.

"I guess we should free up this table for someone else huh?" Alexa said, noncommittally.

"Yeah I guess but I really don't want to go back home yet. I mean, I'm still on city time and it's still early. You want to take a ride and drive around, or head up to Daiker's for a drink, or possibly take a ride by your house?"

"No thanks, it's not my family home anymore. It would just make me sad seeing another family living in my childhood home so I'll pass on taking a drive by if that's all right with you.

"Say," Alexa said, suddenly smiling, "why don't we check out that bistro that I mentioned when we were coming through town earlier."

"I've been in there a few times and it's really nice inside; so sure."

Hitting the gas and cranking her truck in a U turn, Maren headed down 28 toward the center of town. Her timing was perfect as she pulled into a spot that had just been vacated. Both Alexa and Maren put yet another coat of lip stick on and fluffed their hair as they exited Maren's truck and headed toward the entrance.

They entered the Bistro and were immediately hit by sensory overload. The smell of jasmine, cinnamon and a faint hint of lavender was immediate. The scents were welcoming, not overpowering. Alexa turned to the source of the music and noted the small yet serviceable platform that the violinist was perched upon. Her long white billowing dress was a sharp contrast to her raven black hair that hung to her waist. As she listened to the crisp notes, she realized that the woman looked like a fairy or better yet, a mythological goddess as she serenaded the audience with Bach, Beethoven and Bruhn. Not necessarily a classical buff, Alexa still couldn't help but be impressed by the woman's musical talent. As she and Maren stood just inside the doorway that bartender had made his way down the counter and was currently studying them as they studied the violinist.

Alexa was the first to feel the eyes that were burning her skin. She shifted, just enough to find their source, but not enough to make it obvious. But to Luke, it was as if Old Forge shifted off its' continental plain. There was nothing extraordinary about her attire; she and her girlfriend were dressed in casual tank tops and jeans, both toting designer purses and cute wedges. Even in the dim light, he noted that her toenail color matched her earrings, fingernail color and purse. Her hair hung loosely off her shoulders and wasn't hair-sprayed tight to her head like so many of the patrons that frequented. Neither of the women had their faces plastered with makeup, yet both were extremely attractive in very different ways. And when Alexa turned just enough to make eye contact with him, Luke felt something that he hadn't felt since junior high. It felt like someone had punched him in the gut as he looked into the biggest green eyes he'd ever seen in his life. His Anastasia had caused the exact same reaction when he first had been pierced through the heart with her baby blues. It wasn't his Ana's eye color, or this woman's eye color; but the emotion showing in her eyes. Both he and Alexa felt it, immediately and intensely for that one quick second, and then they both simultaneously broke the connection. Neither wanted to feel anything, it was so much easier going through life each day not feeling anything. But then she looked at him again and smiled. And his world shattered for the second time in his life.

"Hi. Welcome to Black Bear Bistro, or the Triple B as it's known by the locals. Can I get you ladies a drink?" he asked, now that he had both Alexa and Maren's attention.

"He can offer me anything he wants to" Maren whispered under her breathe to Alexa, but said it just loud enough that Luke heard. Realizing that he had, in fact, heard her slightly drunk friend's statement, Alexa found herself blushing slightly. Speaking for both of them, she ordered two beers and turned as if looking for a place to sit. Intrigued by the strangers, Luke wasn't quite ready to watch them disappear so he stalled just long enough pouring their beers to allow the couple a few seats down to vacate their two bar seats and promptly set their glasses in their spots and waved his hand toward the seats, welcoming them to sit at the bar. Maren smiled and made her way to the assigned bar stools, followed reluctantly by Alexa. Once they sat on the oversized barstools, with their high backs and overstuffed cushions, they quickly realized why the bar itself was packed. The stools welcomed a person, and the sense of relaxation was immediate.

"Maren, look at this bar," Alexa commented, almost afraid to touch the glistening metal. "Isn't it absolutely gorgeous?"

"It's copper and I know for a fact that the owners all took turns pounding the heck out of it to give it such a distressed look. Do you like it?" he asked, having once again, perched himself in front of the two out-of-towners.

"It's amazing. And the nails that are securing it," Alexa said as she swallowed a sip of her beer. "They almost look like shoeing nails from the turn of the century."

Turning to her, Maren nearly spit out her beer. "Where the hell did that come from? Have you been watching Jeopardy with momma Marsha again?" she laughed. "Shoeing nails, what the hell are they?"

As the auburn-haired friend, who'd originally asked the question, started explaining exactly what the nails were and what they were used for, he smiled and was immediately impressed.

"You are correct. I believe that when the bar was put in, the owner sought to keep the look not only that of a French Bistro but authentic to what an establishment would have looked like here in the mountains at the turn of the century."

Catching the eye of another patron in need of a fill, he excused himself and made his way down the bar. He wasn't five steps away when Maren turned to Alexa and laughed.

"He's hot for you my friend. And oh my God, if I'd have known that there were specimens like that up here, I'd have come home earlier to visit mom. Wow he's gorgeous."

"Yes, he is. And he's very married Maren so cool your jets."

"Married? No way, the way he was coming on to you. He most certainly is not married."

"Well, the platinum looking band on his left fourth finger says otherwise," Alexa countered, as she looked over once more at the bartender. "You're right, he is gorgeous, and seems really sweet. But all bartenders tend to flirt Maren. That's how they get bigger tips silly. Come on, drink up and let's just enjoy the music."

Moonlight Memories: An Adirondack Love Story

They stayed for another round of beer as the music flowed. The bar tender, that they learned was named Luke, made small talk with them and the other patrons seated at the bar. Alexa took in the nostalgia that was sprinkled throughout. She saw dried wildflowers in a few vases here and there, antique snowshoes hanging near the rest rooms, and personalized touches everywhere. The owners had gone to great length and expense to create not only an illusion of luxury, but also hominess. The atmosphere was comfortable with the tables spread just far enough apart to provide privacy, yet all the booths faced the front of the bar, and the platform that the musician was still performing on. The hand stamped copper bar was by far the center of attention. As she occasionally glanced toward the constantly moving and very organized bartender, she quickly deduced that he was most likely the center of attention on more than one night, despite his wedding band.

When the violinist was finished, and their beer glasses were empty, Maren and Alexa decided to call it a night and get home before they drank more than they should. They said their goodbyes to the few people still left that they knew and as they made their way toward the door, Luke shouted to them.

"Good night ladies. Thank you for brightening up this place. Make sure you visit us again. Oh hey," he shouted as he quickly made his way toward the door that they had just exited. "I don't even know your names."

"Maren," Maren shouted back, lifting her arm above her head and using her index finger to point downward, "and my gorgeous, single friend is Alexa," she shouted back, as Lexi nudged her in the side.

~Chapter 8~

They slept soundly, despite the silence. Having lived in the city and surrounded by constant noise for the last 10 years, Alexa had been concerned that Marsha's home would be too quiet to sleep. That was not the case, compliments of the IPA's that they'd consumed the night prior. Both woke rested and only slightly hung over, to birds chirping outside Maren's bedroom window. Alexa brushed the hair from her eyes as she rolled over in the single bed that she was currently sharing with an oversized orange Tabby cat named Garfield. Maren's mother had a soft spot for animals, with cats being her favorite. Maren vented to Alexa every time that she learned of her mother's most recent rescue, with Alexa only shrugging and laughing at her frustration. Marsha currently had four cats of her own, while she fostered two more until they could find forever homes. Luckily for Alexa, Garfield was friendly and not nearly as needy as the others in residence; which was a good thing as she didn't really care for cats.

"Move your fat ass over cat so I can use the bathroom and brush my teeth," she said, throwing back the covers. With the air still chilly, Alexa quickly ran into the tiny bathroom down the hallway while Maren remained asleep and snoring.

She made her way toward the kitchen after washing up and was greeted by Maren's mom who was already showered, dressed and focusing intensely on the Sudoku that came with the morning paper. She knew that it wasn't her daughter before she even looked up.

"Well, good morning, honey. You don't look any worse for wear. How's my girl this morning?"

"Good morning. I'm not sure how she is quite yet since she's still snoring away in there. I'd forgotten just how loud she can be when she's in a deep sleep after a night of drinking," Alexa joked.

"I figured you two must have had a grand old time by the noise that you were making when you came home," she winked. "I could also tell by the appearance of my kitchen this morning when I got up. Had yourselves a little midnight snack now didn't you my love?"

"What?" she said, joining her mother and best friend in the kitchen. "What in the hell are you two doing up at this god forsaken hour? The sun isn't even up yet," she continued as she started the coffee maker, and waited impatiently for her cup of Joe to brew. "God I hate mornings," she added for good measure.

"Glad to see my girl is so delightful on this beautiful spring morning," Marsha teased as she walked over to her only daughter and took her into a bear hug.

"You never were one to like mornings despite your father's insistence that it was the best time of the day. Go on, drink up and I'll make you girls one of my special omelets, guaranteed to fix any hang over in a jiffy.

"Mom, I don't want you mixing any weird ass herbs into our breakfast. I've told you before, we never know if and when they're going to do a random drug test and I don't need some cannabis type chemicals showing in my bloodstream or urine sample!"

"Relax my dear," Marsha teased, as she put her hands on her daughter's shoulders. "Have I ever led you astray?" she teased.

"Oh God, we're screwed," Alexa chimed in, walked over to her best friend and surrogate mother and joined their group hug. "I love you two, and I so needed this."

Separating from their embrace, Marsha simply smiled.

"You are welcome here anytime, and for as long as you need, and I expect you to remember that. Should you ever relocate back home where you both belong, I might add," eyeing her daughter as well, "there is always room for one more and you my dear are welcome."

"First of all, mother, my "home" is now New York and that's where I'm staying. Second, if even I were move back home, which I won't, I sure as hell wouldn't share a room with her," she said, pointing at her best friend. "She snores," she laughed.

"Oh no you don't," Marsha quickly intervened. "Before this argument goes any further, you two go wash up and get ready for breakfast! Oh, and Maren, Alexa won't be bunking with you. She'll use the spare bedroom until more suitable living arrangements are available."

Not saying a word until they got into the bathroom, the two women left the tiny kitchen as instructed. The second the door was shut and Maren was brushing her teeth, Alexa started.

"Maren, are you aware that your mother made that declaration in the present tense, not a hypothetical speculation. It's as if she knows something that we don't know."

Trying to answer with her mouth full of toothpaste, Maren put her finger up indicating to give her one minute to rinse, and after doing so, answered her best friend.

"My mother knows a ton, and yes she's extremely intelligent; we both know that. But do you honestly see yourself moving from the bling of the city to the fireflies of Old Forge? Seriously Lexi, that ship sailed a long time ago, and I have no desire to return back to this boring town. Do you?" she asked, suddenly turning serious.

"No, but," she started and was promptly cut off.

"Correct, the answer is no. We're city girls now and there's no way in hell that I'm moving back to this one-horse town."

"There are many worse places to live Maren, than in our home town. Sometimes the city gets too crazy, you know? Don't you miss watching the Fourth of July fireworks from a boat while chilling on Old Forge Pond? Or spending the day on the Moose River kayaking the way we used to? Oh my God, remember the time we had the entire senior class float?" Laughing, Alexa continued, "Actually I don't remember too much of that trip, compliments of that damn Boones Farm you stole from my brother. But I know we had a great time."

"Great time my ass, you puked in our kayak!"

Pretending to be indignant, Alexa defended herself. "I did not puke! I spit up the mosquito that I had accidently swallowed!"

"Bullshit!"

"That is the truth! No honestly Maren, admit it, don't you miss the laid back attitude that you find in a small town like ours? And doesn't the hustle and bustle of the city get to you from time to time? Waiting in line everywhere you go and having it take 20 minutes to go less than a mile because you're in bumper to bumper traffic. And the constant noise; that gets to me the most. Sometimes it seems like I can't escape it and that there's never a place where I can find solitude in the silence."

"I honestly didn't know you felt that way Lexi. I thought you loved the fast-paced life, and the excitement. You are actually considering leaving New York, aren't you?" Maren asked, suddenly very worried that she might be losing her best friend.

"No. It's not that I am actively looking to leave New York. It just feels like something is missing. And I'm not sure what it is that I'm looking for, but I feel unsettled and won't know what's missing until I find it. Does that make any sense whatsoever?"

"Do you think you're still hung up on Bradford?"

"Still hung up on Brad? No, absolutely not. Looking back now, I realize that he was wrong for me in so many ways and that's why I never said yes to his proposals. Yes, he could have financially provided me with anything that I asked for or wanted, but he would never have fulfilled me emotionally. Quite honestly, an emotional connection is far more important to me than how fat a man's wallet is. And before you say it," Alexa kidded, "I know, I know; money can't buy you happiness, but it can buy you everything else. I want the whole package Maren. I want someone who is my equal and has the same values and morals that I do. I want someone who isn't afraid to get dirty or leave the house not looking absolutely perfect, yet says that I look that way regardless. I want someone who would kayak the Moose River with me, or chase fireflies like you mentioned earlier. I want someone who loves and respects me for me; is that too much to ask?"

"No it's not Lexi. But when you find Mr. Wonderful, make sure that he has a twin brother for me too, okay?" she teased. "We'd better get our butts back to the kitchen because I can smell the bacon from here and momma will be hollering if we let her breakfast go cold."

They finished changing into yoga pants and t-shirts and joined her mother in the kitchen. The aroma was inviting with the smell of not only garlic and onions but peppers and bacon in the air. Knowing that everything Marsha was using to cook with, most likely came out of her garden, Alexa anticipated not only a scrumptious meal but a healthy one as well. For as long as Alexa could remember, Marsha had raised chickens, with each of them having very distinct names. Maren's mom hadn't been a flower child but was the daughter of one, and thus, carried on much in the same way she had been raised. She practiced yoga daily, ate only organic food, sewed majority her own clothes, and prided herself on being completely self- sufficient. As a child, Alexa always had been intrigued when Mrs. Wilson had kidded with her daughter that her self-sufficiency would one day pay for her college education. She and her husband had installed a wood furnace in their tiny home, without the mortgage companies' knowledge, and also took advantage of a grant to have their home equipped with solar panels long before they were in vogue. They'd raised pigs and chickens and had a garden the size of a football field. Marsha bartered with others, trading eggs and vegetables for firewood and other essentials. Looking back now, Alexa realized that the woman had been ahead of her time and had been right; the amount of electricity that she sold back to NiMo every month that was produced by her solar panels had nearly paid for Maren's education. While others had placed a panel or two on their home, Marsha had negotiated with the state to have them not only encompass the entire roof of her home, but also her barn, thus producing twice the voltage. When she'd first installed them, everyone said that she was crazy and that they'd be useless and simply an eyesore as upstate New York wasn't exactly known for continuous sunshine. But then again, they'd scoffed at her when she installed a windmill on her property as well. Now, it was Marsha who chuckled when she passed by windmill after windmill throughout Madison, Herkimer and Oneida County. She never considered herself a forward thinker, just "a think out of the box" kind of woman; and that was enough for her.

Marsha smiled as she turned to find her girls ready for the breakfast that she'd prepared. Her iron skillet was steaming and filled to the brim with three huge omelets. Maren poured more coffee as Alexa quickly grabbed plates from the cupboard where she knew they'd been kept for three decades. They all sat down as the aroma of the meal permeated their senses.

"Glad to see you haven't forgotten how to cook Mrs. Wilson."

Looking around, Marsha pretended to be searching for someone. "Mrs. Wilson, where is she? I didn't know my mother-in-law was arriving today?" she kidded. "I'm too young to be called that, and you're family so either you call me Marsha or Mom, but certainly not Mrs. Wilson. And I know we've had this very same discussion before, so don't make me repeat myself Alexa Rose."

"Yes mam, I mean mom," she chuckled, and started eating the omelet in front of her.

They ate in relative silence, each nearly inhaling their meal. Finally, it was Maren's mom who started the conversation.

"So what are you two doing this weekend for fun? If you're heading into town to do some shopping, I suggest that you do it today before the tourists arrive. Oh, and the parade is tomorrow at one so plan around that as well."

"What do you want to do today Maren? I was thinking that maybe we'd take a ride past my home, and then maybe take a ride around and see if anything's changed and what new construction has gone up. We haven't gone cruising on back roads in over a year, I don't think," she added as if she needed a bargaining tool.

"Yeah, sure, that sounds great. But what exactly do you think actually changed in the big metropolis of Old Forge Lexi? Same day, month, year around here; only the tourists' faces have changed," Maren answered honestly, yet somewhat bitterly.

"That's not necessarily true Maren. We certainly saw some eye candy last night, and we've certainly never seen him before."

"Where'd you go out last evening girls? I thought you were heading into town to grab a pizza and wings."

"We did Mrs., I mean Marsha," Alexa responded. But then we stopped in at the Black Bear Bistro since we hadn't been in there in a few years."

"Oh, the Triple B?" she asked inquisitively, already knowing who must have been bartending during the evening, but continued to play along. "Was it crowded?"

"Actually yes," Maren answered. They had an amazing violinist, and most of the tables were filled, which was surprising for a Thursday night, I thought. And the cutest bartender ever," she added for good measure.

"Cutest married bartender," Lexi corrected. Marsha listened but didn't correct Alexa regarding Lucas' marital status but stayed in the conversation.

"So Sam wasn't bartending last evening?"

"Who's Sam mom?" Maren asked, now at full attention. You have a "friend" in town named Sam? Holding out information on me mother?" she teased.

Not quite ready to divulge to her daughter that Sam was short for Samantha, and someone who'd become not only her best friend, yoga partner, and close to soul sister, Marsha played along.

"Actually yes, Sam and I have become very close; especially since Sam is part owner of the Triple B and one of my closest friends. I stop in there often for their Lentil soup. You really should try it sometime."

"Mom, is Sam a friend with benefits?" Maren asked, not entirely sure if she wanted to know the answer. Even though her father had passed away near a decade before, she thought of her mother as simply a mother, not a woman who still might desire a sexual companion.

"I don't think you should be asking your mother such a personal question, now do you Maren?" Alexa asked, trying to break the embarrassing silence.

"Absolutely I should ask, especially if my mother's having sex and I'm not!" she answered, laughing.

"Settle your jets ladies, my uterus and all of its' other associated parts were put out to pasture the day that your father died; and there's no one on this planet that could make me desire a man the way I desired him. So in answer to your question, no, no I most certainly am not having sex. But Sam certainly would get a chuckle out of this conversation."

Pushing herself back from the table, Alexa quickly got up and carried her dishes over to the sink. After the table was cleared and the remaining dishes were washed, both she and Maren decided that maybe they should attempt to run off part of the calories that they'd just ingested so they changed into running attire and were out the door.

They no sooner were out of sight when Marsha dialed up Samantha's cell.

"Hey, good morning."

"Good morning to you as well. It might be wishful thinking, but I have to ask you something, something very much on the QT."

Hearing her best friend's quiet but very excited tone, she became very serious. "Shoot, what'd you want to ask me?"

"When the board had its most recent board meeting, didn't you say that there were six or seven teachers retiring at the end of this school season?"

"Yes, why do you ask?"

"Call it a hunch, or maybe just completely wishful thinking, but I get the feeling that maybe, just maybe, my baby girl is finally getting sick of the city and might be ready to come back home. Don't say a word to anyone, but please tell me that one of the teachers retiring is at the elementary level. She currently teaches 5th grade and has always taught at that level. And I was thinking that maybe if there's an opening, that maybe she'd apply for it. I know best friend would move back here in a New York minute if given the opportunity."

"Marsha, she's been gone a long time and I would hate for you to get your hopes up and get disappointed if she has no desire to move back north. Our world here in the mountains is vastly different than the life she leads in New York. You know that as well as anyone. Believe me, Logan tells me all the time that we live in the twilight zone. He'll never leave New York. But in answer to your question, yes, three of the positions are at the elementary level, and one of them is Mrs. Hornsworth, who teaches 5th grade."

"Yes!" Marsha responded, even surprising herself with her burst of jubilation.

~Chapter 9~

"I don't know why I can't go with you when you run your errands daddy."

"Because Kels, maybe I was planning on picking up a few surprises for you for our big camping trip."

"You mean like a puppy, Daddy?" she asked, with her eyes growing big with excitement.

"Oh baby, no, not a puppy. We've had this conversation how many times? We can't get a puppy because grandma is allergic remember?" he said, pleadingly.

Pouting, Kelsey looked directly into her father's eyes. "Then what daddy? There is nothing better than a puppy and you promised that someday we could get a puppy. When, daddy, when?"

"I promise you Kels, I solemnly give you my word, you will get a puppy someday," he said, taking his daughter into his arms.

Hugging him back, Kelsey looked into her father's eyes. "I know dad. I just really would like a puppy before Christmas. Wouldn't a puppy be a nice Christmas present?" she asked innocently.

"Yes baby, that would be a great present and I'll make sure to tell Santa that a puppy is a top priority okay?"

"Okay. But I still want to go with you today to run your errands. And what does solemnly mean?"

Laughing, he pulled out his cell phone and dialed his mother.

"Hey mom, Kelsey wants to ride shot gun with me so you're off the hook today. But mom," he said sincerely, "Thank you anyways."

"You're welcome honey. Enjoy your day with my favorite granddaughter."

"I will mom. And remember, she's your only grandchild."

~Chapter 10~

Alexa and Maren actually made it much farther than either of them had anticipated. They ran the equivalent of a 5K, a feat that neither would have thought possible just a few short hours before. Feeling somewhat hydrated, despite their respective hangovers, they chatted and laughed their way along the bumpy road near Maren's childhood home. As they walked back towards her mom's house, they were surprised by the number of cars on the road for a workday. Neither paid much attention to the local traffic, and simply waved at the honks and whistles that they heard along the way. When a dark colored Dodge Ram flew by them with country music blaring and its' occupants singing along, Alexa felt the hair on the back of her neck rise as she caught a quick glance at the man and the woman in the vehicle. Since she hadn't lived in the area in nearly a decade, she couldn't begin to guess who might be commandeering the truck. She let the feeling fade as the truck rounded the bend and sped out of sight, kicking up dust as it went.

"Who was that daddy?"

"I don't know baby. Probably just summer people up for the holiday weekend."

"You know what Dad? I was talking with Jessica the other day and we both agreed, school should only be Monday through Thursday. I mean, think about it. Us being off from school today means that I can help you all day long," she smiled. "And Jess and I were thinking that since we're both turning eleven, we really should have our own phones. I mean, don't you think that it's important that you can reach me and I can reach you at any given time?" she gently persuaded.

He looked over at his daughter and couldn't help but feel proud. She was becoming everything that he and Ana had hoped for from the moment that they realized that they were becoming a family. She was smart, fiercely independent, and growing into her looks. She had been a cute baby, adorable toddler and preadolescence had only reaffirmed what her parents had always known, Kelsey Rose was going to be a knock-out when she grew up. As he continued down the road, he kept glancing over at his daughter who was busy snap chatting with her girlfriends on her father's phone. It always startled him, when he'd glance quickly and see her sitting there; her resemblance to her mother was becoming much more pronounced and apparent. Sometimes he missed her so much that he found it hard to breathe, but other moments like now, he knew that she was still with him and would always be. Their daughter would always keep Ana's memory alive.

"We'll see about the phone young lady. How about you help me all day and we'll see if you're responsible enough to have a phone okay?"

"Deal. I am Dad, you'll see. But," she added, thinking now might be the time to broach the subject, "If I'm responsible enough for a phone, which I am, then I should be responsible enough to take care of a puppy. Just saying. Oh, and how come we can't leave to go camping today Dad; why do we have to wait until tomorrow?"

"Kelsey."

"I know, I know. You have to work. I really do hate that people have to work all the time. When I grow up, I'm going to work from my house Dad. I'm gonna have six or maybe eight dogs, and a cat, and rabbits, and chickens maybe; and I'm going to stay home all day and play with them and work only when I want to," she proclaimed, eyes still glued to her father's cell phone.

"Sounds like a great idea Kels. But how are planning on making money to support your family of animals?"

"Oh that's easy Daddy. I'm going to invent software that helps people like me read better. I don't know how yet Dad, but when I figure out how to get smarter and become a better reader, I'm going to design something to help others get better as well. You said that there are lots of other kids who have reading problems like mine, and they're not dumb either; so I'm going to make it easier for them to feel smart too. Isn't that a good idea, Daddy?" she asked sincerely.

He willed the tears away as he responded. "I think it's a splendid idea, Kels. I have no doubt that you'll invent something that makes a huge difference in this world. And just so you know, I couldn't have ever asked for a better daughter than you. You know how much I love you right, Kelsey," he said, holding back his emotion.

"Of course I do dad. Dah. I just sometimes wish that you had someone to love you too; I mean other than me and grandma."

Very surprised at her statement, he looked over at his daughter.

"I have all the love I need Kelsey. You and your grandma give me more love than any man deserves, and you ladies are the only ladies that I will ever need in my life."

"What about momma's spirit? You still want her around don't you?" she asked, suddenly very sincere and focused.

"Oh course baby. You momma was my first and only love and I want her around always. But she was needed in heaven, and I am needed here on earth with you and grandma. But some day your mom and I will be dancing under the stars again, you wait and see. You know you're beginning to look more and more like your mom, and she was the most beautiful woman on earth."

"Really?" she asked quizzically.

"Really, you have her eyes, and lips and you definitely have her stubborn streak," he laughed.

Your grandma even commented how you walk like her and your laugh is exactly like hers was."

"I miss her a lot dad. And sometimes I get scared because I can't remember things she said or did and I don't want to forget her, ever," she said as tears welled up in her eyes.

"Oh baby, you'll never forget her. I will always remind you of things she said or did, and we'll look at our picture albums more often okay?" he promised. "Did you know that your mom loved camping?"

"She did?"

"Yup. We went camping for our celebration of our high school graduation and our wedding. She knew that she was pregnant with you and she didn't want to take any chances flying, so I told your mom that I'd take her anywhere she'd like to go and you know what she told me?"

"No what?"

He smiled. "She told me that she'd like to go tent camping at Fish Creek, which is up by Tupper Lake and Lake Placid. You've never been there, but," he said as the brain storm hit him. "I was thinking that it's about time that you, Miss Kelsey Rose get introduced to real old-fashioned camping and if you're game, I was thinking that we'd camp at Fish Creek this weekend. How does that sound?"

She nearly burst with excitement. "Really, like tent, tent camping? Not Uncle Logan's camper, but camping in a real tent and cooking in the fire pit and everything? Oh my God, wait until I tell Jess, and Ashley and Meghan. They're gonna be so jealous!"

Now that he had her hopes up, he prayed that he could get a site reserved on such short notice at his childhood campground. It was a holiday weekend after all. But he'd gotten caught up in the moment, and carried away by her excitement. And now, his daughter was expecting the camping trip of a lifetime; so, come hell or high water, he'd deliver just that.

~Chapter 11~

Once back at Maren's moms, they took turns showering in the one full bath that the house afforded. Unlike the mega-mansions that spread across the Fulton Chain of Lakes like patchwork, many of the year-round residents lived in more modest homes. Maren's parents had purchased their little bungalow back in the 80's before the housing market exploded in the mountains. Back then, waterfront homes were still affordable, and raw land was easy to come by. They'd purchased their 1100 square foot house from a widower who was moving in with his daughter, and over the years, turned it into a home. Marsha was eclectic in her design and if nothing else, her ingenuity was unique in the personalized touches that she'd put in her home. It was functional and practical, but mostly, it was fun; simply a fun house to be around and in. Maren had been raised to appreciate mother earth and all that she had to offer, but also hadn't lacked in basic necessities. Where Marsha chose to sew her own clothes, she always made sure that her daughter didn't go without and made sure that she had the same staples that all the other kids her age had. Even though she and her husband might prefer a more organic lifestyle, they didn't want their only child ostracized at school. But the most important thing they stressed when purchasing the must-have articles of clothing to start a particular school year, was for her to be true to herself and not always go along with the crowd. They'd raised their girl to be independent and head-strong and to always follow her dreams, and she'd done exactly that. And Marsha had no one but herself to blame for assisting her daughter in flying the coop nearly a decade before.

It was times like this, looking into her living room and seeing her daughter's best friend sprawled out on the couch, that she missed the most. She'd give anything to have her daughter living closer to her in Old Forge, but would never tell her that. She'd wanted to fly and she never stopped her. For now, she was just so appreciative every time Maren returned home, even if only for a few days.

"So have you two figured out what you're doing today?" Marsha asked casually.

Alexa was the first to speak up. "I was going to ask Maren if she'd like to climb Black Bear or Rocky Point while it's still cool out."

"Great idea," Marsha commented.

"Yeah, I'm still not much into shopping during tourist season and theoretically, today does mark the beginning of the summer season up here if I recall. Besides, growing up here, what could the stores possibly offer that I could possibly need?" she asked and stated, all at the same time.

Marsha hesitated for just a brief moment before wording her response. "You are right Maren, I don't think the stores have anything to offer neither you, or Alexa. But don't sell the area short because things haven't changed all that much over the last decade up here. But I think that both of have changed and I think that you might be pleasantly surprised to find that this area might offer you more than you think. You and Lexi just need to be open to the possibilities around you."

Before Alexa could respond, Marsha rose and headed towards her room.

"Hey Maren if I leave before you're out of the shower, I'm heading over to Sam's to do some gardening there and then have lunch. Lock up behind yourself and the spare key is still under the flower pot if you forgot to bring yours, and you ladies return before I get back. Oh, and Lexi, you know it's been weighing heavy on your mind, so do it. Take a quick drive by your homestead. Maybe you'll like the work that's been done to it and you'll like what you see. Remember Lexi, I love you almost as much as I do my own girl and I know you're not happy in New York anymore. Follow your heart, not your head sometimes and you'll realize just how much happier you can be. And pound that same thought into my girl's head as well okay?" Marsha left Alexa standing alone in the living room, lost in her own thoughts.

It was only a few minutes from the time that Marsha went outside to organize her truck for her day, to the time that Maren appeared from the shower, looking refreshed and ready for the world. She found Alexa bending over, lacing her hiking boots and smiled. From her attire, she knew that her best friend wanted to find a trail and head into the solitude of the woods.

"I guess I know what we're doing today."

Looking up, Alexa stood up after finishing double knotting her boot.

"I was hoping, if you didn't mind, we could go climb Bald, Black Bear or Rocky Point, your choice. And then I was kind of thinking that maybe I'd like to take a drive by my old home, that is if we have time and you don't mind."

"Why would I mind? It's not like we're on a time schedule you idiot!" she kidded. "But, I am absolutely not climbing Rondaxe if the parking lot is full. There is nothing more annoying than assembly line hiking, following a bunch of first time tourists pretending to be hikers," she answered, her tone dripping with sarcasm.

"So true," Alexa agreed, pretending to be in total agreement.

"The damn tourists can be so annoying to us locals, you know. I just can't stand them," she exaggerated her movements, "taking pictures every 20 feet, wearing their inappropriate footwear, chitty-chatty the entire way, and holding us locals up. I couldn't agree with you more," she laughed at Maren, who by now had caught on to her kidding.

"Kiss my ass. You know exactly what I mean Lexi so don't judge me for speaking the truth."

"True, but honey, we're technically not locals anymore. We've spent over one-third of our lives away from here, so at some point, we have to resign ourselves to the fact that we too, are tourists."

"Screw that," Maren exclaimed. "I might not live here anymore, but I will never be labeled a tourist or summer person; not there's anything necessarily wrong with either," she added for good measure.

"But we were born and raised here, and our roots will always be here so that makes us locals, and no one can insinuate otherwise."

"Agreed. We will always be home-grown girls. Maren," Alexa asked, suddenly turning serious. "Do you ever wonder what would have happened to us or where'd we be today if we'd come back home after college and got teaching jobs in Old Forge or Inlet? You ever wonder what life would be like for us or how different things would be?"

Maren answered the only way that she knew how, and that was with honesty.

"What would life be like Lexi, that's easy. We'd probably be married, each have a couple of kids by now, and most likely teaching in one of the classrooms that we sat in as children. We'd be going to the same church that we were both confirmed in, and probably be part of the PTA," she continued. "And we'd probably be wondering how we ended back up where we started."

"Maren, it's a gorgeous area and we both had a wonderful childhood here, don't you think? There certainly are worse places to raise a family. But what the hell, I don't know why I'm getting so mushy; I don't even have a freaking boyfriend, let alone a family," she laughed. "Maybe the thought of going by my childhood home has been weighing on my mind and that's what's got me so sentimental. I don't know, it's just weird sometimes when we return to visit friends and your family, it truly feels like home to me."

Not quite sure where she was going with her statements, Maren turned serious and shifted towards her best friend.

"You're not seriously missing this place enough to move back, are you? Our lives are in New York now Lexi, not here. Hey, look, why don't we skip driving by your old house? We can climb whichever trail is less crowded and then let's take mom's boat out on the lake for the afternoon? We can pack a lunch, head over to the sandbar and relax with a good book, some tunes and a bottle of wine. It's supposed to reach the upper 70's today, and by Adirondack standards, that's a heat wave for Memorial Day Weekend, so let's take advantage of it," she said, trying to convince her girlfriend to forget about taking any more drives down memory lane.

"That sounds great Maren. I'd love to go out on the boat! But I really need to take a ride by my house if that's okay. If you don't want to come, I could grab your mom's bike and take a ride by."

"Lexi, that's nearly twenty miles round trip! We already ran this morning so stop acting like you're training for a triathlon. Of course, I'll go with you to ride by your house and then we'll swing by the grocery store to grab some fruit and munchies for the boat. You want to take a drive by now so we can get organized for the afternoon?"

Smiling, she locked arms with her best friend. "Come on, let's go."

They loaded up their truck with Marsha's tote bags to use at the grocery store; each grabbed a water bottle and the short grocery list and said their good byes to Maren's mom who was also on her way out to meet Samantha. She still hadn't revealed to her daughter and surrogate daughter than Sam was actually not only her best friend, but a woman, not a man. She chuckled at the aspect of the two of them speculating on what she'd be doing all afternoon with her "date."

They made their way down Maren's road to the intersection of Route 28 and turned toward town. Northbound traffic was already steady and an early indication of what the rest of the holiday weekend would be like in their little town in the mountains. Maren make their way through town and headed toward Inlet. When she saw three vehicles all turn left down Rondaxe Road in front of her, she made the conscious decision to keep on going and drove to the turn off for Black Bear and Rocky Point. Once parked in the designated lot for hikers, she turned toward Alexa who was already exiting the truck.

"Your call, Rocky Point or Black Bear?"

"Black Bear," she answered without hesitation. "I know it's longer and steeper but the morning is still young and we've got the time. Besides, I'm hoping since it's a little longer hike, maybe there will be fewer on the trail."

"Okay then. Let's get going," Maren agreed wholeheartedly.

They had chosen well. Being experienced hikers, and in great shape, they made the round trip in under 90 minutes. Hot and sweaty, they collapsed into Maren's truck, taking off their hiking boots and socks immediately upon completing their hike. They had met only three other hikers while on the trail and had been pleasantly surprised to have had the mountain nearly to themselves. When they saw the number of vehicles in the parking lot when they descended, they realized that the majority of the hikers must have opted for the shorter hike. Finishing off their last bottles of water, they packed up their gear, and headed toward Lexi's childhood home.

    The road to the home that Alexa had grown up in was still a quiet dead end street with just a handful of homes sprinkled along the way. Even after all these years, the road surface had never been paved and the crusher run was noticeably thin in places. Maren drove slower than she probably needed to, but since her truck was less than a year old, with payments higher than some people's mortgages, she chose to err on the side of caution and proceed down the road at a snail's pace. As they rounded the last bend to what had been home for 18 years of Alexa's life, they were surprised to see not only four pick-up trucks on the lawn, but also a large moving van backed up to the front door.

Curious, Alexa instructed Maren to pull into the already crowded drive. Everything in Maren's psyche told her to turn around and return to the village, but she did as her best friend requested, despite her intuition telling her otherwise. As soon as the truck was in park, Alexa was out the door and marching, not walking toward the front door and the source of the commotion, with Maren quickly falling in behind her. As she bounded up the front steps, a flashback of doing exactly that same thing countless times as a child hit her. Now standing there peering through the door into what had been her living room brought back an influx of mixed emotions. She hated the color that had been painted on not only the walls but the beautiful hardwood trim, and someone had had the audacity to cover the gorgeous hickory floors with a disgusting plaid carpet. The house reeked of smoke, and whether or not her parents were theoretically the owners of the house, Alexa knew that they would never have consented to allowing renters to smoke on the premises, let alone inside the home. Thoroughly pissed and ready for a fight, she walked inside the home looking for a confrontation. And it only took her less than ten seconds to find one.

"Hello, anybody home?" she yelled. "Hello?"

"Yeah, who's there?" a burly sounding voice responded. Within seconds, a man appeared from the rear of the house, arms loaded with kitchen appliances, including the microwave that she knew belonged to her parents.

"Who are you and why are you in my house?" he asked indignantly and definitely irritated.

Before Maren could intervene, Alexa was on the verbal attack.

"I'm Alexa and I own this house, including the microwave that you currently have in your arms. So, I suggest that you put it back where it was and tell me what's going on here."

"Fuck you lady. The landlord of this dump lives down south in North or South Carolina and she's a hell of a lot older than you are, so get lost."

Maren knew Alexa's temper and could tell that the current tenant was probably as much of a hot head as her best friend, so she quickly excused herself and went out onto the porch to make a quick call.

"Fuck you?" she repeated, indignantly. "I'll give you fuck you, you redneck little twit. First of all, this place certainly is not a dump, or at least it wasn't before your fat ass moved in. Are you the idiot that painted over the crown molding and door trims because if you are, then you're even stupider than you look! Are you moving out or simply robbing the place?" she added, still steaming. "And what gives you the right to smoke inside? I can guarantee you that that act of stupidity cost you your security deposit!" she continued, indignantly, as she found herself getting madder and madder.

"Look lady, I don't know who you are or why you think you've got a right to be up in my business, but yeah I'm moving out. Piece of shit house ain't got no central air, the water pressure sucks, and it just ain't big enough for us no more."

Just as Alexa was about to defend her childhood home, an extremely pregnant blond made her way cautiously down the stairs, carrying several boxes.

"Jason," she called out, sounding extremely out of breath. "What is going on down here? All I hear is your screaming and carrying on. What's the matter?"

Even with her face obscured, Alexa would have known the voice anywhere and quickly raced over to the landing to assist the woman with the load that she was trying to balance. Maren entered the room just as Alexa was taking the boxes. As soon as she saw who was assisting her, she shrieked with joy as she glanced from one side of the room to the other, seeing her former classmates and former best friends.

"Alexa, Maren? Oh my God, is it really you?" she exclaimed, holding her very rotund belly as she laughed. "What are you doing here? Have you finally decided to leave that horrible city and come back home?"

Alexa was the first to answer but not before getting an evil glare from the man she'd just confronted.

"Oh my god, Molly, I had no idea that you were back in town! I mean, obviously, I knew that you weren't in the city any longer, but I never realized that you'd moved back to Old Forge and into my parent's home for that matter! How long have you been back, and with him?" she added, nodding her head toward the jerk that she still wanted to deck.

Knowing what a temper her boyfriend had, and now putting the shouting together, she went to his side in his defense, putting her arm around his waist.

"Oh Jason and I have been together just about a year now, isn't that right honey?" she added, nudging him to respond.

"Yeah, whatever. Guess it's been about seven or eight months I guess."

"Well it looks like you've been busy during that time," Maren added, looking at her very large belly.

Laughing, Molly answered. "Yeah, I guess that you could say that."

Still feeling the tension in the air, she motioned for her former classmates to take a seat on the few remaining pieces of furniture in her living room. They did so as she nudged her boyfriend out of the room. As soon as he was out of earshot, she turned back towards her friends.

"Sorry if he was rude to you earlier. Jason's a great guy, but he is constantly on his conspiracy theories and his paranoia gets the better of him sometimes. If he sees an unfamiliar face, he kind of goes nuts. I apologize for him if he was disrespectful in any way."

"Molly," Alexa interjected. "Don't you dare apologize for someone else's behavior. He was rude and a jerk, but he's no reflection on you or our friendship," she smiled. Reaching over to touch her friend's hand, she asked gently. "Does he treat you well? And what's going on here? Are you and Jason moving out of mom's house?

Do my parent's know that you're leaving? She never said anything to me about you living in our home."

"Yes, I spoke with your mom last week. I love it here but with the baby coming and all, Jason just doesn't think it's going to be big enough, especially since we usually have his twins every weekend," she added coyly.

"Oh," was all Maren could think of saying, while Alexa had a lot to say.

"So who is this Jason and is it serious? And most importantly, are you having a little boy or girl?"

Molly smiled. "I'm having a little girl and we're going to name her Magnolia, Maggie for short. I know I'm naming my little girl after a flower, but they were my grandma's favorite and she was the most influential woman in my life so I wanted to honor her in the only way that I know how," she said, sniffling back a few tears.

Taking her hands in hers, Alexa smiled. "Your grandmother would be so honored to have you name your child after her. And if your little girl grows up to be half the woman you are, then both you and your grandma can be very proud."

"Oh thank you, Lexi! I've missed you both so much. Listen, I've got to help Jason with these boxes, but I definitely would love to get together with you both before you head back to the city. Do you have plans for dinner, or lunch tomorrow?" she asked excitedly.

They exchanged cell numbers before Alexa and Maren made their way towards their truck. Molly formally introduced them to Jason and all five of his brothers. By the time the introductions were over, Jason was more notably relaxed and was apologetic for his earlier behavior and attitude. He assured both women that he wouldn't let Molly do any heavy lifting and that he'd take good care of her. They really wanted to stay and help with the moving, if it meant easing her burden, but once they saw the amount of manpower already working steadily, they reluctantly left, promising to call her in the morning. As they were about to get into Maren's truck, a black blazer pulled in behind them. It took a minute or two to recognize the face but when they did, they squealed in delight.

"Oh my God, this is like a freaking class reunion! Jimmy, is that you behind those tinted glasses? Holy shit, you're a cop? They let you carry a gun James Eugene," Alexa teased, remembering her classmates nickname that he hated.

"Should have known it was a couple city chicks causing trouble!" he kidded back. Molly had heard the commotion and made her way out onto the porch and smiled. The second Jimmy spotted her, he forgot about his former classmates and quickly made his way to the stairs, separating the distance in three strides.

"Hey, Mols. We got a call that there might be some kind of disturbance going on here and I got here as quick as I could. I was on the other side of Inlet so I'm sorry it took me so long."

Looking into her hazel eyes, he melted, like he did every time she gave him a moment of her attention. The look was not lost on them as Alexa and Maren looked on, quickly realizing that there was more under the surface than an officer simply responding to a call.

"Oh Jimmy, I'm sorry you had to race over here and probably take you away from more important things," she said making eye contact with her two friends who were still standing in the driveway.

"Alexa and Jason just had a little misunderstanding, and I assume someone must have heard the raised voices and called the police. I'm really sorry to have bothered you," she continued, apologetically.

"Mols," he reached over, gently taking her hand, "anytime I get to see you is not time wasted. I'm just glad everything is okay here. No issues with Jason that require my attention then?" he asked regrettably, almost wishing there was a reason to arrest the scumbag and bring him in. He had hated him from the moment they'd met, and hated him even more for his relationship with the one woman he'd loved since junior high, though she had no clue.

Molly had been his everything back then, and she'd never known just how much her friendship and kind words had meant to him. He'd been the tall, lanky, acne faced kid who never fit in, in any clique. He wasn't a jock, scholar, stoner, or nerd. He wasn't stupid, nor academically brilliant. He was just one of the invisibles, those kids who don't stand out or get noticed, the kind that sort of pass through school year after year and their presence or absence wouldn't make a difference. That's how he'd always felt, except when he was with Molly. She'd occasionally sit with him at lunch, talk with him at their lockers, which happened to always be next to each other, compliments of alphabetized locker assignments, and she'd make a point of spotting him in the crowd at the basketball games while she was cheering. He absolutely detested watching the other guys play basketball, but attended every home game, just to see her smile. Over and over again, he'd told himself that she was out of his league, but it didn't negate the fact, that he was still hopelessly, and probably eternally, in love with her. Now, ten years later, he still looked at her, with the same longing and admiration. He would do anything for her, anything; but for now, like back in school, he had to accept that he was just her friend. She was with Jason, scumbag or not; and he was still alone, idolizing her in silence.

"No, I'm good, Jimmy. But," she squeezed his hand, "Thank you. It was nice to see you. And, Jimmy," she said, as she let go of his hand, "Stay safe out there," she added, with a look of genuine concern. The look did not go unnoticed by either Alexa nor Maren.

"I will." He turned and walked back to his other former classmates and spoke quietly for just a moment. "So I take it you met Jason? Piece of shit," he added.

"Yeah, he's a real piece of work alright," Maren agreed. "Why would Molly be with someone like that" Alexa asked, confused why their fun-loving, always happy girlfriend would be with someone so miserable.

"I wish I knew," was the only response he could give them. As he started towards his truck, Alexa grabbed his arm just hard enough to gain his attention. As he turned toward her, she smiled.

"Just tell her Jimmy. Tell her how you feel."

"She should know by now Lexi; but she's still with that asshole," he added, feeling his heart sinking, the same way it did, every time he had to walk away from the love of his life. Looking not only somber, but genuinely sad, he walked to his patrol vehicle, got in and backed out, leaving the women with nothing to do but do the same.

 They made their way in and out of the only grocery store in town, purchasing munchies for the boat, along with a 12 pack of beer. As soon as they left the crowded parking lot, they maneuvered their way through town and turned onto Hollywood Road. Maren's mother kept her boat moored at the member's only beach at Hollywood Hills. Even though she didn't live in the home within the Hollywood Hills community, she still had her membership there and had stored her boat at the same slip for nearly two decades. Maren parked her truck and they jumped out. The sun was high in the cloudless sky and extremely warm for May in upstate New York. As they carried their belongings and cooler down the hill to the boat, they actually felt hot and sweaty which was unusual given the month of the year. As soon as they were loaded, untied and ready to launch, both pulled off their T shirts, enjoying the warmth on their skin. The lake was already busy with numerous kayaks, jet skis and pontoon boats already out on the water. Growing up in Old Forge had afforded both Maren and Alexa the luxury of being familiar with operating boats, and having grown up being out on the water every weekend, both knew the idiosyncrasies of the Fulton Chain of Lakes well. Maren navigated her mother's Baja as if she'd just driven it yesterday.

~Chapter 12~

With Kelsey riding shotgun, Luke completed not only his mandatory stops, but also managed to fit in grocery shopping and a few last minute supplies that he'd thought they might need for their camping adventure in the morning. He'd lucked out when he was finally home and able to pull up the Reserve America website on his laptop. Afraid that Fish Creek might be completely booked, he grabbed the first available site. Campsite number 70 was not only a perfect location, located in a quiet loop and on the point, but also was one of the larger sites which afforded privacy between the neighbors on sites 69 and 71. Luke secured the site with his credit card and when the transaction was completed, smiled in victory. He looked around, and swore he could feel Anastasia's presence and approval, but knew that it was just wishful thinking. Putting his credit card back in his wallet, he stood to go outside and it hit him. The scent of lilacs was so strong that it nearly accosted his senses, and he knew. Somehow, some way, his Ana was there or at least giving him a sign that she was. They were her favorite flower, her favorite scent and in that moment, he simply stood, frozen in the moment; taking in what was offered. In the years since she'd passed, Ana had come back several times to make her presence known. Little signs were always present, things moved from where he'd left them, missing items appearing where they should have been when he or his daughter searched for them, the cap in the toothpaste falling off or set next to the tube of toothpaste, like Anastasia was notorious for doing. And then there was her signature scent. It could be the middle of winter, and he'd smell it. Unlike today, usually it was just a faint whiff, a millisecond of acknowledgement that her love was still alive, even though her body was gone. He'd always do the same thing after each occurrence; he'd walk to the nearest window and look outside. After Ana passed, and he and Kelsey had eventually moved into the home they currently resided in, they'd planted a few lilac bushes in her honor. Each spring, he'd allowed Kelsey to choose which color she wanted and they'd planted two or three more to welcome in the start of summer. Now, bursts of color could be found in nearly every corner of his property. In the spring and early summer, his yard was alive with purple, pink and white flowers everywhere. No matter what direction he looked, her memory was there; and he wouldn't have it any other way. He'd do anything in order to keep her alive for his daughter.

He stood frozen until the scent finally dissipated, and then silently thanked her, and left the room in search of his daughter. He found her in her room, packing. She'd neatly laid out her clothes for their camping trip and was currently debating on which duffel bag she should attempt to cram them all in. He noted, by the overabundance of clothing currently covering her bed, that she was prepared to spend three or more weeks, not days, camping; but he didn't have the heart to discourage her. He simply smiled and encouraged her independence.

"Hey kiddo. It looks like you've got your packing organized so I'll let you continue. Just don't forget to bring your hiking boots, sandals for the shower, and warm PJs for sleeping because it might be cool up there at nighttime, okay?"

"I know dad. I'm not a little kid you know!" she exclaimed, sounding exasperated. The music blared from her I-Pod as she went back to the task at hand, leaving him standing there laughing.

"No Kels, you're certainly not a little kid anymore."

He left her in her room, and made his way to the kitchen where his mother had been kind enough to let herself in and drop off his requested meals. He opened his refrigerator to find not only Chicken Riggies, but Beef Stew, and Chicken and Biscuits. She'd made homemade sugar & cinnamon donuts, which were Kelsey's favorites, along with sourdough ones, that he loved. She'd already precooked a pound of turkey bacon and wrapped it in aluminum foil so all he'd have to do was throw it on the fire to reheat, and had made a dozen blueberry pancakes, again, wrapping them in foil for easy warming. He made a mental note to call and thank her. He didn't know what he'd do without his mother's assistance in not only raising his daughter but for always being there for him. Maybe he'd send her flowers or pick her up some chocolate, but no gesture ever seemed worthy enough to express his appreciation for her selfless dedication. If not for the Bistro, he'd invite her to go with them. But, with it being a holiday weekend, he wouldn't feel comfortable unless either he or his mother, his partner and co-owner of the Triple B, was at the helm. He trusted his employees whole-heartedly; it wasn't that. It was just that he took pride in everything that he and his mother had worked for, and to date, one of the two of them had been behind the bar every day since they'd opened three years prior. This weekend would be no exception. They'd even elicited the assistance of his twin every 4th of July, when he made his semi-annual trip to the mountains. Logan tried to avoid venturing north of the Catskills, but in order to see his family, he make the trek up to the mountains at least two or three times a year. He'd made a working vacation out of the Fourth of July week for the last few years and being able to work anywhere, as long as there was internet service, he'd gradually expanded his length of stay every summer. Both Luke and his mother were aware of the fact that though he claimed to hate life in Old Forge, he surprisingly was staying longer and longer with each visit. Lucas never challenged his twin, nor questioned what was going on in his life that drove him away from his life in the city. He simply enjoyed the time that he was able to spend with his identical twin brother.

When Logan was in town every July and offered to help out bartending, it was always a memorable event. Their appearance might be the same but their mannerisms and temperaments couldn't have been more opposite. Where Luke had been forced to be responsible and mature at a very early age, Logan was much more free spirited and impulsive. Logan was more like his mother, while Luke was the calm, logical one who always analyzed and overanalyzed every decision that he made, a trait that was the only thing that he and his mother had argued about over the years. Samantha had never once questioned his parenting ability while Anastasia had been alive, nor after she'd died. Luke was a wonderful father to his daughter and did the best that any man could, to try and provide his daughter with the both a nurturing environment and one that promoted self-assurance. But in Sam's opinion, he never relaxed and could never chill out long enough to simply enjoy life. From outward appearances, her son appeared to be friendly and fun loving but she knew that even though his smile, his mind was always racing and unsettled every moment of every day.

The closest he ever came to being the happy go lucky child that she remembered from his youth, occurred every July when Logan came to town. It was a hoot seeing the two of them bartending together. They were basically fire and ice together, polar opposites but completed each other and were a blast to watch working both ends of the bar. The Bistro was typically busy during the week of the 4th with both tourists and locals. Once word got out that Logan was back in town and bartending, it seemed that every single lady within a twenty-mile radius made their way to the Black Bear Bistro, in hopes of leaving enough of an impression on him to convince Logan to return to the mountains permanently. While Logan soaked the attention up, Luke politely blew off each and every advance, whether they were subtle or not. He explained to both his brother and mother, that he didn't have time for a relationship and had more than enough women in his life, with Kelsey and his mom. Samantha had, on more than one occasion, attempted to introduce and/or fix him up with single women his age but each attempt had been politely declined or thwarted if she'd brought the young lady into the Bistro in person. Luke did not want another woman in his life and had made it very clear that he was totally okay being alone; but his mother knew otherwise. Samantha knew that someone, someday would walk into her son's life and never leave. She just hoped that the day came sooner, rather than later.

~Chapter 13~

He spent most of the afternoon organizing and packing what he could pack into his truck. Their tent, sleeping bags, folding chairs, portable stove, and cookware didn't take up much room in the bed of his truck so he decided to throw their bikes in, just in case they wanted to ride around the 10-mile loop that circumvented Fish Creek Pond and Square Pond. They'd only have three days and two nights there, but Luke was determined to provide his daughter with a camping trip she wouldn't soon forget. There was nothing in the world that he wouldn't do to make his little girl happy, and if camping was what it took to see her smile, then he'd give her the camping adventure of a lifetime. He found their fishing rods, and tackle boxes in the garage, covered in dust; reminding him that fishing was just another thing he'd let go by the wayside. He used to love to fish and thinking about it now, he couldn't remember the last time he'd taken his rod and reel to his favorite fishing hole. As he dusted them off and added them to the growing collection of items in his truck, he realized just how much he'd given up when he had been forced to become both mother and father to his only child. Never once had he regretted having Kelsey, and abortion had never been an option when Ana had told him that she was pregnant. But, he was the first to admit that sometimes, only very occasionally, he found himself mad at God for taking away his Ana and leaving him to raise their daughter alone.

Before either of them was ready, it was time for him to head over to the Bistro to start another shift before their mini-vacation could commence. His mother was currently helping his daughter choose between the two-piece bathing suit and a new dark blue one piece that still had the tags on it. As he gave his daughter a hug and said his goodbyes, he couldn't help but cast his vote for the one piece, citing that it brought out the blue in her eyes, a line that neither she nor her grandmother bought. In the end, she simply packed both and stuffed the last of her clothes in the over-sized bag. Samantha listened intently as her only granddaughter excitedly spoke about all of the adventures that she and her father were going to have during their three days in the woods. It warmed her heart to hear Kelsey so animated and happy about spending time with her father. What she didn't know about was the surprise that her grandmother had planned for her on their way to Fish Creek.

"Hey Kels, you're not afraid of heights are you?"

"Of course not grandma, why?"

"Well, I just thought that maybe you and your father might want to see what a bird sees when he's soaring above the tree tops."

"That crazy grandma, because we can't fly."

Pulling out the brochure and two tickets that she'd been hiding behind her back, she handed them to her granddaughter and smiled.

"Maybe you can't today Kels, but you certainly will be able to tomorrow morning if you and your daddy stop at The Wild Center in Long Lake on your way to Fish Creek."

Her granddaughter immediately snatched the brochure out of her hand and started looking at the pictures. Her eyes grew as she viewed one picture after the next.

"We seriously can do this grandma? I mean walk up that trail across the treetops? And grandma, did you see the Wild Walk's Snag? How cool is that? The bridge walks right into the inside of the tree and it's four stories off of the ground. And the nest that we get to climb into," she continued, barely containing her excitement. "How freaking cool is that?" she exclaimed as she launched herself into her grandmother's arms. Pulling away, she became very serious.

"But there are only two tickets grandma. How come you're not coming with us? I mean, wouldn't you like to see it?" she asked, sadly.

"Oh I'd love to see it Kelsey Rose, but someone's got to take care of the Triple B while you and your father go off on your adventure. Tell you what, you guys go and have fun tomorrow, and when you get back you can tell me all about it and if you love it there, we'll all go back together in the fall. Deal?"

"Deal!"

Once they'd brought her bag and other camping essentials into the family room, Kelsey helped her grandmother start supper. They both sang along to every song that emitted from the radio, with Kelsey laughing when her grandmother purposely sang off key.

"Yes," Samantha thought, "she'd been so blessed to have two wonderful sons and such an amazing granddaughter. Life was good, life was definitely good.

~Chapter 14~

Alexa and Maren spent the entire afternoon and early evening on the water. They'd run into a few classmates and they, along with old friends and new acquaintances, hung out at the sand bar on First Lake for much of the day. They swam, drank, sunbathed, and drank some more as the sun beat down. Before the afternoon was over, all had taken their turn climbing up the embankment on the island and swinging out over the water on the rope swing that hung proudly as it had for years. The water was freezing, with several yelps, gasps and screams being heard as one after another took the plunge into the 51 degree lake. When the afternoon turned into evening, Maren decided that it was probably time to call it a day and slowly headed back toward Hollywood Hills. They were cold, tired and hungry as they docked and emptied her mother's boat. By the time they got back to her mother's home, the only thing on both of their minds was a hot shower and warmer attire.

They pulled into the drive and noted that her mother's truck wasn't parked in its usual spot. Maren immediately drew the conclusion that her mother must still be with Sam, whoever the hell he was. She knew nothing about her mother's new companion, yet she disliked him on principle.

Once they were both done showering and changed into warmer clothing, Alexa joined her girlfriend in the living room where she was met by a serious glare.

"What?" she remarked as Maren sat, cross-armed with a puss on her face.

"What do you mean what?" she said accusingly. "My mother's still not home and is probably with Sam again," she responded, very frustratingly.

"Okay, and?" Alexa said, not quite sure what the issue was.

"What do you mean okay and? My mother is with God knows who, doing God knows what," she exclaimed, soundly truly distraught. But instead of siding with her, Alexa just burst out laughing.

"What?" Maren asked, now very frustrated.

"I'm laughing because you're getting mad because your mom might be getting some and neither of us are, and that's what's pissing you off!"

"Screw you Lexi! That's my mother we're talking about here and she's not supposed to be getting any, period! Oh my God, do you think that's what's she's doing? I cannot think about my mother doing the nasty. I mean, she's a woman and all and she probably has needs just like we all do but she's my mother and I just do not want to think about her doing THAT. You don't think that's why she's not home yet? Oh God, I think I'm going to be sick," she added, wrapping her arms around her waist and bending over.

"Relax Maren, she's pulling into the drive right now."

Jumping up, Maren ran to the window and once she saw with her own eyes that her mother was, in fact, walking toward the house as she looked out, she quickly raced toward the kitchen to meet her mother at the doorway.

Marsha walked in, smiling. "Hey girls, how was the lake?" she asked as she carried in her bag and set it down on the countertop.

"Our day was great mom," Maren offered. "And how was your day with um, Sam?" she asked tentatively.

Not catching her daughter's sarcasm, Marsha smiled. "Oh it was a wonderful day as always. We always have so much fun together," she added, not seeing the scowl on her daughter's face.

"Mom," Maren exploded, "I really don't want to hear about how much fun you and this Sam guy had today. You're my mother for God's sake!"

Still not quite understanding where she was coming from, Marsha looked at her only daughter quizzically. "What is wrong Maren and I don't care how old you are; don't you take that tone with me!"

"I won't. But I also don't want to hear about your sex life mom, or who you're involved with. You're still my mother for Gods' sake! Yes, I want you to be happy and I'm glad you've found somebody, but spare me the details okay?"

The light finally came on and Marsha had everything she could do to not burst out laughing. She would never intentionally insult her daughter but she found it hysterical that her daughter assumed that Sam was a new man in her life. She wasn't quite ready to let her off the hook yet.

"Don't worry Maren, I won't say a word to you about my sex life. But I honestly would like you to meet Sam before you return back to New York. Why don't we plan on going out to dinner tomorrow evening, my treat, and before the evening's over, I'll introduce you to Sam."

Reluctantly, Maren agreed. Alexa saw the glint in Marsha's eye and didn't know what she was up to, but knew that there was more to it, than just dinner and meeting her friend.

They decided to catch a movie at The Strand, and the topic of Marsha and her supposed sex life was dropped.

~Chapter 15~

Saturday morning arrived and Kelsey was up and ready to go before her father had even finished his first cup of coffee for the day. Knowing that he wouldn't be about to contain her excitement for too long, he expedited his morning routine and finished packing their cooler with last minute food provisions. Thanks to his mother, they certainly wouldn't go hungry; she'd made enough to feed half the campground. He called her one last time, to again thank her for covering for him over the weekend, and for the tickets to The Wild Center. Knowing that Kelsey was going to absolutely love their adventure, he finished packing as quickly as he could, locked up and they were on the road before nine. If the traffic wasn't too heavy, they'd be in Long Lake, and walking high about the tree tops before eleven. "Yes, the weekend was turning out to be one that neither was going to ever forget," he thought as he looked at his daughter.

He had no idea just how correct he was.

~Chapter 16~

Maren woke shortly before eight. She silently stretched and rolled over to see if Alexa was stirring yet, only to find an empty bed. Thinking that she'd probably gotten up to use the bathroom, she didn't think anything of it as she rolled over, covering herself with the blankets as she did so. The air was brisk but somehow always smelled so much fresher up in the mountains. Here, she had to admit, there was no smog, no odor that seemed to come up through the streets where she lived, no smell of dirty laundry or decaying food. Here, in her little town, the air just smelled clean. As she waited for Alexa's return, she thought about some of the other ways that living in the city and up here in the mountains differed and she had to admit, both had their advantages and disadvantages. When she realized that Alexa must not be returning to bed, she got up to see where she'd gone off to.

She found her sitting alone in her thoughts, outside on her mother's front porch. She was bundled in one of the many quilts that had lined her single bed. She could see how at home her best friend was by her appearance. Knowing that Alexa wouldn't be caught dead in New York in her current apparel, she sat down on the wicker loveseat next to her.

"Gorgeous here, isn't?" she finally spoke, as she leaned her head down onto her best friend's shoulder. Neither spoke further, just soaked in the sights and sounds from her mother's beat up loveseat, as the birds chirped around them. There were robins everywhere, despite the thirty-degree temperature drop that occurred when the sun set. There were blue jays and cardinals, along with ravens as black at night. Priscilla, one of her mother's cats, sat just inside the door frame, tail flickering and scoping out what would hopefully be her morning meal. They sat, taking it all in, both lost in their own thoughts. Their silence was finally broken with the creaking of the antique screen door, as Marsha came outside, carrying a tray and three coffee mugs, whose contents were steaming hot. She handed one to each of the women and then sat down beside them in the wicker rocking chair, painted fire engine red. They graciously accepted the coffee, and sipped on it eagerly.

"I miss these times the most you know," Marsha finally said.

Not quite getting her drift, Maren was the first to respond. "Mom, you can do this anytime you want. It's not like you're on a time-clock with your artwork you know."

"You're right, I'm not. I can paint anytime I choose to. And that's not what I miss. I miss not having you and Lexi here, sitting on my porch the way you are right now; the way you used to all summer long when you were kids. Do you have any idea how many times I served you young ladies pancakes and bacon from that very same platter that just delivered your coffee? Remember how you used to camp out here on the front porch with your sleeping bags and flashlights so that you could watch for shooting stars? Oh, and I know it had nothing to do with the boys who'd come sneaking over so y'all could go skinny dipping in the pond!"

Seeing her daughter's shocked expression, and Lexi's immediate blushing simply confirmed what she'd known all those years before. Laughing, she continued, "You two thought that I was just some country bumpkin, with a little bit of hippie mixed in, now didn't ya? Well, my dears," she smiled, "believe it or not, I too had a wild streak about me before I became such a reserved, dignified lady."

Both Maren and Lexi burst out laughing at her attempt to curtsy. The three women went back to sipping their morning coffee in relative silence after they'd all laughed so hard that it made their sides hurt. Though no one acknowledged it, all three were thinking about growing up in Old Forge during simpler times, happier times when life was so much easier and much less dramatic. Marsha would never ask her daughter to give up her life in the city, but she'd truly love it if her daughter were to get sick of the hustle and bustle and return back home, especially since there was going to be a vacant teaching position tailor made for her. But, Marsha thought, that was a conversation for another time. She'd take what her daughter offered, and be thankful for their time together.

~Chapter 17~

Luke and Kelsey sang the entire way up Route 28 and 30 through Inlet, Blue Mountain Lake, and finally Long Lake. They turned off the main road by the Health Center, and drove into the Wild Center's parking lot moments later. Luke surveyed the lot and was pleased to see that there were just a handful of people already inside. He'd hardly shut off the engine when his daughter bounded out of the truck.

"Let's go dad! I want to be up in the nest before it gets really, really crowded!" she exclaimed excitedly.

"So let's hurry dad, come on!"

And so, part one of their adventure began!

They spent nearly two hours above the trees, walking, running, and exploring. Kelsey loved the giant eagle's nest, pretending she could fly out of it, nearly scaring her father half to death. Luke, on the other hand, was intrigued by the ingenuity of the spider's web, to which he received one comment from his daughter, "Ew, gross!" It took a little coaxing, and after watching a little girl a few years younger than she was doing it, Kelsey reluctantly climbed out onto the massive spider web dangling high above the ground. Once she made it into the center of the web with her father, she spun onto her back, looking up into the cloudless sky, smiling ear to ear.

"This is so freaking awesome dad!"

"Kels," he scolded gently. "What have I said about using that word?"

"What word? Oh, you mean DAD?" she kidded.

"Kelsey..."

"Alright, alright," she laughed, rolling onto her side. "Sorry, I won't say freaking anymore. Or," she added. "I'll try not to say it anymore, but it just slips out sometime dad."

"I know Kels, we all have things slip out now and then. It's okay, just try not to say it, especially in front of grandma."

"K. Dad," she asked, suddenly turning very serious, "Can I ask you something about mom?"

"Sure Kels, you can always ask me anything about your mom."

She hesitated for just a moment, as if she wasn't sure if she wanted to know the answer or not.

"Dad, is it normal or am I just weird; cause I kind of feel like I'm closer to mom, you know, being way up here near heaven. Do you think she knows I'm closer to her, than when we're on the ground? Do you think she can tell I'm so close that I could almost touch her if she knew I was here?"

Stunned by her question, he swallowed the huge lump in his throat, and then slowly responded.

"Oh Kels, she knows and she's here. Baby," he added, gently brushing he hair from her face, "She's always with you, so yes she knows you're here. You Miss Kelsey were her ray of sunshine, and the light of her life and I know that every day when you wake up, she's there with you and every night when you shut off your light to go to sleep, she's there with you as well. Your mom can't walk on this earth with us anymore, but never forget, she's with you."

"How do you know dad? I mean, I want to believe you, but how do you know for sure?"

"Because I feel her everywhere, Kels. And I just know. She loved you more than anything in this world, and I know she's still watching over you from heaven."

As her father finished his sentence, Kelsey put her hand to her face quickly and gasped so loud that she caught her father's attention.

"What is it Kels? What's wrong?"

She turned toward him, tears flowing from her eyes.

"She's here dad! She's really here with me! Can't you smell her? You were talking, and I suddenly felt tear drops hit my nose and cheek. Look dad," she said, smiling, pointing overhead. "There are NO rainclouds above us. I know that they were tears from mom in heaven! She is here dad, I knew it!"

Trying very hard to contain himself, he smiled, and looked up at the cloudless sky, not quite sure what he expected to see. "Of course she is baby. Let's move off this spider web and enjoy the rest of the park with your mom, okay?"

She smiled and sat up. "Okay. Come on mom," she whispered so that no one would know that she was talking to the air. As they slowly made their way out of the giant spider web, the distinct smell of lilac was everywhere around them.

The finished their adventure by stopping for ice cream in town before continuing toward their final destination. As they sat at the intersection of 30 and 28N, Luke spoke up.

"Remind me to bring you back up this way sometime and we'll take a drive out to Newcomb and the abandoned town of Tahawus."

"Abandoned, like in ghost town?" her eyes lit up at the prospect of a ghost town.

"Yes. I'm not exactly sure how many ghosts there are still lurking around the place. But I do know that the residents of Tahawus simply packed up their belongings and left their homes and whatever was left, behind. It's actually kind of sad Kels. One day the town was up and running and the next, it was essentially deserted. You see, Kels," he said as he continued driving through the little hamlet of Long Lake, "the town began when iron ore was first discovered back in the early 1800's I think. The town was called Tahawus or Adirondak, but not spelled the way we're used to spelling Adirondack. The town dissolved once they realized that they couldn't mine the ore due to impurities that they eventually realized were caused by titanium, but by the time they figured out how to efficiently mine the ore, it was too late for the little town. From what I remember when your mom and I went there, when you were still small enough to be in a baby carrier on my back," he smiled remembering the adventure as if it were yesterday and Ana was still with him, "many of the homes still stand, though it wouldn't be safe to venture inside them. It's actually a really cool place to see; and the Macintyre Furnace that still stands is over 50 feet tall. I remember walking inside the blast furnace, with you on my back, and it was so tall inside it, that I couldn't touch the ceiling. If I remember correctly," he paused, as if trying to access some long forgotten crevasse of his brain, "when the town was up and running in the 1820's, there were 16 homes, a school, a church, a hotel and a store. Now, all that remains is the massive stone furnace and what's left of a few of the homes that remain standing. But I think that it would be cool to explore sometime if you'd like too."

She started laughing out loud, never saying a word, but laughing so hard that she was snorting.

"What?" he asked, questioningly.

Still laughing, she finally responded. "You just sounded like grandpa used to sound. I mean, with the history lesson and all," she continued.

"I used to love it when grandpa would tell me the silliest of facts. It always seemed like useless junk ya know, dad. But I really wish that he was still around to tell me more of those dumb facts. He used to be so proud of me, dad," she sniffled, "when I could remember everything that he told me. He always made me feel so special, so smart. I really miss him."

"I know baby; I miss him too. He loved you with every ounce of his being. And Miss Kelsey Rose, don't you for a minute forget that you are very smart. You just learn things a little differently than some people do. And," he said as he continued driving north, eyes straight ahead. Someday, someone is going to figure out how to help you with your reading difficulties and once he or she does, then you'll read and learn just like everyone else does. It'll happen Kels, I can feel it. It'll happen soon, I promise." Changing the subject, he turned to her when he saw the exit on the left-hand side of the road. "Hey Kels, do you know what that is?" he asked excitedly.

"Um, a campground dad, duh."

"Yes, it is Kelsey. And that happens to be the exit to Fish Creek Campground. So, in a minute you're going to see the campground store on the right and then right after that, we'll be there! I don't know about you, but I can't wait!"

She didn't respond but sat up straighter and looked out her window for the store, and then out the front windshield for the entrance to the park. As soon as it came into view, she nearly jumped off her seat.

"Dad, there it is! We're here, we're finally here."

They turned into the campgrounds, registered, and within minutes, Luke was backing into the forty-foot-wide site that was going to be home for the next three days.

~Chapter 18~

Alexa and Maren spent the day shopping, catching up with friends in town, and just enjoying the relaxing atmosphere. They laughed, talked, made a quick visit to the cemetery, a ritual that both women insisted on, whenever they were in town. Ironically, both of their families' plots were next to one another. They planted flowers and weeded around the headstones as the sun beat down on them.

Finishing up, they found Marsha at home when they returned. They convinced her to join them for another day on the water, to which she eagerly accepted but not before making a few quick calls. The three women enjoyed cruising and tanning in the unseasonably hot sun. Marsha convinced the girls that she'd like to take them out to dinner in the evening, in order for them to meet Sam. Alexa was all for it, while Maren took a little more persuading. Once in clean, more appropriate attire for going out, they set off in Marsha's truck toward town. Maren remained very reserved, which was very uncommon for her; while Alexa talked the entire way to the restaurant, trying to pry more information about Sam. Marsha just laughed and remained tight- lipped as she drove into the center of town. It wasn't until they pulled into the parking lot beside the Black Bear Bistro that Maren spoke.

"Is this where we're meeting your friend, mom? Lexi and I were in here the other night and the menu looked really good. What time is he meeting us?"

Smiling, Marsha continued to string her along; at least for just a little bit longer. "Oh, I bet Sam's already inside, and expecting us." They entered from the rear of the building and made their way towards the front and the greeter. Surprised that the young girl knew her mother's name, she quickly surmised that this Sam fellow and her mother must frequent the establishment a lot. They were seated and much to both Maren and Alexa's surprise, not only was Marsha's date nowhere to be found, but the greeter who seated them had only provided three menus. Thinking that her mother and Sam must be serious enough to have her mother order for him, or they were going to share the menu once he decided to show up; either way, Maren found herself getting irritated and quite frankly, bitchy. She didn't realize it until that very moment, that while she wanted her mother to be happy and not have to continue going through life alone, she wasn't quite sure how she felt about her mother being involved with a man at this stage of her life. Trying to restrain herself from saying what was on the tip of her tongue, she simply stared at the menu as if there was going to be a test later.

"Wow, the poached salmon sounds wonderful. Have you ever had it here Marsha?" Alexa asked, breaking the silence.

"Oh yes, it's wonderful. They have it flown in from Alaska this time of year and it's about as fresh as it could possibly be. Have it with their wild rice and you'll be in heaven," she added. "I'm going to have their brisket. I worked hard this morning and burnt a lot of calories so I'm going to indulge myself in not only their amazing brisket but also their mashed potatoes and gravy."

Nearing slamming her menu down, Maren glared at her mother. "Burnt a lot of calories. Seriously mother, do you honestly think that I need to hear about how you and Sam worked up a sweat enough to burn a lot of calories. Really?" she continued, with a look is disgust on her face.

Remaining calm, Marsha simply looked up and responded. "Here's Sam now. She stood up and hugged her best friend and confidante. With her arm still around Sam, she smiled.

"Sam, I'd like you to meet my beautiful daughter Maren and her best friend, who's equally as beautiful," she winked at Alexa, who was staring at the matronly looking woman in front of her. Her blonde hair was a sharp contrast to the sleeveless jet black knit top and black dress slacks. She wore simple silver hoops and several silver and bronze bangle bracelets on her right arm which jangled when she lifted her arm to welcome them. Alexa noticed that she wore minimal makeup except for a hint of green eyeliner and shadow which accentuated her cat green eyes even more than they already were. Alexa guessed her to be approximately the same age as Maren's mother, give or take a few years and from the look of her biceps, she was in very good physical shape. Alexa was the first to comprehend that Sam was in fact, a woman. She stood and put out her hand in welcome.

"It's very nice to meet you Sam, and I assume Sam is short for Samantha?" she added as she smiled.

"Oh yes, Samantha Gene and it's very nice to meet you both," she said, looking at Maren, who still remained silent.

Collecting her words, Maren looked back and forth from her mother to her "date" and burst out laughing. "You're a girl!" she exclaimed, smiling. "And unless mom has changed more than I realized, you're just her friend, not her lover! Look Lexi, she's a girl!"

"I assure you Maren, your mother is still very much heterosexual. And yes, she is not only my friend, but my best friend and confidante and she's obviously told me much more about you, than she's told you about me," she laughed, still seeing the slightly confused look on Maren's face. "But I can assure you that I have never, do I ever have, any desire to be your mom's lover," she teased a little more with Marsha laughing as well.

"You honestly thought that when I mentioned Sam, that Sam was a man and my lover? Seriously, Maren, I have told you how many times, my only lover was your father and I'll never have another. So now that we've got this silliness over with, let's order and enjoy our meal and then we'll head over to the bar and join Sam. Sam is the owner of this fine establishment and will be our bartender for the evening."

Instantly both Maren and Alexa looked toward the bar, realizing that the hunk of a bartender they'd met earlier in the week wasn't behind the bar. Refusing to show disappointment, Alexa smiled and looked up at Samantha who was still standing beside Marsha.

"You must be really proud Samantha. You have a really nice bar and restaurant here. I love the name and the ambiance is very inviting. How did you come up with such a fun name?" she asked.

"Oh," she chuckled. "My son actually came up with the name when we first moved to Old Forge. After he kept encountering the same black bear every time that he went for a run in the morning. At the time, he was quite terrified of bears, but eventually after encountering the same one time and time again, he still is leery of them, but has developed an appreciation and respect for the big teddy bears that we have up here. So long story short, when we decided to open the bistro, it was his daughter who said that we should name it after his morning companion. Hey, look, I'd better get back to the bar before the patrons get testy. Enjoy your meal and head on over to my side of the restaurant when you've finished. We have a great folk rock band playing this evening and I'll save you three seats."

And just as quickly as she'd blown in, she was gone.

Maren turned to her mother with not only an attitude but a look of embarrassment. "You're so proud of yourself, aren't you mother? Leading me to believe that Sam was a guy and you, well, you know. All this time, Sam is actually Samantha and a girl. Good job mom," she laughed. "Here I was thinking I was about to meet a potential step dad, and he's a she!"

Remaining calm and monotone, Marsha responded as the waitress approached to take their order.

"I never once said that Sam was a guy. Any assumptions are on you my dear," she smirked.

They ordered their entrees and within moments, were enjoying a warm loaf of French Bread and their salads. They made small talk about life in the city, the children in their respective classes, with Marsha filling them in on what had changed and what was new in town. After what seemed like just a few moments, their meals arrived and everyone dove in. No one was disappointed in their meal choice and after paying their bill, they made their way over to the bar, just as the trio starting playing their first number. As promised, Sam had three bar stools waiting for them. They ordered another round of drinks and made themselves comfortable in the oversized chairs, with Alexa once again commenting how much she loved them. Samantha explained that her son had actually spotted them in New York in a café, and once he found out who the manufacturer was, ordered them for the bar the same day. She went on to say that he'd commented on how they seemed to welcome a person in and make them feel at home, a sentiment shared by Alexa and everyone who'd ever sat in them.

The band played their first set with everyone just enjoying the music, atmosphere and the alcohol. Once they took a quick break and the room was quieter, Sam approached them to check on refills. Maren, who was beginning to really feel the effects of her Dirty Martini's, was the first to speak.

"Hey Sam," she said, only slightly inebriated, when Lexi and I were in here the other night, there was a hunk of a man bartending. I think he said he name was Larry or Luke or something like that. Where's he tonight?"

"Doesn't matter where he is Maren, he's married, remember," Alexa responded, in a hushed tone.

After bartending most of her life, Samantha had become a near professional at reading lips and had understood every word that Lexi had said to her best friend. Smiling to herself, and thinking for just one fleeting moment how perfect Alexa would be for her son, she answered.

"Oh Luke, he's off tonight. He took his little girl camping up near Lake Placid." Glaring at Marsha in order to keep her silent, she continued. "He works here full time but I'm covering for him so that they could have a special father-daughter camping trip. He's a great father, but his work schedule doesn't allow him much time to get away with her. She's 10, closing in on 11, and the cutest thing ever."

Alexa spoke first. "Camping, that's really sweet. I used to love camping when I was a kid, and some of my fondest childhood memories were of camping at a place called Fish Creek and Rollins Pond. Remember Maren, you used to come with us all the time?"

Before Maren could process what Alexa had said and respond accordingly, Samantha answered.

"How ironic! That's where Luke is camping right now! Small world isn't it?"

"Yes, very," Marsha answered. "Hey Sam, you never finished telling me at lunch today how the school board concluded? Did they actually accept all of those resignations from the teachers? I mean, I realize that half of them are as ancient as some of the fossils found in the ADK Museum, but how can the board allow so many to retire all at once? How will they replace all of them by August?" she asked, trying to plant the seed but not be too forward. Her attempt at subtlety failed miserably.

"Mom," Maren said, in a low whisper, still smiling, "I'm not moving back here so don't waste your breath. I like living in the city and Lexi and I are very content right where we are, right Lexi?" she asked, for reinforcement.

"Yes, we are," Lexi answered in agreement, but definitely with less enthusiasm. "Out of curiosity, why are so many retiring this summer and what grade levels will be affected?"

"Who cares Lexi! It doesn't matter nor pertain to us, so let it go. Let's talk about something more interesting, like, is Luke single?" Maren asked.

She heard her question, but refused to be pulled into that particular conversation. Sam didn't directly answer but responded honestly without providing much detail.

"Luke married Anastasia when they were only 18, and besides his wife, their daughter Kels is the love of his life." Samantha had purposely phrased her statement avoid disclosing her son's marital status. Instead she chose to address Marsha's question.

"At least three of the teachers are at the elementary level. I know for sure that we are losing one 4th grade and one 5th grade teacher," she added casually as she put shot glasses in front of the three of them.

"Here we go ladies, I think we all need to be meet Mr. Fireball up close and personal," she laughed as she poured four shots and lifted hers up in salute.

"To old friends and new, and to new adventures for all. Salute!" Following her lead, the others lifted their shot glasses in salute. They downed their shots, each enjoying the burn. Sam poured another round and this time, it was Marsha who made the toast.

"To my gorgeous daughter and her best friend; may your life's paths always bring you happiness, fulfillment and joy. And always remember that if something doesn't bring you pleasure and a sense of contentment, then you're just wasting your time. And time is too precious a commodity to waste. Love you both to pieces and will miss you before you're even gone! Salute."

Hearing the sincerity in her words, Alexa smiled warmly. "This will always be home Marsha. You know that. And I for one, know that if life's journey doesn't bring me in the direction that I want it to go, this will always be home, and I'll always know my way back home," she smiled warmly.

Samantha stood back, allowing the interaction between the women to continue. After a few minutes, she added her opinion of the town.

"My son and I moved here after we lost someone very special in our lives," Samantha said. "And from the first day that we planted roots in this town, this felt like home. We knew only a handful of people, yet we were greeted by strangers and welcomed into the community. This town embodies what the world needs more of. The townsfolk here would give you the shirt off their back, argue with you like family, and will do anything for you or simply give you space if you need it. Yes, the tourist industry is what helps keep this town alive but whether it's a full time resident, summer person or simply a tourist spending a week or two in our little hamlet, each becomes part of the fabric of our community. I couldn't imagine living or running my Bistro anywhere else," she added.

They dropped the subject and they continued chatting about more neutral subjects with everyone weighing in with their opinions. Alexa participated in many of the heated subjects, never afraid to offer her opinion; but continuously her mind kept circling back to what Samantha had said about her home town. She wasn't exactly sure how long Samantha and her son had resided there, though she presumed less than four years since the Bistro had only been open that long. Yet Sam seemed to understand the town better than most who had lived there all their lives.

"Yes," she thought silently, "there were far worse places to live than Old Forge," and at that moment, sitting on the high-back chair, looking down at the stamped tin bar, she made her decision. She was coming home.

The rest of the night became a blur. Maren, her mother and Alexa laughed, sang and danced the night away. They caught up with old friends and made new ones, got a little crazy when they took the band's challenge and got up on stage and sang Pat Benatar's "Hit Me With Your Best Shot" and helped Samantha close up after last call. Marsha had stopped drinking long before the girls did and she laughed as they piled into her truck. Neither was completely smashed but both were feeling the effects of the evening. They sang the entire way home and as Marsha wished them both pleasant dreams, both gave her a big hug and kissed her good night. It was Maren's one sentence that brought tears to her eyes and the reason she'd stay up half the night praying to Saint Michael.

"I love you mom and who knows, maybe someday I'll come back home for good after all."

The rest of the holiday weekend flew by. Monday morning arrived before anyone was ready to accept the fact that they had to made the arduous drive back toward the city. Maren knew that they needed to head out early to avoid majority of the holiday traffic, and while Marsha and Alexa knew that she was right, neither was quite ready to say their good-byes.

Alexa had phoned her parents on Sunday afternoon and spoken with them in private for several minutes before Maren walked into the room. Alexa then abruptly ended the conversation, telling them that she'd call them once back in her apartment Monday afternoon or evening. Maren had thought that it was peculiar but didn't read too much into it. They packed the few items that they'd brought with them in silence after breakfast, with Alexa finally breaking the silence.

"Maren, I have to tell you," she said, as she stuffed the last of her clothing into her Victoria Secret overnight bag. "I've been thinking about it, and just for kicks, I might at least look into the upcoming open teaching positions up here. I mean, it's not like I HAVE to move back this way, but you know, without Bradford to think about anymore, and the fact that I'm not fully tenured yet, and the ridiculous amount of money that it costs us every month just to live near the city; I was thinking that it wouldn't hurt to at least think about the possibility of teaching somewhere else."

Maren didn't respond for what seemed like eternity. Alexa valued her best friend's opinion and would welcome any advice that she had. But at the moment, she was holding her breath in anticipation for what she expected her reaction was going to be. Instead, Maren neatly folded the sweater currently in her hand, and placed it gently in her bag before responding. Alexa thought that it was as if she were formulating the correct response before opening her mouth.

"Sounds like you've been giving this a lot of thought," she stated, showing no emotion in her voice.

"Actually, yes I have. I mean, I thought I'd at least look into what the position entailed, what the pay scale would be, and then weigh my options. That was part of the conversation that I was having with mom on the phone. I mean, with Molly moving out, and our home sitting vacant; I thought that maybe now would be a good time to try something new, something that I would never have considered five or six years ago. I love it up here in the mountains Maren. I know we all complained about living in a small town while we were growing up but I absolutely loved living here as a kid and maybe at this stage in my life, this is what I've been looking for. You know, a sense of home. Maybe I just need to sever all ties with the city, and the crazy pace that we live with there. I don't know, maybe I just really need a fresh start after Bradford. Either way, I'm at least going to look into the position and go from there. If it pans out, mom and dad want me to move into their bungalow so it doesn't sit vacant. And they insist that their mortgage is paid in full so I'd only have to pay for the heating cost and cable. Mom even mentioned that maybe you'd come back and move in with me since it's a big house for just one person," she added, smiling.

"Lexi, you never adapted to city life the way that I did. I love living with all the noise, the hustle and confusion, and the insanity. I could never move back here, but if it's what you think you need to do, then I'll miss you terribly but I'll also support you 100%. You're my best friend and I want you to be happy, that simple."

"Ah, thanks, Maren," embracing her. "I really think it might be exactly what I need. And I'm so glad you understand. If I actually do this, then you'll have two places to bounce back and forth between when you come home to visit. I'll even let you decorate one of the bedrooms anyway you'd like so it's truly yours whenever you're in town," she added for good measure.

"Let's not get carried away, Lexi," she joked. "I said I'd support you and I'd come to visit but I don't need a bedroom with my name on the door quite yet. Come on," she said, lifting her bag onto her shoulder, "it's time to hit the road and start heading south."

They said their tearful good-byes to Maren's mom and pulled out of the driveway just before 11. Alexa sat quietly in the passenger's seat and looked at building after building, business after business as they passed through town. It was as if she were looking at them for the first time. Many of the brick buildings had stood the test of time, through the depression, through wars, the recession and the good years when businesses prospered. They lined main street on both sides of the road and were a testament to the resilience of both the town and the towns' people.

"And there," Alexa thought, "there was the big red school that had been her alma mater, a place she loved and loathed at times. It was a place where she'd been challenged and pushed by her teachers, but only pushed because they'd seen her potential, even when she hadn't. She stared at it as Maren drove by as quickly as the traffic allowed.

"Maybe I was wrong all those years ago," she thought to herself. "Maybe I will set foot back inside that building again, after all."

Surprisingly, the trip downstate took less time than either had anticipated. They talked, ate and sang their way nearly to Poughkeepsie and before they knew it, Maren was dropping Alexa off, reminding her to bring her gym bag for their class in the morning. As Alexa entered the townhouse that had served as home for several years now, she looked around and couldn't help but find herself critical of everything about it. Funny, she thought to herself as she set her bag down and glanced around. The place had always suited her needs, but now as she gazed around, it just felt sterile and boring. During the ride home, in her mind, she was already decorating and remodeling her childhood home. Realizing that maybe she was getting very ahead of herself, she tried to push Old Forge out of her head and focus on unpacking, laundry and tending to the stack of mail on her counter.

~Chapter 19~

Kelsey had been a trooper. She never complained once during the entire camping trip that she and her father experienced together. The Wild Center had been a huge hit, and they were fortunate enough to get their tent set up before the deluge started. Though it hadn't been a total wash out, Luke and his daughter had discovered many things about camping together, in a tent, in the rain, for three days and nights. Luckily, he had the foresight to bring a 10 x 10 easy up screen house, that at least gave them an area in which to sit and eat, that was out of the elements. He'd taken every tarp that wasn't needed to keep his tent from leaking, and rigged them to his canopy to provide some protection, at least on two sides from the wind and on occasion, rain that came down sideways. They'd played more games of rummy and go fish than he cared to remember, and both had read every magazine and book that they'd brought with them. When it felt as if the walls of the tent were closing in on them, they had thrown on raingear and had gone fishing, which Kelsey had absolutely loved; almost as much as she'd enjoyed the hot shower afterward. They'd spent part of Sunday afternoon in Lake Placid and when the sun came out briefly, they took the opportunity to visit Whiteface Mountain, with Kelsey insisting that they climb the last stretch to the summit, despite the ominous looking clouds overhead. All in all, both he and his daughter had enjoyed their first official camping trip together without Ana. Despite the weather, he felt that, thanks in part to his mother's wonderful pre-made dishes, the overall trip had been a huge success. Kelsey talked about their adventures the entire way home, and made him promise that they'd make it an annual Memorial Day tradition, to which he reluctantly agreed. As he pulled into his drive roughly two hours after leaving the campground, all he could think about was a long hot shower, and an even hotter cup of coffee from his Keurig. Knowing that his mother either had ESP or an uncanny knack for knowing when he was home, he wasn't at all surprised to see her pull into the drive just as he carried the rain soaked tent into the garage. She filled him in on the weekend's business, and current events that he'd missed while out of touch. She'd simply smiled, with an occasional giggle escaping her mouth while she listened to his commentary of their camping trip. Just when she was about to head into his home in search of her granddaughter, Kelsey came bounding into the garage looking for her father.

"Oh hey Grandma! Did dad tell you about how much fun we had camping? It was awesome Grandma, and next time you've got to come with us okay? We had so much fun! It was really cool sleeping in a tent, and dad said that once it dries out, cause it's really wet right now; we can put it up in the backyard and I can have my friends over and we can have sleepovers in it this summer. Maybe you can come over and sleep in it with me," she added.

"Well it sounds like you had quite the adventure there, Kels! How about you and your dad come over this evening and tell me all about it over supper okay? I've made your favorite," she teased.

"Lemon meringue pie?" she asked, suddenly very excited all over again.

"Yup. And I might have gotten around to making Chicken Francoise as well," she added, knowing that it was her granddaughter's favorite.

"Yes! We can go right, dad?" she asked excitedly.

"Yes, we can go. As long as I can sit my tired ass, oops, I mean butt, in a chair and relax for at least a few minutes first. And I think we need to give some serious thought to starting a couple loads of laundry. I think everything that we brought back is either soaking wet or covered in mud or sand, or both!" he added, laughing. "Kels, I left all of the clothes on the floor in the mud room. Do you think you could run in and start the load so I can have a minute with your grandma?"

"Sure dad. I'll see you soon, grandma. Don't start eating the pie without me," she shouted back as she ran out of the garage and into the mud room.

Turning back toward her son, Samantha saw not only the fatigue but the sadness in her son's eyes. Knowing that the rain was not the reason, her heart ached for her eldest son.

"Sounds like Kelsey thoroughly enjoyed herself, despite the weather," she gently started. "Was it hard for you Lucas? I mean, being there knowing that the last time you camped there was with Ana?"

"It wasn't that it was hard mom," he confided. "It's just that I felt her everywhere. We were up in the clouds at the Wild Center, which by the way was a major hit with your granddaughter; and Kels asked me if her mother was closer since we were up in the sky closer to heaven. It just sucks sometimes mom. My daughter is growing up and she needs her mother, and I still need her too," he added, in barely a whisper. "I still miss her so much, and sometimes I swear that I can feel her with me."

"I know Luke. You've had enough sadness to last a lifetime, that's true. But you've also been given the greatest gift so instead of dwelling on the past and something that you can't alter or change; maybe it's time to start thinking about the future. You're right, Kelsey is getting to the age where she's going to need the influence of a mother. She's going to need someone in her life daily to confide in, someone to talk about boys to, and your daughter will need a woman around when her body starts changing more than it already is, if you get my drift."

Color draining from his face, he stopped mid stride and looked at his mother. "She has you mom. Developing?

Seriously, I swear I hadn't noticed. She's only ten. She can't possibly be getting ready for her, Oh God mom. I can't do this on my own."

"You most certainly can do it! I don't want to hear that sentence or attitude again! But being able to and having to are two different things. I don't expect you to ever forget your Ana, but she's been gone a long time and it's time that you and Kelsey consider having a woman enter your life. I'm not saying marry the first one you meet; I'm saying keep an open mind. That way, if someday, somewhere, someone special enters your life, you'll be open to the possibility of finding happiness again."

"Not gonna happen mom. I've got all the women I need in my life, with you and Kelsey. But you're right. Ana's been gone a long time, even though it still feels like yesterday. It's not that I'm not open to finding someone mom. It's just that living in a small town like this, there's not exactly an overabundance of single women. And of that group, how many of them would be interested in dating a single father? Besides, I'm not going to grab the first woman who looks my way just so that Kelsey can have a female influence. We're a package deal and if someday I meet someone, she has to love Kelsey as much as I do, or it won't go anywhere; that simple."

"Oh honey, I couldn't agree with you more," she said, putting her arm around her son as they made their way inside. "Don't give up hope. I firmly believe that someone is out there who would be perfect for both you and Kelsey. It's just a matter of time before she walks into your life."

~Chapter 20~

"I can't believe the school year is over with already, and you're leaving next week," Maren said, over the humming noise emitting from her elliptical as she and Alexa worked out.

"Mar, you know that I needed a change and I think that the timing was right for me. I just wish that you'd considered applying for one of the vacancies. But I understand," she added sincerely, "You adapted to the city far quicker and better than I did. Guess I'm more of a country girl than you," she laughed. "But you'll be up for the fourth in less than two weeks and hopefully by then, I'll be somewhat settled in the house and we'll catch up, and go boating and hiking, just like we always have during the summer. You'll see, it'll be as if nothing's changed."

"Stop kidding yourself Lexi, you're moving back to Old Forge and I'll be down here alone. Molly's gone, Frank is ancient history and now you. Maybe I should have snatched that teaching position out from under you so you'd be forced to stay here," she chuckled. "You don't even like teaching 5th grade because you told me that the girls all start getting too hormonal at that age. Remember when we were kids, none of that stuff started until 6th or 7th grade? Now these poor kids are getting their periods and wearing bras, and make up for that matter, by the time they reach junior high. I kind of feel sorry for them you know. You sure you're ready for that drama my friend," she teased, knowing full well that her best friend could probably handle any dilemma that was thrown at her.

They finished their workout and went into the locker room to gather up their belongings before heading home. Both remained quiet as they walked toward their vehicles.

"Hey Mar, why don't you come over tonight for a late dinner. We can order take out, I was thinking maybe Chinese if that sounds good, and we'll drink one of the bottles of wine I was given at my going away party. Okay?"

Resigned to the fact that nothing was going to change her best friend's opinion, Maren smiled and responded.

"Sure, that sounds great, Alexa. You want your usual? I can pick it up on my way over. What time works for you?"

"Around 7?

"Yeah, sure. I'll see you tonight around 7, Alexa."

"Great, see you then." Alexa had been so preoccupied, focusing on how she could make her apartment look more presentable; that she hadn't heard the sadness in her best friend's voice. She'd already packed three quarters of her belongings in boxes, and had them labeled and stacked in the living room. At least she'd only filled half of the room, and had the foresight to pile them neatly. Her kitchen was down to only having a few bare essentials at her disposal for cooking, and she had been relying on take out and freezer dinners for days now. She was very excited about her new teaching opportunity, and when the school had not only met her salary requirement, but allowed her to carryover her years of teaching experience to their school and have it count towards her tenure, once her probationary period was up, it was a no-brainer decision. Her best friend had been right, she definitely preferred teaching fourth grade over fifth but she'd adjust. After all, it was just a one-year difference and it wasn't as if she were going from teaching kindergarten to junior high.

She got home, dumped her bag on her bed and set about organizing for her impromptu company. When she finally sat down with her first glass of wine of the evening, she opened up Facebook on her phone and started perusing the postings, killing time before Maren arrived. Two minutes into surfing through the various posts that included recipes, endless pictures of her friend's children and pets, self-help quote after quote and other topics that didn't necessarily peak her interest, she came to a post that not only caught her attention but nearly made her spit out her wine. There, in bright color, lighting up her phone was Bradford and his new fiancée, who happened to be none other than Brittany, his former girlfriend. All smiles with their porcelain veneers, they looked like the perfect WASP couple, color matching shirts and all. She didn't know why it mattered to her, but she couldn't help herself. She slowly clicked onto each picture of the smiling couple, their smiling families and friend's reactions and lastly, a ring with enough bling to light up the Empire State Building. There on the future Mrs. Pendington's finger was a marquise cut diamond that had to weigh in at four or quite possibly five carats, or more. The baguettes on each side added to the overall glitz and in Alexa's opinion, must also have added another couple carats to the already overpowering ring. If Bradford had been going for flash, she thought to herself; then he definitely accomplished his mission. She stared at the ring for just another second or two. Briefly, just briefly, she thought about what a ring of that caliber would look like on her finger. As quickly as she allowed the thought to enter her mind, she pushed it right back out again. She thought the ring was not only gaudy but ostentatious and not at all what she would want. She allowed herself to think about what cut of diamond she would have wanted, if she had said yes to Bradford, or anyone else for that matter. There, sitting on her couch, looking down at her fingers, she decided that someday, if ever given the opportunity again, she would prefer an emerald cut chocolate colored diamond. Not too big, like the one Brittany was currently drooling over in the pictures, just big enough to know it was there, located on a certain finger. But right now, that was a pipe dream and nothing more. In less than a week, she'd be leaving the life that she'd known, to start another chapter in another area. She was going home and going there solo.

~Chapter 21~

Truck and U-haul trailer loaded, Alexa looked around at her friends that remained outside her now vacant apartment. Maren was standing next to her, forming an unconscious alliance with her best friend. Alexa promised to come back down and visit often, but everyone standing in attendance knew that that wouldn't happen. They had all accepted the fact that their friend was returning to her roots and putting her life in the city behind her. When everything was said except the good-byes, Alexa took a deep breath, hugged her friends, former co-workers and lastly Maren. She looked at her street, and the building that had been home for nearly seven years, and with that, got into her truck and waved one last time before putting it into drive and heading toward her new life. As she drove down her one-way street for the last time, she didn't second guess herself, didn't feel sadness, and never looked back.

She made surprisingly good time as she made her way north. She had texted her mother from a rest area and told her approximately what time she expected to make it to Old Forge. When she initially told her parents that she'd accepted the teaching position, they'd been ecstatic for her, and supported her decision to move back to Old Forge whole heartedly. They'd insisted on making the drive up from South Carolina to help her get settled. What she didn't know, was that they'd elicited the help of her brothers to meet them at the homestead a few days in advance of her arrival. They'd stripped the hideous wallpaper that the tenants had put up sometime in the span of the last ten years. They meticulously restored the bannister, crown molding and window trim back to its' original natural wood, scrubbed layer upon layer of grease, grit and dirt from every cupboard and countertop and lastly, painted every room a pale cream color, giving Alexa a clean slate in which to start. Unbeknownst to her, was the fact that not only her parents, but her brothers would be there waiting for her arrival and the start of her new journey.

    She made her way cautiously through town, with trailer in tow. She had become comfortable towing it on the wide highways and the Thruway, but it made her slightly uncomfortable as she navigated her way through the car lined streets of town. Once she rounded the bend by Souvenir Village and made her way toward Water Safari, she felt almost home free, knowing that she was almost there. Turning onto her road, she finally took a deep breath, which up until that point, she had had no idea she was holding. She proceeded slowly, trying to familiarize herself with each home, and who lived in them now. It was funny how she'd grown up on this very same street, yet it was if she were seeing each home for the first time. She registered each to memory and as her little bungalow came into view, so did the commotion in front of it. She recognized her parent's Subaru, but the two black trucks were unfamiliar to her. As she pulled up beside what she believed to be her parents fifth or sixth Subaru they had owned, she saw the front screen door fling open and her mother practically spring out to greet her.

"My baby is home! Well would you look at you and how wonderful you look!" Alexa couldn't help but laugh at the southern twang that she detected in her mother's voice. They'd only been living down south for just about a decade, yet from listening to her speak, most people would have thought her to be a native. She got out of her truck, trying to comprehend what was going on around her. Upon seeing her father and brothers exiting the front door behind her mother, it took her only a second to figure out why everyone was there. Knowing her parent's eclectic taste, she prayed that they hadn't done anything that she couldn't undo. Smiling, she walked towards the front porch, bounded up the stairs and into the warm embrace of family. After what seemed like eternity, they finally let go of their only daughter and everyone entered the living room for what was about to become Alexa's home for the second time in her life.

She was given the grand tour by her mother as the men finished picking up the last of the paint cans, stains and brushes. Once all were carried to the basement and the last broom, mop and dustpan was out of sight, they set about helping Alexa unload her very full U-Haul, refusing to take no for an answer. Very physically fit and still full of energy, her brothers and father had the entire contents of the trailer unloaded in no time. Marsha, Maren's mother had stopped in just to say hello and welcomed Alexa home with a huge tray of homemade Italian cookies, and a massive tray of lasagna and garlic bread to serve as the evening's meal. She stayed only a few minutes and upon leaving, added that she could only take credit for the cookies. The gelato, and main meal had come from The Black Bear Bistro, she added as she left as quickly as she had breezed in.

The rest of the weekend flew by, with Alexa finding herself saddened to see her brothers depart and go off their separate ways, followed by her parents. She hadn't expected them to do the amount of work that they had to make her new residence home. Her mother had insisted that while they had the help, they should paint. Before her family left to return to their respective homes, not only did her bathroom have a new coat of yellow paint the color of a sunflower, but her living room, dining room and kitchen also had a face-lift. She'd chosen warm earth tones to compliment the dark mahogany colored stain that enveloped her windows and crown molding. Her floors had been stripped, sanded and polyurethane applied to bring out the natural color of the hickory wood, and they had turned out beautifully. She looked around at what they had accomplished and Alexa realized for the hundredth time that weekend, how truly blessed she was to be part of such a wonderful and supportive family. She walked room to room once she was alone and took in the feel of each area. She purposely hadn't painted the bedrooms or the master bath yet because she felt that she needed to live in the house again to get a vibe for the color palate of the most intimate rooms. The house seemed so quiet now that her family was gone. Actually, everything seemed so quiet now that she no longer lived within the confinement of the city. She knew that if she needed noise and commotion, she only had to venture out to the end of her street and she would find it; but for now, she was simply enjoying the lack of any form of stimulus whatsoever. She realized that sleeping in pure silence in the evening might be another story since she'd lived with sensory overload for the last ten years of her life.

Luckily, she'd been wrong. She found herself sleeping better in her wrought iron bed than she'd ever slept back in the city. She loved hearing nothing but the crickets, and an occasional loon or coyote. She loved being able to sleep with her windows open, with no fear of anyone breaking in. Even though the crime rate was virtually nonexistent in the little hamlet of Old Forge, Alexa still erred on the side of caution, locking both her truck and her doors at night. After the third night in her home, she decided that once she got settled into her new classroom and made sure that her move was, in fact, the right decision and a permanent one, she'd visit the Humane Society back in Utica and pick out a companion. She knew that a cat would be the easiest choice and less responsibility than a dog, but she already had her heart set on a dog. Nothing too big, or too small; just a puppy or grown dog who needed love. But adopting a dog would have to wait until another time.

~Chapter 22~

Alexa found herself getting reacquainted with the area, and found it very enjoyable running into old friends and classmates alike. She had bumped into Molly at the grocery store, who was pushing a very full cart with two twins in it. Jason was nowhere to be found and Molly looked exhausted and ready to have the baby at any second. Alexa chatted with her during the remainder of her shopping, pushing her own cart aside so that she could push Molly's. When it came time for checkout, she insisted on helping her former close friend out to her truck to not only load up the boys, but the numerous grocery bags that were brimming over the cart as she pushed it across the lot. The parking lot was very busy with out of towners and local residents alike.

"Here, let me help with those," a voice from behind her said, as she was trying to juggle two bags at a time. Before she had time to respond, she felt both bags being removed from her arms and hoisted into the rear of Molly's truck. Molly was on the passenger's side of the truck attempting to strap two rambunctious boys into their car seats and hadn't noticed the truck beside her. Alexa didn't argue with the man who'd come to her aid, and since he had what she assumed to be his daughter with him, she didn't question his motive either. When they were all done loading up the last of Molly's grocery, she turned once again to thank the stranger and his daughter, who'd pitched in to help.

"Oh hey, Luke," Molly yelled. "Hi Kels, you enjoying your summer vacation?"

"Yes, but it's July already and we'll be stuck going back to school in two months." Changing the subject, Kelsey eyed Molly's very rotund belly and asked as only a child would do. "You're like really big! Are you going to have that baby soon?"

Shocked by her very accurate observation and subsequent statement, Luke informed his daughter that asking someone that type of question wasn't appropriate, to which Kelsey responded, "Dad, if I was that big, I'd want someone to ask me when I was going to be skinny again. Molly's belly is huge!"

Both Alexa and Molly couldn't help it, and burst out laughing, only making Luke more embarrassed by his daughter's remarks. Molly quickly introduced the two of them and got into her truck with two very impatient boys and headed home. Alexa followed both Kelsey and her father back into the store so that she could resume her shopping, but not before her new acquaintance commented.

"That was a nice thing you did back there. I'm not too sure how much assistance my friend gets at home, so you were very kind to help her out."

"So were you," she responded as they walked into the store and went their separate ways. He watched her turn left while he and his daughter entered to the right. For some reason, she had familiar eyes, sad eyes. He wasn't sure what there was about them; maybe it was the deep green hue or the way she'd made direct eye contact with him, but he knew that she had a story to tell. Shame that he hadn't had another minute to quiz Molly after they'd loaded up her truck. "Oh well," he thought to himself, as he and Kels started their dreaded shopping odyssey.

    The days flew by and Alexa spent her time biking around town, rearranging a few of her rooms, and tons of yardwork. She hadn't realized how overgrown the yard truly was until she was standing there, surrounded by weeds, downed branches and meadow mole holes throughout the rear yard. She worked daily on the mess, until either her back ached too much to stand up straight or her blisters grew additional blisters. But by the time Friday rolled around and Maren was supposed to arrive for the holiday weekend, she'd not only cleaned up the mess, but planted flowers in the shadow boxes out front, put down mulch, reseeded the yard, and removed all of the debris and rubbish from the yard and surrounding area.

Maren's mother had swung by twice, unannounced and unexpected to check in on her progress and to offer her assistance. On both occasions, she had invited Alexa out to lunch, which she had politely declined, citing that she wanted to get her yard cleaned up prior to her best friend's arrival. So, Marsha decided after a second day of rejection, that if she couldn't get Maren to the bistro; then she'd bring the bistro to her. She casually asked what time she expected Maren to arrive and then proceeded to order take out for the three of them.

Maren arrived very close to her expected time-frame and after settling in, the three women enjoyed a bottle of Pinot Noir, appetizers and entrees from The Triple B that Marsha had the foresight to order. She'd hoped that Luke would deliver the feast but realized that he must be either swamped at work or possibly off that day. Either way, she had conspired with Samantha and between the two women, they knew what was meant to be and what they needed to do to achieve their objective. Both women knew that they shouldn't meddle, but both felt compelled to do so anyway. Marsha wanted her daughter to find happiness as well, but trying to play match maker when her child lived in another part of the state was even too much of an undertaking for her, so she'd do what she could to help Alexa.

Saturday was filled with sleeping in, their obligatory run, and simply catching up. Maren hadn't realized how much she'd actually missed her best friend until Alexa had pulled away and not returned. Gone were the days when she could simply stop in unexpected to share a pizza with her best friend, or vent about a disastrous date, bitch about work or sweat at the gym together. As she looked around, she saw that not only had Alexa settled in nicely to her new surroundings, but it appeared as if she had already completely forgotten about the life she left behind in New York. She had to admit it, her best friend belonged back in their home town, and was not destined to be a city girl after all.

After lounging around most of the morning, the girls decided to take Marsha's boat out for the afternoon. Marsha met them at the dock and after helping them load up their cooler, towels and bags, she politely declined joining them.

"Thanks girls but Sam and I are in a golf tournament that starts in an hour or so. You two go out and have a great time. But remember, be back in time for the four of us to go out to dinner this evening okay? My treat."

"Okay mom. Where are you taking us?" Maren asked inquisitively.

Laughing, she quickly replied, "Well if Sam's joining us, it would probably be rude to go anywhere other than the Triple B don't you think? Besides, Samantha has a surprise at the bar this evening that might make the night even more enjoyable!"

Now curious but still cautious knowing her mother's past history, Maren looked her square in the eyes.

"Mother, promise me you're not trying to play matchmaker again? I live in New York and I have no interest in being introduced to some local that I probably went to high school with."

"Chill Mar, it's all good," Alexa spoke up. "In the short time that I've been back, I've come to look at the town in a very different light and where I once saw it as a dead end place that was nearly impossible to escape from, I now realize that the people who choose to stay here post-graduation maybe already knew something that we didn't. I love the slower pace, the fact that people look you in the eye, hold open the door for the person following them into a store, and when they say "Good Morning", they really mean it. And no, I'm not saying that the same type of behavior can't be found in the city, but face it Mar, we know it's not as common as in small town America."

Knowing that she was right and finally back where she needed to be, Maren smiled at her best friend. "You're right Lexi. It was a great town to grow up in and I can see how happy you are to be back, and I am truly and sincerely happy for you. Living in small town USA isn't for me but it obviously suits you. I know that the town of

Webb School District has gained an awesome 5th grade teacher who will make a huge impact on so many children's lives."

Hugging her best friend, she smiled warmly. "Now let's fire up this baby and hit the water."

They said their good-byes to Marsha, promising to be back at the house before six and ready for dinner on time. They'd barely left the dock before Marsha was already dialing Samantha's number.

"Hi Sam. Just checking in to make sure we're still all set for dinner this evening."

"Oh hi, Marsha. Kelsey and I are elbow deep in sugar cookie dough. Yes, yes we are all set for this evening. Kels is spending the night with Ana's parents so yes, both Luke and I will be at the Bistro this evening. The girls don't know what you're up to, do they?"

"Absolutely not. But they don't know what's best for them and if I can nudge them in the right direction, then there's nothing wrong with that," she added, as if trying to rationalize her actions in her head, and justify her meddling into two grown women's lives. "Besides, they're out on the water for the afternoon, so I won't see them until it's time for me to pick them up for dinner."

~Chapter 23~

"It's a great day to be outside soaking up the sun. The boys are out in Luke's boat today as well. Kels didn't want to go with her father and her uncle, so she's helping me whip up a batch of the best sugar cookies around. Isn't that right Kelsey?" she asked her granddaughter who was waiting impatiently to turn on the Cuisinart.

"Yes grandma. But hurry up," she whispered, but not quite quietly enough.

"Okay then, I had better let you go before your little chef loses her patience," she kidded. "See you at the Triple B this evening. Oh, and fingers crossed."

"You have no idea how much they're crossed Marsha. Fingers and toes," she added before saying good bye.

Alexa and Maren honked at a few boats they recognized as they made their way toward the sand bar. Already nearly filled to capacity with jet skis, party barges and ski boats, Maren expertly weaved her way in and around the bobbing boats, and mooring lines that were strung out in all directions off bows and sterns as far as she could see. The water was shallow in the area where the cove and sand bar were located. Anyone who knew the lake, knew that there was always enough of a current and wind to not only turn a boat around but move it into deeper water if not properly anchored with two lines. Once Maren found an area that she considered suitable, both she and Alexa dropped their anchors and shored up the slack. They'd grown up on the water and had done the same routine dozens of times. After they confirmed that the anchors were solidly secured to the sand bottom and that they weren't going to drift anywhere, they set about getting settled and comfortable. They quickly looked around at the boats and people in their immediate vicinity and after not recognizing anyone, they stripped down to their bathing suits. Maren was touting a black bikini with metallic gold trim, while Alexa's was emerald green with silver colored rhinestones accentuating each strap. Both made a statement, whether they realized it or not. Both women wore their respective bathing suits very well and the hours they'd spent sweating in the gym had not been in vain. While neither woman paid much attention to their surroundings, they certainly hadn't gone unnoticed by a few boats, especially the ones filled predominantly with men.

"Hey Luke, check out the black Baja that just pulled up. Damn those young ladies are quite the eyeful. Hey, check out the one in the green suit fixing her hair. Come on baby, bend over and fluff that hair," he said, never taking his eyes off of her and she leaned forward, not to fluff her hair as he'd hoped but to pull it up into a pony tail before putting a ball cap on. They were just far enough away that not only couldn't he make out the insignia on her baseball cap, but he couldn't make out many details of her face. But at the moment, he wasn't looking at her face but enjoying the view of the rest of her.

"Jesus, Luke, those chicks are smoking! Let's move over their way before someone else hones in on them," he pleaded with his brother.

"We are not moving Logan. Drink your beer and shut up so I can read will you? And if you want to hook up with either of them, feel free to swim over," he added, tipping his beer up to his lips, but not before he subtlety turned to see what his brother was all worked up about. The blonde in the black bathing suit had a body to die for, but also appeared to have an attitude to go with it from the way she was over-exaggerating her movements. He quickly moved past her and when his eyes latched onto the auburn colored siren in the emerald green bikini, he felt something awaken inside him. Dismissing it as simply a testosterone induced reaction, he forced his eyes back to the book that he was reading, but not before admiring her entire petite package. She couldn't be more than 5'4" or possibly 5'5" he thought to himself, and was probably approximately his age. As quickly as he allowed himself to appreciate how nicely she filled out her bathing suit, he then just as quickly chastised himself for even bothering to look.

"Okay, you're right," he said casually to his twin. "They definitely know how to accentuate their assets so to speak. But a lot of good that does us," he added to defend his argument. "They're here on holiday and will be gone when the weekend is through. So stick your tongue back in your mouth and relax. Besides, there must be plenty of single women down in the Big Apple for you."

"There are, but it's been awhile since I saw one look like that. Wow they're both hot. And how do you know that they're from out of town?" he asked casually, still enjoying the view.

"Because that's Marsha's boat, so suffice it to say, that the blonde is most likely Marsha's daughter who is up here for the weekend on vacation. Just like I said earlier. And the auburn haired one is her friend that always comes with her when they're in town."

"And you know this how?"

"Look Logan, they live down near you. Somewhere down by the city. And I know this because I had the pleasure of meeting them when they came home to visit Marsha over Memorial Day weekend. They came in for dinner and stayed to listen to the band. Found out after the fact that they were visiting from New York."

"Then you have an in. Let's go," Logan encouraged.

Just as Luke was about to respond to his brother, his cell rang. Seeing his mother's ID come up on the screen made his heart leap for just a split second. He'd had to teach himself not to panic every time a call came in. But whenever his daughter wasn't within his range of sight, he felt that immediate sense of dread. The call had come over six years ago telling him of Ana's accident, but he couldn't help it; sometimes it still felt as if he'd received it just a few weeks ago.

Immediately he answered his phone. Instead of it being his mother on the other line, it was his daughter's voice that he heard.

"Hi Dad. Grandma and I were just wondering how your afternoon is going? And we were wondering if you were coming back soon since we've made more cookies than you can believe! And Grandma says that it's a wonder that I don't have a belly ache with how much raw dough I ate," she added. "I kind of do have one but don't tell Grandma or she'll tell me that she told me so."

"You okay, Kels? You need me to come home now and pick you up?" he asked, with his voice showing concern.

"If that's okay dad. Yeah, I'd kind of like to go home now. I told Grandma that she could drop me off and I'd be okay alone. But she said no, not until I have a guard puppy to be with me when I'm home alone," hoping to play on his sympathy.

"She told you that huh?" he asked, dumping what was left of his beer into the lake. Not sure what was going on, Logan followed his lead and started picking up the boat. Even though he and Luke no longer lived in the same area, nor had lifestyles even remotely similar to one another; they still were twins, identical at that, and still had a strange sort of telepathy. Seeing the concern on his brother's face was enough to know that something was wrong at home and they would need to get there post haste.

Their sudden movements did not go unnoticed. Alexa and Maren weren't the only single women currently enjoying the day on the water. And while Luke and Logan were hastily packing up and lifting the anchors, they had more than one boat paying attention. Once finished, Logan put his T-shirt back on, much to the dismay of his female admirers. Both were the same height and build but with Luke's cropped haircut and very muscular build, he looked more military than Bistro owner. Logan, an attorney by trade, was definitely the free spirit in the family. He wore his hair longer, allowing the natural curls that both boys had been blessed with, to form ringlets just above his collar. He drove a Harley while sporting Armani suits and Hermes' shirts, and while the other attorneys frowned on his unorthodox appearance and attitude, they couldn't deny that when it came to Real Estate law, he was one of the best in the city. He'd worked his way up through the ranks quickly during the few short years that he'd been practicing law and had made partner in record time. Monday through Friday, he was all business; but he certainly knew how to party on the weekends. His carefree lifestyle didn't sit well with the women who had tried to tame him over the years. He'd told his brother years before, that someday, when he found his Anastasia like his brother had; then he'd settle down. Until then, he'd live life the way he chose.

Logan tried to make it up to his mother's home at least three or four times a year to spend time with the only family that he had. He was Kelsey's favorite uncle, spoiling her with not only gifts, but also his undivided attention when he'd stay with them. He tried to evenly divide his time between staying at his mother's house and his brother's. Even though he didn't have any children and rarely got exposed to the children of the women he dated, he still had an uncanny way of making a child laugh and feel comfortable around him. It wasn't that he didn't want children someday, he'd just never gotten that far in a relationship to think about the possibility of settling down, marrying and having children. So for the interim, he took advantage of the time that he could spend with his favorite ten-year-old.

As Luke started the engine, Logan looked over at his brother. "What's up?" he asked casually, never one to overreact.

"Seems that Kels might have eaten more dough than she made into cookies and now has one giant sized stomach ache."

"Shit. That stinks, poor honey," he added.

"Mom said she hasn't thrown up yet but is looking kind of green so to speak. Hope it' a quick thing because I can't bring her to Ana's parents if she's throwing up," Luke responded, already trying to come up with a plan for the evening.

"If she's sick, I'll watch her."

"How many times have you taken care of a puking, hormonal girl in your lifetime Logan?"

"Um, never. But I've had my fair share of women in that condition, and let me tell you, it's never pretty."

"Exactly," Luke responded. "Tell you what, if she's feeling rotten and miserable, I have no choice but work this evening since it'll be one of our busiest nights of the summer. Why don't you help me behind the bar and mom can stay home and take care of Kelsey? That is, if she's still feeling blue."

"I'm an attorney not a mixologist Luke. And other than knowing how to pour a mug of beer without head, I don't know how to mix drinks. I'd be useless behind the bar, as evidenced by some of the previous occasions when I stepped in to help."

Looking ahead as he drove across the lake, Luke responded in the form of a challenge. "You own an I-phone correct? And you are fairly intelligent correct? And you'd do anything for your niece and mom correct?"

Irritated and even though he knew he was being baited, he answered, "Yes, yes, and yes. So?"

"Then it's settled," Luke answered smugly. "If Kelsey is still ill, she'll stay home with mom and you'll be behind the bar with me. Your phone has an app for every mixed drink known to man so you can use it to make any drink that a young lady requests. That simple."

Knowing he'd walked right into his brother's trap, he didn't argue. Instead he reluctantly agreed, thinking that it couldn't be that hard to mix up a few drinks, pour a few beers and who knew, maybe he'd end up scoring a few points with the ladies who frequented his brother's establishment. Always the strategist, he smiled as if in defeat.

"Sure Luke, I'll help you out," he smiled. "Anything for the greater good," he added.

"Thanks, Logan. Oh, and just for the record, my waitresses are off limits while they're working. Agreed?"

"You got yourself some hot ones this summer huh? Well, didn't this just get interesting," he said, specifically to get under his brother's skin.

Pulling up to his boat slip, Luke turned toward his brother.

"Yes I did. And they're still off limits Logan."

Logan jumped out and assisted his brother in tying off the boat. He might live in the city and was unable get out on the water often, but he still knew his way around a boat. Once everything was secure and unloaded, they made their way to Luke's truck and headed towards their mother's home.

They walked in the front door to find Kelsey curled up on the couch with their mother sitting beside her. She had a hot water bottle against her granddaughter's stomach and a cup of green tea on the TV table beside her. At first appearance she didn't look any worse for wear but as he approached his daughter, he could see how pale she really was. Even though her eyes lit up upon seeing her father, she didn't lift her head.

"Hi, Kels. How are you feeling?"

"I'm okay dad. But the stuff that grandma made me drink made my belly hurt worse and I almost puked," she added, eyeing her grandmother.

"I know sweetie. Grandma used to make your Uncle Logan and me drink the same thing whenever we had a stomach ache too. It tastes nasty but it usually does the trick and prevents you from throwing up. Is your stomach feeling any better?" he asked, gently pushing the hair out of her eyes.

"Yeah, I think so. But it still hurts when I move too much. I want to stay here on the couch dad. I don't want to go to the baby sitter's or my nana and papa's tonight. Can you stay home with me?"

Before her father could even respond, it was Logan who came to his rescue.

"Hey Kels, whenever your father and I were sick, we had the absolute best person to take care of us. She always knew what to say to make us feel better. Grandma always knew what to do for us to make the pain go away; and usually did so before we even asked her to. It was like she was magic or something. Now I know that your Dad could stay home and be with you but he's not the one you really need today. What you need to feel all better, is a little TLC from your grandmother right here. And mom, before you say a word, I'm going to bartend with Luke this evening so it's all settled. It'll be fun and you can work your magic on our little patient here," he said, winking at his niece. "So if it's alright with you Kelsey, I'll go to the Bistro and help your father since he obviously can't handle the place on his own," he said, rolling his eyes for her benefit, "and you stay right here on the couch with grandma and let her take care of you. Deal? Oh, and I was thinking that tomorrow we'd go race go-carts if you're feeling better," he added for good measure.

"Deal," she said, already looking perkier.

Luke wasn't sure what exactly was going on but from the Chester-cat, almost smug grin on his mother's face, he was starting to doubt the acuteness of his daughter's stomach bug. She looked pale but didn't look overly sick. It was as if she and his mother had conspired to get he and his brother together for the evening. But before he could give his conspiracy theory any credence, his daughter jumped up and raced towards the bathroom, with his mother close behind. Hearing his daughter in the bathroom, he silently chastised himself for even considering the thought, albeit briefly, that maybe she'd been faking it.

It had taken a few minutes before she exited the bathroom but only took two strides for her father to be at her side. He'd tried to gain access while she was in the bathroom throwing up, but his mother had flatly refused him entrance. He crouched down eye level with his daughter who by now no longer looked pale, but flushed from vomiting. He took her into his arms and felt the tears. He hated to see the most important person in his world sick. As she held on tight, he scooped her up in his arms and carried her into his mother's spare bedroom. Logan had already picked up her pillow and hot water bottle, along with her now cold tea and stepped in behind his brother in silent allegiance. Samantha stood back, watching her two boys, her greatest accomplishments in life, unite in solidarity to take care of their own. She had truly loved her daughter in law, and still ached for her sons' loss. Seeing her two sons together and alone in life, only made her pray even harder that someday the two of them would both find their soulmates.

She waited until they both exited the bedroom, with Logan gently closing the door behind him; then she motioned them over to the kitchen table. At first she didn't say anything, simply looked at the two men sitting across from her and smiled.

Feeling paranoid, Logan spoke first. "What? If we're in trouble, it's Luke's fault. You know I was always the good one and it was always Luke who got us into trouble."

Samantha burst out laughing at that statement, knowing full well that whatever Luke got caught doing, his brother had put him up to it and was the instigator. Lucas had always been her reserved, serious one; while Logan had been the hell raiser from birth, actually even while in utero. Their facial appearance and mannerisms were exactly alike, but their personalities couldn't be any more opposite, if they tried. Her Lucas had been her cautious, over analyzer while his twin had been the free spirit, much like herself; carefree and never serious. So when Logan had decided that he wanted to go into law, everyone was shocked. The epiphany had come after sparring with a certain young lady in debate class during his junior year. Now all these years later, he couldn't remember her name, but had never forgotten the class. He'd made up his mind at the age of sixteen that he had a future in law and there was nothing or no one that could change his mind. Both of her kids were good students, so it didn't surprise anyone that Logan finished his four-year degree in three, and continued his education at Albany School of Law. Now, a partner at one of the largest firms in Manhattan, Samantha could only imagine the kind of money that her son must be making, but never once had she observed him flaunting his good fortune, nor had his personality changed as he climbed the social ladder. He was still her free spirited gypsy child and probably always would be. Just like her Lucas would never allow himself to be carefree and irresponsible, to any degree.

"Neither of you are in trouble," she commented, after she finished laughing. "Unless there's something that you're not telling me," she added, knowing full well that there wasn't. "I just wanted to take two minutes to tell you both how incredibly proud I am of you and how blessed I feel to have raised such fine men. And, Logan," she said, making direct eye contact with her city boy, "Thank you for pinch hitting for me this evening. It's going to be busy and probably trial by fire for you, so be ready. Traditionally we're packed on holiday weekends so even when it gets crazy, just smile and turn on your charm and you'll do fine. And you Lucas," she said, shifting her eyes from her one son to the other. "You need to promise me that no matter how insanely busy you get this evening, that you won't snap or complain to your brother if he's not as quick with the cocktails as you are. Remember, he's offered to help you out and is there because he wants to be, not because he has to be."

"Yes mam," they both responded in unison.

"Oh, and another thing, I had planned on joining Marsha, her daughter, and her daughter's best friend for dinner before helping you behind the bar. Please make sure their meals are on the house and send them my regrets for me, will you? Marsha's daughter lives down your way Logan and I know is only up for the holiday weekend."

"Um, okay," Luke said tentatively. "Of course we'll take care of them, but why don't you just call her on the phone and explain why you can't meet them. Why have us play middle man?"

"No reason. Stop reading things into everything I say. If you explain why I can't be there, it'll make them less likely to no argue about paying their tab, that's all," she responded. There was no need to explain to her knuckleheaded sons that she had her reasons for insisting that they meet.

They stayed and visited with their mother for another hour or so. Lucas fixed her leaking sink while he was there, whistling as he did so. Once the afternoon started drifting toward the supper hour, they said their goodbyes to both she and Kelsey and headed back towards Luke's home to get ready for what would most likely be a busy evening. Both were ready within 20 minutes and out the door two minutes after that. It wasn't until they were inside Luke's truck that he noticed what his brother had put on. His ensemble included boot cut jeans, which were totally acceptable for behind the bar; but his brother had chosen what appeared to be a very expensive looking tailored silk shirt. It was dark cranberry in color, looked great with his lighter colored hair, and Luke was certain that the ladies would love it. Only problem was, with the color and texture of the fabric, Luke was certain that every splash of liquid would leave an ugly water mark on his brother's fancy shirt. But Luke chose to keep his opinion to himself; until he saw his brother's choice of attire on his feet. He'd chosen cowboy boots, a choice that made Luke cringe. Knowing what it was like to stand for hours on end, Luke knew that his brother's feet would be killing him before the night was over. Concrete floors were unforgiving.

"Nice boots," he said casually.

"Thanks, they're python," Logan responded proudly.

"Sure you don't want to wear something a little more comfortable this evening? I would think that sneakers might be a better option for the night?"

"I don't look sexy in sneakers, mate. How am I going to impress the ladies if I'm frumpy like you?" he teased.

"Suit yourself, but unless you're planning on dancing on the bar, I don't see how the ladies are going to see your feet anyway," Luke retorted.

"Hey, you never know. Remember that bar in Albany that I told you about back when I was in law school? Everyone danced on the bar there, sort of like in the movie Coyote Ugly. It was a blast! So dear brother, you never know how the night might turn out. And if I end up on your bar dancing, at least I'll have great attire on my feet!"

"You're not dancing on my copper bar," was his only response as he rolled his eyes, envisioning his brother attempting to do what he was threatening, and knowing full well that he'd probably be doing just that before the night was over.

As soon as they entered the rear of the bistro, there was action. They were met at the door by one of their beer suppliers who regrettably had to inform him that he'd been unable to secure the quantity of specialty beer that Luke had ordered and that the delivery wouldn't be in for another two days. Next, they were met by Luke's full time dishwasher who currently was up to his elbows in suds and water, sweating and swearing profusely that the commercial dishwasher that currently was in his kitchen, was a piece of crap and broken again, forcing him to wash everything by hand. Luke placated the obviously very irritated man by promising to look into replacing the very old and now dysfunctional appliance as soon as possible. It, like most of the equipment had come with the place and had seen better days. It just wasn't in the budget to spend nine or ten thousand on a new one.

Once they made it to the bar and dining room, Luke gave Logan a quick rundown of the set up. He introduced his brother to the waitresses as they arrived, and subtly reminded him that they were still off limits, no matter how intrigued they were with meeting their boss's twin. Before anyone was ready, the doors opened and they were off and running. As the patrons trickled in at first, Logan smirked and felt that his brother had tried to intimidate him needlessly. Just as his confidence increased and a tad bit of his cockiness started to come out, the dinner crowd hit and before anyone knew it, the place was packed and complete ciaos ensued.

~Chapter 24~

As promised, Maren and Alexa were back at Alexa's house and ready for their dinner date with Maren's mother and Samantha by six. They both had chosen to wear sundresses, partly because they'd both gotten a little too much sun and the thought of wearing tight fitting attire with sunburns didn't sound at all appealing to either. Maren had gone for the glam look, applying just enough makeup to make her blue eyes pop even more. With naturally curly hair, she completed her look by teasing her hair just enough to give it body, volume and attitude. Alexa on the other hand, had chosen a softer look. She wore minimal makeup; just enough to make her jade green eyes look even greener. She'd swept her hair off her shoulders and secured it with a clip, allowing a few strands to fall. Her white sundress was simple, but form fitting and flattering. She wasn't heavily endowed in the chest department, but filled out the dress perfectly.

When Samantha arrived to pick the girls up for dinner, both were ready and came bounding down the stairs towards her truck. She watched them approach and it brought back a flood of memories of them doing the exact same thing as children. They'd been best friends practically since birth, and here they were, still soul sisters despite the miles between their homes. She silently prayed that Alexa's returning home would prompt her daughter to consider returning to the nest as well. She missed her husband and the way life had been before he passed away, but he'd been gone for years, and she'd gradually moved on with her life. Her daughter was a different pain, a dull ache that always simmered just below the surface. She missed them both so much that it actually hurt but would never tell Maren how badly she wished she'd come back home. She was an adult, living her life, and who was she to meddle in her daughter's affairs. For now, she'd simply cherish each and every moment she got to spend with her when she returned home for a visit.

They jumped into her truck, Maren riding shotgun, with Alexa sliding into the rear seat. Both looked so radiant, happy and rested; along with a little sunburnt.

"Well don't you two look fantastic! I take it the sun was hot out there today?"

Eyeing her mother, who was also sporting a sundress, though not nearly as revealing as the one she was currently wearing like a glove, she smiled.

"Mom," she said sincerely, as if seeing her mother, really seeing her for the first time. "You look stunning!"

Blushing, Marsha, put the truck into reverse and backed out of Alexa's short drive. "We're going to have a splendid time tonight! I just know it!" And they were off.

They were surprised to see that the parking spots in front of the Black Bear Bistro was already taken, and the parking lot to the rear of the Triple B was half way full and it was barely 6:15.

"Wow, they're hopping tonight."

As they parked and exited her truck, Alexa looked around at all of the restaurants along Main Street and noticed that each of them seemed to be pulling in a decent crowd. Even when she'd lived in the city, she'd tended to gravitate toward the independently owned stores, bars and diners. She tried to avoid the chain stores whenever possible, citing that she preferred to help keep the mom and pop type stores afloat. If tonight's crowds were typical of what summer tourism in the Adirondacks was like, then she felt confident that each business would survive another year. They made their way in the front door and the aroma, noise and energy hit them as soon as they passed through the threshold. Jessica, the hostess, greeted them warmly with Marsha immediately looking around for Samantha, who was supposed to meet them there. Jessica, signaled Luke upon their arrival and he made his way over. He gently pushed through the crowd, with an occasional "hi" here, hug there, and one pat on the rump by a slightly inebriated patron who looked at him like raw meat to a tiger. Alexa happened to catch the pat as he discreetly pushed the young ladies' hand away. He hadn't even made it to the door, but he'd already known it was her, the girl with the green bikini from earlier at the cove. Even though she had been wearing aviator sunglasses and a baseball cap, he knew that it was Marsha's daughter and her friend that had caught his eye while out on the water. He'd never let his brother know that he had in fact noticed them, but now standing here, next to them, he was certain that the two women on the Black Baja were in fact, the same ones currently standing in front of him.

"Welcome ladies. Nice to see you again." He leaned in and gave Marsha a quick kiss on the cheek. "Marsha, you look stunning this evening. We're going to have to beat the men off with a stick the way you three look. Regrettably mom won't be able to join you this evening. She currently is playing nurse and asked if she could please take a raincheck." He didn't elaborate anymore, nor did they ask any questions. Alexa looked into the eyes of the man standing just a few feet away. She immediately recognized him as the driver of the Ski Nautique that she'd seen earlier. Wondering why he and his passenger only stayed at the sand bar for a brief stay, she looked at him, really looked at him, and saw an obviously very nice looking man, but also a very serious, cautious one. She got the hint that even though he was being jovial and friendly enough, the man currently talking to her best friend's mother, was all business and obviously one to never let his guard down. Alexa saw past the exterior facade and saw sadness. As they stood talking, none of them noticed as he approached, and it wasn't until Logan was standing next to his brother that Maren gasped.

"Holy shit! There's two of you! I mean, one of you is great, but hot damn Lexi, there's two. They're twins." Turning towards her mother, she continued speaking. "Mom, you never told me they had gorgeous bartenders like this up here. And twins to boot!"

"You never asked. Besides, you don't live up this way anymore, remember. Alexa, Maren, I'd like to introduce you to Sam's other son. This gorgeous hunk, she teased, "is Logan. He lives in the city and is up visiting his brother and mother for the weekend."

Smiling, Logan laughed as he put his arm around Marsha's waist and drew her near. "I only come up to flirt with you, my love," he said as he jokingly kissed Maren's mother on the cheek. "And I'll keep returning until you finally agree to run away with me."

Marsha hugged her best friend's son as she laughed. "Honey, you keep asking, because you're starting to wear me down," she teased back.

Coughing slightly at her mother's overt flirting with a man half her age, Maren extended her hand. "It' nice to meet you Logan. I'm Maren and this is my best friend Lexi."

His eyes went back and forth between the two of them and then lit up in recognition.

"Black Baja. Black bikini," he pointed from Maren to Alexa, "Green bikini with baseball cap," he smiled, proud of himself to make the connection. "You were at the sand bar this afternoon."

Alexa extended her hand and smiled. "Yes we were. Good eye, Mr. Ski Nautigue," she responded, seeing the quick flash of surprise come and go from his twin's face.

Luke spoke up. "How'd you know what type of boat we were in?" he asked tentatively.

"I'm psychic," she joked. Seeing Luke pale, she quickly added, "I'm very observant and have always made a point of being aware of my surroundings. After living in the city for years, I might not necessarily make eye contact with everyone in my immediate area. But you can be certain that I know who and what's around me."

It was Maren's turn to hone into the conversation. "So Logan, you live in the city? What borough? Lexi doesn't any more, but I'm in Yonkers."

"Really?" he said, genuinely surprised. "What do you do in Yonkers?" he asked, over exaggerating the k-e-r-s just to tease her. He wasn't quite ready to reveal where he lived or what he did for a living so he kept the conversation centered around the two beautiful women standing in front of him. Luke remained present taking in the conversation without saying anything. He was studying Alexa while Marsha was studying the dynamics unfolding in front of her, and already scheming on how she could bring the four of them together.

"Alexa and I are teachers and we both attended college down there, along with Molly. She left immediately after school, but Alexa and I loved the city so we stayed. I teach 5th and Lexi teaches 4th grade."

In the conversation, Maren failed to mention that her best friend no longer resided in New York nor taught in the same school district as she did; a fact that didn't evade her mother.

"That's awesome!" he said, with a smile big enough to light up the entire room. "It was very nice meeting both of you, and I hope that y'all enjoy your dinner here. Consider it on the house," he added. "My treat. But I'd better get on back behind the bar or I might get fired," he added, winking at Marsha. "I heard that the owner's a real hard ass." And with that, he turned and walked away.

The three stood momentarily motionless, watching him depart. Even Marsha couldn't deny the fact that the man knew how to make an entrance and an exit. Between the perfectly fitting jeans and the cowboy boots, Logan might be big city, but the boy knew how to get back to his roots and at the moment, had captured nearly half of the women in the room's attention. Luke simply rolled his eyes and addressed the three, breaking the spell that his twin had obviously put them under.

"Jessica will seat you, and as Logan offered, everything is on him, so make sure you order the most expensive items on the menu," he joked. "I'd better get back as well. No guessing what he'll screw up if I'm not there to bail him out," he teased. "Good seeing you again Marsha, and very nice seeing you both again as well. Don't be strangers. Make sure you stop in whenever you're up here visiting."

Before either could respond, Marsha answered for them. "Oh they will. I'll make sure of it."

Chapter 25~

The rest of the holiday weekend flew by and before anyone was ready, Maren stood by her loaded truck saying her good-byes. Marsha didn't ask her to stay. She didn't need to. The hesitancy and reluctance to leave was clearly visible in her daughter's eyes. They'd had a fantastic week together, with she and Lexi practically attached to each other's hips, the way they were back in school. Marsha had spent every day with the two of them and by week's end, it was as if they still both lived in the area, with both zigzagging between both homes. The three of them had finished stripping the remainder of the horrid wall paper in Alexa's little bungalow, and Maren prided herself on helping her best friend hang new mini-blinds, and curtain rods. By the time Maren was ready to leave, Lexi's home looked exactly the way that she'd envisioned it would. Maren had mentioned on more than one occasion how lucky she was to be finally settled in something that was hers, and not just investing her money in lining a landlord's pocket. Lexi missed her best friend and was dreading saying good-bye, but she also knew that deep down, Maren was destined to always be a city girl. If she were to move back to the area, the slow, relaxed pace of country living might make her stir crazy. So as she hugged her best friend, she allowed the tears to flow; promising her that she'd make a trip down to visit her before the school year started. After many hugs, and several tears, Marsha and Alexa watched Maren drive away and head south.

The rest of the summer flew by with Alexa continuously busy with one project or another on her home. Her oldest brother came to visit three times over the summer and each time, she found numerous projects for him to assist with. He was always jovial and willing to help, and never once complained. Alexa appreciated his expertise and offered to compensate him after each visit, which he adamantly refused. By the end of his third visit, it dawned on her that he appeared hesitant to leave.

"I love you and I love that you've come to visit and help me around here. We wouldn't be sitting on this amazing deck if you hadn't helped me. But Grant, something's going on between you and Andrea, so spill it."

His little sister didn't need to be clairvoyant to see the sadness in his eyes and pain that he'd been trying so unsuccessfully to mask.

"It's nothing Alexa. Really, I'm fine."

"Liar," she responded, as she bit off another piece of the string of red licorice that she was enjoying. She didn't make direct eye contact with her brother; simply extended out her arm, offering him a bite. He didn't look at her, knowing that she'd read his mind if he did, so he just snagged the licorice and stuffed it into his mouth.

She didn't remark, simply waited until he was done chewing and ready to speak.

"She moved out. She moved out Alexa, and filed for divorce. Nothing more to say, don't you think?"

"Her loss," was the only response Alexa offered. She got up, leaving her brother alone in his thoughts. She went inside, and returned with two beers in hand. Sitting down next to her brother, she took a swig and continued staring ahead. They sat in silence, enjoying the tepid weather and silence of the night. She waited for him to speak, and when he continued to remain silent, she pried only once.

"Do mom and dad know yet?"

"Yeah, I told them before I came up here. Figured they would find out soon enough so I wanted them to hear it from me you know?"

"Yeah. How'd they take it? I mean it's not like you had a lot of options right? Oh Grant, I'm so sorry."

They remained silent, sipping their beers. It took him a few moments before he felt that he could contain his emotions and respond.

"Please don't give me your sympathy Alexa. I need your love, but not your pity. You know what mom said when I told her?" he smiled, holding back a laugh. Before she could respond or comment, he continued.

"She said the hell with Andrea and told me that I should move up here with you," he chuckled.

"She's worried about you living way out here by yourself," he outright laughed. "She's obviously forgotten that for the last how any years you lived alone in an apartment in the city. And now she's worried about you living alone, here in town, in Old Forge! I didn't laugh at her but oh my God, Alexa, she was serious. She loves that you're living back here in our home town, but she's paranoid and worried about you living at the end of this dead end road. She won't let on to you, but she let it slip that she and dad were considering moving back north, just so you won't be alone. They said that their lease is up at the end of the year, and if you're still alone and single by the end of the year, then either I or they should move in with you. So consider yourself warned," he finished.

She loved her parents very much, actually adored and respected her mother for her concern. But after being on her own for so long, she had no interest in once again sharing a home with her parents. She finally had her childhood home updated, modernized and decorated the way she wanted, and the thought of having to move out if her parents moved in, was very unsettling. Her brother could see the surprise, and immediate fear in her eyes, so he offered her one last word of advice. "Hey, just find yourself a man, and have him move in with you by the end of the year. That'll satisfy mom and keep them down south. I'd love to help you out sis but my life is in Wilkes Barre now Lexi. Otherwise I'd start over, up here with you. Even with Andrea gone, my home, work and circle of friends is in PA. But you know, and it goes without saying, you need anything, anything at all; call me, and I'll be here in under four hours. I love you sis."

She reached over and touched her big brother's hand. "I love you too."

~Chapter 26~

Alexa sat and stared at the four walls that would become her second home for the next nine months. Sitting there, looking at the miniature desks and chairs, at the ivory colored walls and oversized green chalk board brought back memories of two decades ago when she was on the other side of the room facing the teacher, not being one. She was nervous, excited and just a little terrified as the reality of her impromptu decision finally sank in. She'd been very settled and comfortable in her old school and knew the routine as one year rolled into another. Kids were kids and teaching whether it was here in Old Forge or back in the city was essentially the same, yet Alexa found her stomach tied up in knots and what she assumed was a panic attack, taking hold of her psyche. Just as she felt herself starting to sweat, a familiar face peeked inside her classroom, breaking the downward spiral that she'd felt herself slipping into.

"Well don't you look all grown up and professional sitting there," Marsha announced as she walked into the classroom.

"I mean, I know that you and my Maren are seasoned teachers, and I couldn't be more proud of the two of you. It's just that I'm used to seeing you in sweats or bikinis on my boat, not all spiffy and grown up like you look here sitting in your classroom. Oh how I wish your momma were up here right now to see you like this! She'd be so proud of you; more of course, than she already is," she added for good measure. "Say," she said, making her way into the classroom, looking around at the way Alexa had decorated, utilizing astrology as her theme.

"Would you care to join Jacqueline and I for lunch?"

Still a little shaky from the partial panic attack that she'd been suffering, Alexa rubbed her hands up and down her arms, as if she needed warmth.

"Who?" she asked, not quite sure who Jacqueline was.

Laughing, she answered Alexa. "You'd know her as Mrs. Murphy. You probably had her as your teacher when you were in first grade with Maren. She used to teach at the lower level but has been a sixth grade teacher here for years now. We get together with Samantha over at the Bistro or the golf course at least every other week to have lunch and a few cocktails. Would you care to join us?"

"Um, sure, that sounds great! As long as I'm not invading your luncheon," she added.

"Not at all. Do you have a preference as to where we dine? If not, I was thinking that a nice cucumber salad on the upstairs deck of the Triple B would be enjoyable."

Having no clue as to Marsha's sudden change in venue, Alexa happily agreed.

They picked Jacqueline up at her home and headed toward the Bistro, and after the formal introductions were over, reintroductions to be exact; Marsha and Jacqueline talked practically nonstop all the way through town. Alexa answered appropriately when asked a direct question, but for the most part remained silent in the passenger's seat. When Marsha pulled in next to a large black pickup truck, Jacqueline commented that Lucas must be working, which caught Alexa's attention; not only because of the statement but because she'd seen that same truck somewhere over the summer but couldn't quite pinpoint where. They made their way inside and were greeted warmly. Marsha noticed the ever serious Luke completely change his demeanor, if only for a moment, when he noticed who was in their company. The change went unnoticed by Alexa, who greeted him the way she would anyone else. What wasn't evident from her external posture, was the way the butterflies were once again flipping inside her stomach. She seen Lucas at the Bistro many times over the course of the summer, and he'd always been cordial and friendly, but nothing more. As far as she knew, he was married, as evidenced by the ring on his left hand. She'd never asked about his wife, nor had the topic ever come up in conversation. Still, she felt some type of connection to the man behind the bar, with the sad eyes and sadder smile. But knowing he was married, was enough to push whatever she was feeling out of her system, and look at him for what he was; the owner of the Bistro and Samantha's son.

"Well, look who is gracing my doorstep," he kidded. Not only the prettiest women in town, but also what I hear is our newest teacher," Lucas said as he wiped his hands, as he came out from behind the bar to give Marsha and Jacqueline big hugs. Then looking at Alexa, he extended out his hand in welcome to her as well. Knowing it would be rude to avoid him, she smiled and reached out to shake his as well. Taking his hand, she felt the jolt of electricity pass between them almost immediately. He saw the surprise flash in his eyes as well as he obviously had felt it too. It was then that he looked into her eyes, and pierced her soul.

Suddenly very uncomfortable with whatever was happening in that split second between them, she immediately let go of his hand. But even without the physical connection of their hands touching, Alexa couldn't deny that she still felt something that she couldn't explain. She knew that she would chastise herself later; but at that moment, she knew that she had to learn more about the man with the sad eyes.

Once Samantha was freed up, she joined them at their corner booth, sliding in next to Jacqueline and directly across from Alexa. The waitress took their order and everyone enjoyed the warm sunshine and ice cold beers. Alexa felt more comfortable now that they were seated on the upstairs deck, and away from the bar. She didn't like the way that looking at Lucas made her feel, and wanted nothing more than to forget that he was just one floor away. She pushed any thought of him out of her head, and when his name came up in conversation, she cringed.

"Sam, it never ceases to amaze me what an amazing job you and Lucas have done in turning this restaurant into such a thriving business. I mean," Jacqueline said, in between sips of her beer, "he only relocated up here by you, what, five or six years ago?" she asked.

Remembering the day as if it were just yesterday when she'd received the call that changed her life forever, she stared at her beer and simply answered.

"It's been six years since we lost Anastasia and Luke moved to Old Forge."

She knew she shouldn't be asking, and knew that she already knew the answer; but Alexa couldn't help herself and asked anyway.

"Samantha, who was Anastasia?" Alexa asked innocently.

"Ana was Luke's wife and she was killed in a car accident when she was barely 23 years old. She died on her way home from Old Forge, returning to their home in Forestport when a deer ran out in front of her. She died almost instantly, and Luke never got to say goodbye to her, and has never forgiven himself for her accident."

Alexa took a moment to digest what she'd just heard. She now understood the pain and sadness that flickered in his eyes when he let his guard down. The otherwise tough looking man with the piercing eyes, lived day by day filled with guilt and a broken heart. She felt immediate sadness thinking about how hard his loss must have hit him, especially at such an early age.

"Why would your son blame himself for her accident?" she found herself asking, even though she had no right, nor business asking.

"I've asked him that myself a million times, and the answer is always the same. He thinks that it's his fault that he never put his foot down and insisted that they relocate here to Old Forge. He hated her driving alone on 28 so late at night but she insisted that they were content in their tiny cabin in the woods in Forestport and she refused to consider moving up here. He feels that it's his fault that she was on the road that night and if he'd moved her to Old Forge, she'd still be alive."

Alexa felt the lump grow in her throat, looking into Samantha's eyes. It was then that Marsha spoke up.

"I never realized that Lucas has kept that pain inside him all these years. Hank told me when it happened, that the deer came out of nowhere and your poor daughter-in-law never even had a chance to react it happened so fast. I am so sorry that our Lucas had carried that guilt all these years," she added.

"I lost part of my son the day I lost my daughter-in-law. She was pregnant at the time also, so we lost Ana and he lost his baby as well," she said, in a near whisper. Samantha could have taken the opportunity to tell Alexa about her son's daughter but reframed. She, nor her son wanted anyone's sympathy, just empathy and a little understanding as to why they both were so protective of Kelsey.

Everyone remained silent for just a moment, absorbing the information. Marsha was the first one to speak up.

"Luke has certainly been through a lot in his life, yet he is one of the sweetest men that I know. He's been through such sadness, and I certainly hope that in time, he not only forgives himself for his wife's accident, but also finds love again. Nobody should go through life alone. So I would like to propose a toast, and then move on to happier subjects." Raising her half empty bottle of Corona, Marsha smiled.

"To everyone finding love and happiness, and to people who belong together, finding each other."

They all clanked their bottles in salute and then dove into the appetizers that had been placed on their table in front of them.

The talk ranged from what life had been like for Alexa and Maren living in the city, to what she'd done to her childhood home, to what she could look forward to during the upcoming year teaching for the Town of Webb School System. She surprised them when she let it slip that she'd already accepted a position coaching the girl's modified soccer team. Jacqueline applauded her for diving right into her new job and environment, while Marsha encouraged her to consider signing up for one the many courses that were offered at the art museum. She went on to explain that she and Samantha taught a fundamental basket weaving class that she might enjoy. Samantha casually also let it slip that her son taught a wildlife photography seminar twice a month at the museum. Alexa didn't catch on to the women's subtle prompting and just thought that they were offering her suggestions to help her settle into her new environment. Jacqueline sat back, listening to the banter back and forth, and as an outsider listening to Marsha and Samantha, it didn't take long to see where and how they were steering the conversation. She quickly deduced that her best friends thought that possibly Alexa and Samantha's Lucas would be a good match. "Well," she thought to herself, "if they were encouraging it, then she'd have to get to know her fellow teacher a little better, and give her a little push from inside the classroom as well."

They talked, laughed, ate and drank their way through the meal, enjoying each other's company. When the food was gone and they'd consumed their beers, they hesitantly allowed the outing to come to an end, but not before Marsha insisting that they follow Samantha back into the restaurant proper, to have one last drink at the bar before calling it a night. Everyone noticed Luke's eye drift to Alexa as she entered the room with the women. This time, now that she knew that he was no longer married but in fact widowed, she allowed herself to look at him as well. And now she understood the reason for his sadness.

~Chapter 27~

Labor Day came and went. Alexa couldn't believe that she was already getting dressed for the first day of class for yet another school year. As she sipped on her tea, she glanced around her kitchen. She'd never felt so content, so happy and it wasn't until that moment, that she realized that this is where she was supposed to be all along. The city had been fun, a great place to attend college and enjoy the nightlife that it offered. But here, in her childhood home, in the quaint Adirondack town where she'd grown up, was truly home and not only her place to find refuge; but also, pure contentment. She was incredibly proud of what she and her brothers had done to the home to fix it up and make it shine once again. Sitting there in her tiny kitchen, in her parent's bungalow, she was proud of what she'd become as well. And with that, she brushed her teeth, took one last look at her ensemble in the mirror, and headed out the door to start her new school year as a teacher for the Town of Webb.

~Chapter 28~

The first few weeks of school flew by and as Alexa got to know the sixteen students in her classroom, she also became comfortable with the routine and flow within the walls of the school itself. Almost every teacher within the district had taken the time to welcome her, offer tidbits of advice that they thought would make her transition smoother, and allow her to become more comfortable in her new setting. Some had inquired about her previous teaching environment, while a few appeared hesitant to accept "the fancy teacher from the city." It only took a week for all to realize that even though she might have lived and taught in a much larger area, the newest member of their faculty was a country girl through and through. Alexa owned many designer labels, and while she dressed very professionally for her new job, she also dressed conservatively, and never flashy. A few teachers realized within that first week how wrong they'd been in judging her and quickly accepted her for what she was, a great teacher.

As she got to know the students in her class, she realized that there really wasn't much difference between teaching fourth vs. fifth grade, with the exception of introduction of puberty. At first, she wasn't quite sure what she, as a teacher, was supposed to address and how detailed she was supposed to get. She asked Jacqueline during their lunch break, and after she finished laughing so hard that her side hurt; she answered Alexa's questions. Both chuckled at the realization that Alexa was not only uncomfortable, but a little terrified at the thought of having to answer questions about the birds and the bees. Jacqueline reassured her that most of the kids already knew way more than they should regarding the topic of sex, and the school nurse would be a great resource for any remaining questions.

"So, other than the hormone issue, how different is teaching 5th grade here from teaching 4th grade down state?"

"No difference really. The kids are the same, but I have to admit, I'm really enjoying the smaller class size. Already, I feel as if I know the kids better than I ever did at my old school. The challenges are the same, but having a smaller more intimate class size definitely has its' advantages," Alexa concluded. "The only thing missing is my best friend. We used to work out nearly every day after work and I miss the company, and her pep talks to get me motivated after dealing with kids all day," she kidded.

"You're welcome to work out with us anytime," Jacqueline offered. "There are several of us who go to the gym at least three times a week so you should join us sometime. And while I realize that I'm old enough to be your mother; there are plenty of young people at the gym."

"Thanks Jacqueline. But I assume that you go right after work, and currently I'm tutoring twice a week and have soccer practice the other three days. But once soccer season is over, and the snow starts to fly, count me in."

"Oh, Alexa dear; you truly haven't lived up this way in quite some time now have you," she chuckled. "I guarantee the snow will fall prior to soccer season being over." They laughed, not at Alexa's expense; but at the fact that winter in the mountains was just around the corner.

She'd put off giving her class any tests, but as she handed out her first test, a two-page multiple choice one, she heard the not so subtle groans. Being the new teacher in school, she had reframed, until this point, but knew that she had to meet the same standards as the other 5th grade teacher and test taking was required. She'd warned her kids and had basically gone over the entire test the day before with her verbal question and answer session, so she felt confident that her students should all do very well on it. Now, as she graded each paper, it became very apparent that either three of her students hadn't paid attention or had rushed through the test. The two boys and one girl all had no issues when it came to the homework that they'd handed in daily. But as she reluctantly gave them failing grades on their first quiz of the school year, she knew that she'd have to individually speak with each of the students and help rectify whatever had gone horribly wrong on their first test.

She considered calling their parents to introduce herself and offer her assistance, should they need it, but then chastised herself for reading too much into one bad test result. Besides, they were only two weeks in and they'd have parent teacher conferences before too long.

She'd been living in Old Forge for less than four months, but found that she was already in a comfortable rhythm. She talked or texted with Maren daily, and forced herself to go for a run nearly every morning, despite running solo and in the brisk fall weather. After class, she stayed behind to grade papers or offer assistance to any child who asked for it, and then she joined her team for soccer practice. When she'd reluctantly agreed to help coach the girl's team, she had no idea that she'd end up the head coach. Once the initial shock wore off, she realized that she absolutely loved coaching! The young ladies on her team were not only pleasant to coach, but extremely talented and Alexa found that she was getting just as excited for their first game as the players were.

By Wednesday afternoon, she could barely contain her excitement. Marsha, Samantha and Jacqueline promised her that they would be attending her inaugural game, and all had reassured her that she'd do fine. And they'd been right. By the time the first quarter ended, not only was Alexa almost as tired as her players, but she was as into the game as the players and fans. They were up three to two against one of their arch rivals and even Alexa couldn't believe how much the town came out to support not only the varsity and JV teams, but also her modified team. She'd known that soccer was very popular but she'd had no idea that it would draw such a crowd.

~Chapter 29~

"Grandma, I'm not so sure why you think I'm gonna like watching a soccer game," she stated flatly as she'd rode over in her grandmother's truck after school. Samantha had asked her son to pick Kelsey up at the soccer field, which seemed like an odd request from his mother, but he didn't argue. It wasn't until Kelsey was watching the girls doing their warm up exercises, that she spotted her and in that moment, Samantha saw what she'd hoped and prayed she would see. The second Kelsey realized that her teacher was out on the field, and dressed like the players, sans the numbered jersey, she gasped and nearly spit out her soda.

"Grandma, that's my teacher! How cool grandma, Miss Greenwood is their coach. Look at her out there! She doesn't look like a teacher anymore, does she?" she asked seriously. "Can we stay and watch the whole game" she asked, suddenly full of enthusiasm.

"I can't think of anything I'd rather do, Kelsey," she answered, as she subtly checked the time and wondered how long it would take to get her son there as well. Not that she was playing match maker, she said to herself. It couldn't be helped if she was guilty of putting them both in the same place at the same time. She'd provide that opportunity, and nothing more, she reassured herself.

Lucas could never be mad at his mother for asking him to deviate from their usual routine. But today, absolutely nothing had gone smoothly and at the moment, he was not only running behind schedule, but was irritated and tired. As he made his way through town, for the fourth time today, and after driving to Utica to meet with a supplier; all he wanted was to pick up his daughter and go home. He wasn't sure why his mother had insisted that he meet her at the soccer field at school, but again, he wasn't one to challenge or question his mother's decisions. He would meet her there, grab his daughter, go home, and work on the books for quarter end. His mother managed the staff, he the books and supplies, and his brother was their legal counsel. The three made a pretty good team, despite being family. As Luke searched for a parking space, he reminded himself to calm down and not look annoyed when he found his mother and daughter.

Out of the corner of her eye, Alexa noticed the black Dodge Ram pass by but thought nothing of it. It wasn't until it went by in the opposite direction, and then back again, that caught her attention. The truck's tinted windows afforded the driver obscurity and Alexa couldn't tell if it was a man or woman driving. She made note of the make and model, and would ask Samantha after the game. Alexa was definitely not an alarmist of any sort, but since she'd seen the same truck at least four times since moving back to the area, she concluded that it must be a local and possibly someone she knew. Not overly concerned nor interested, she focused her attention back to the game that was currently tied.

After finally finding a parking spot, he made his way toward the field and the bleachers where he saw his mother and daughter, along with several other people he knew. His direct path to them was interrupted several times by people he knew from the Bistro, neighbors, and even an old classmate from Adirondack School. By the time he finally sat down next to his mother, who he noted was very into the game; he was completely irritated, despite promising himself that he wouldn't be. He caught himself when he nearly snapped at her but remained composed.

"Hi. Hey, Kels, you ready to head home?"

"Hi Dad! We can't leave now! There are like only five more minutes left and the game is tied! We can't leave until we win," she exclaimed enthusiastically.

"Kelsey, honey, I really have a lot of work that I need to do at home tonight. I never knew that you even liked soccer?" he asked, almost pleadingly, to persuade his daughter to leave with him right then.

Samantha spoke up and silenced the conversation once and for all. "Lucas Mathew! Your daughter has been sitting here watching this entire game and you are not going to drag her away from it when there are less than five minutes left in the game. The books can wait, so make yourself comfortable and enjoy the game. And as far as soccer goes, there are a lot of things that your daughter has taken an interest in. One of them is school; thanks in part to the soccer coach who is currently running down the sideline. Your daughter has been really enjoying the game and watching Miss Greenwood coach the girls. Kelsey was just telling me how Alexa has been tutoring your girl during recess and after school two days a week, and for the first time ever, she is starting to enjoy reading and schoolwork. Isn't that right Kelsey?"

"I don't like school grandma but Miss Greenwood is helping me read just like the other kids. Daddy, she's really nice and oh," she screamed, watching the breakaway heading towards the other team's goal. "Run! Take the shot!" she nearly screamed, completely caught up in the game.

Luke couldn't help himself. He found himself not only caught up in the game, but also in the realization of who had been teaching his daughter for the past three weeks. Sure, he knew that his daughter's teacher was Miss Greenwood, and that she was a seasoned teacher and new to the Town of Webb School System. What he hadn't known was that Alexa, whom he'd met over the summer was Miss Greenwood. Now, sitting there, watching her run up and down the sidelines as her players did; he found himself suddenly very interested in soccer. When #7 scored for the home team, he jumped up in elation with the rest of the spectators on the bench.

Kelsey, Lucas and Samantha remained seated until the final three minutes on the clock ran out and Old Forge finalized their win over Adirondack. As they stood to leave, he continued to watch Alexa interact with her team. They huddled together, embracing in their first win of the season. He couldn't help but think that her tiny frame and attire made her look more like one of the students, not their coach. He caught himself enjoying the way she looked in her spandex leggings and quickly focused his eyes elsewhere when he realized the reaction that was occurring. After things settled down in his crotch, he couldn't help himself, and found himself searching for her again. It didn't take long to find her, since she was walking towards he and his daughter, as they made their way down the bleachers.

She made her way directly towards Kelsey and smiled when they made eye contact. Then she looked up at Kelsey's father and stopped mid stride. Trying to rebalance herself, she searched his eyes for answers.

"Hey, Kelsey," she greeted her warmly. "Did you enjoy the game? Thank you for coming out to root for the girls. You were cheering for Old Forge, right?" she kidded.

As her teacher spoke directly to her, as if she were one of the adults, Kelsey suddenly felt very grown up. She stood a little taller, trying to elongate her growing torso just a little higher. She smiled at her teacher's question and responded, rather indignantly, "Oh course I'm cheering for Old Forge! They're the home team!"

Samantha had silently watched the whole exchange and bantering back and forth between her granddaughter and her teacher. She might not be a psychologist, but she knew affection and admiration when she saw it; and the bond already formed between the two of them was very evident. As they continued to kid each other back and forth, Sam looked over at her son, who remained silent and nearly gasped. Whether he knew it or not, standing there, in the cool fall air, she saw a spark in his eyes that had been snuffed out years ago. The way he was currently looking at his daughter's teacher, was the way he used to look when his wife would enter the room. Seizing the moment, she gently coughed, drawing attention to herself.

"Great game, Alexa! From what I saw out on that field, either you're a natural at coaching or the girls are just amazing athletes." She didn't allow Alexa to respond. Instead, she kept on talking, thinking it was now or never; and if her opinion was correct about her friend, the revelation wouldn't be earth-shattering.

"Alexa, you remember Lucas, my son? And it appears that you must have my granddaughter in your classroom? She's told me all about Miss Greenwood this, and Miss Greenwood that; but I'd never put two and two together, until now," she lied. She'd known even before school started that her granddaughter was in Alexa's class. She'd spoken with Jacqueline and insured which classroom her granddaughter would be assigned, before the rosters had even been sent out. Call it a hunch, but upon meeting Alexa, she honestly felt that her temperament and dedication to the profession were exactly what Kelsey needed. And from the way that they were interacting, her hunch had been right. Now, looking at the way she caught her son looking at Alexa, she couldn't be happier.

Alexa looked from Kelsey to Luke and back again, and as she studied them, saw the similarities. When she finished processing the information, she looked up at Lucas. "I didn't know she was your daughter," she said innocently.

Suddenly very protective, he gently laid his hand on his daughter's shoulder, as if in solidarity. He smiled, "Yup, this one is mine."

"I guess I never put two and two together. She has a different name; I assume she uses your wife's last name," she asked gently.

"Anastasia insisted that Kelsey take her last name, along with mine; sort of as an honor to her parents since Kels is their first grandchild. She wanted the name to be carried along for at least another generation. When she died, I just sort of thought Kelsey should go by her mother's last name, in her honor, so we unofficially dropped my last name."

He had just revealed to his daughter's teacher, more than he had to any other woman who'd entered his life since his wife's passing. She hadn't pried or interrogated; yet he had freely opened up to her and spoken about his family. He stood waiting for her to say something, anything, to break the now awkward silence.

"I'm so sorry for you and your daughter's loss. I'm sure that Anastasia is very proud of her daughter and the fine job you're doing raising her." She winked at Kelsey, and smiled. "I can't say it too loud, but she's definitely one of my favorite students in my class. She asks so many questions and challenges me to come up with answers to such a variety of topics. I'm not sure what goes on in your home, but I do know that you both," she said looking back at Samantha, and then Luke, "must be very active role models in your daughter's life, and must read to her incessantly, because our Miss Kelsey here is a wealth of knowledge on so many subjects. Her recollection of history is astonishing!"

Hearing the praise and sincere compliments melted not only Samantha's heart but also pierced her son's. He loved his daughter beyond words, and for this relative stranger, who'd only had his daughter in class for less than three weeks, to see his daughter's potential, meant the world to him. Kelsey, who'd remained quiet during their exchange finally spoke up.

"Dad, Miss Greenwood's the best teacher there is," she exclaimed enthusiastically. "She lets us chew gum in class before lunch, and we get to have competitions against the stupid boys, and we can don't get treated like little kids, like in 4th grade," she added. "Oh, there's Manda. Can I go see her dad?" she asked before taking off. Just before she scooted off to catch her classmate who was currently exiting the bleachers on the opposite side of the field. "And Miss Greenwood told me that I know how to read really well Dad; it's just my brain does jump rope sometimes too fast, right Miss Greenwood?" she said, smiling at her teacher.

Now completely confused, Lucas answered his daughter. "Go, get out of here," he kidded. "Go see Manda, and we'll meet you at the truck in a few minutes."

Kelsey didn't respond, except with a quick "Okay" and "Bye", and raced off to catch up with her girlfriend, leaving the three of them in her dust. Samantha saw one of the waitresses from the restaurant, and feigned the need to speak to her about something work related. She quickly said her good-byes, and left Lucas and Alexa standing there, now in awkward silence. Not one to be uncomfortable in most situations, Alexa looked up at the man who appeared restless standing alone with her. She now had so much to process about the man whom she'd only known as Samantha's son, the bartender and part owner of the Triple B. She'd known that he was a complex man; had figured that out from their first meeting. But now, standing here in his faded jeans, slightly wrinkled t-shirt and plaid button down shirt, rolled up to his sleeves; she realized that she hadn't really known him at all. He was gorgeous, in a kind of moody way. When she'd thought he was married, he'd been safe to flirt with at the bar, knowing that it was all in fun.

Now, standing here in front of her, realizing that he was not only single, but the father to one of her students, changed the way she looked at him, and for once in her life, she was the one uncomfortable, and it was Lucas who spoke first.

"Nice game," he said, smiling.

"Thanks. I played back in school and a little pick up in college, but have never officially coached a team before. I have to tell you; I was terrified out there! Thank God those girls are amazing athletes, have played together for years, and knew what they were doing. They're the reason we won, not me," she stated, believing every word exiting her mouth.

"Oh bologna," he snorted, surprising them both by his quick defense of her coaching skills.

"I watched you out there, and you were amazing. Those girls not only listened to you, they respect you and your coaching ability. So, don't ever sell yourself short Alexa. You did a great job today," he added, searching her eyes for acceptance of his truth.

She felt her heart quicken at his proclamation. Having just gotten out of a very painful relationship, she refused to allow a few kind words to soften her position on the male species. She wasn't about to let a pretty face, gorgeous body and a few compliments melt away the protective barrier she so firmly placed around her heart when she'd left Bradford and New York behind. Single or not, he was still off limits. Besides, she had his daughter in her class and refused to have there be any type of conflict of interest during her first year at her new job.

"Thank You," she responded sincerely.

"No, thank you. Thank you for the kind words about my daughter. But, I have to ask you; what on earth is she talking about? Her brain playing jump rope? She lost me on that one," he said, looking at Alexa for answers.

Not one to sugar coat anything, Alexa didn't explain herself or try and justify what Kelsey had said, she simply spoke.

"Your daughter is very intelligent, but she has a reading issue, and I'm sure that I'm not the first person who's picked up on that fact. It isn't that she can't read," she added quickly when she saw his body tighten up at her words. "It's just that her mind processes the words in a book or the projector differently than the way we see them. I've been tutoring her during recess and lunch for the past few weeks, and occasionally after school when Sam is running late, and she's already made amazing improvements in how much she can put together at one time."

Searching his eyes for acceptance of what she was saying, she continued. "I explained to Kels that her brain is just as smart as everyone else in her class, except that her brain plays jump rope faster than some of the other kids. I used that analogy so she'd understand better what I think is happening. I'm no doctor, nor reading specialist, but from what I've been seeing in the way she reads, it's like she knows what all of the words are, but her mind jumps around as she's trying to read them in a sentence. So, I have been working with her to slow the jump rope down, and hopefully, eventually stop it from jumping all together," she concluded.

"I hope you don't mind that Kelsey has been missing part of her recess so that I can help her. I asked her if she wanted me to set up a time after school to meet weekly for me to give her a hand, but she told me that she didn't want you to know that we're working on straightening out her reading. She had wanted it to be a surprise for Christmas. So please don't tell her that I told you, okay," she asked, with almost pleading eyes.

Lucas didn't know what to say. The woman whom he'd only met in passing twice in his life, three times if he counted the time he saw her in that wonderful bikini out on the lake; had not only picked up on his little girl's disability, but was taking time out of her schedule and her free time, to work with his daughter to help her overcome her reading problem. She'd already done more to help his daughter than all of the other therapists and reading experts combined. And she'd done it not because she was getting paid to, but simply because she'd saw the need and wanted to help. He felt the lump in his throat that wasn't his Adam's apple, and wasn't quite sure what to say. So he simply said what was in his heart.

"Thank you, Alexa. You have no idea how much that means to me. Of course I don't mind. But if you're taking time out of your schedule to tutor my daughter, I insist on paying you, and I won't take no for an answer," he smiled. "And I guess it goes without saying, that drinks are on the house whenever you stop by the Triple B," he winked.

She laughed, genuinely laughed. "Be careful what you offer Lucas, I happen to have an iron stomach, and happen to like top shelf liquor. You might not be able to afford me," she kidded back. "On a more serious note, I'm not helping your daughter because she's your daughter, which I must say was an obvious lack of observation on my part. Now that I know who her father is, the resemblance is definitely there and I was foolish to not see it earlier. But, I bet her self-assured, confident attitude comes from her momma," she added.

"How'd you know?" he asked.

"I just did. Kelsey is a very intelligent young lady, but her reading disability is a very contentious source of frustration for her. She is a pleasure to teach, but I could also tell from the first day of class, that she is embarrassed that her reading isn't quite on the same level as her peers. Yet, she doesn't let anyone in her class see how much she struggles when she attempts to read. That is a sign of a true warrior in my eyes. She has been taught to be independent, confidant and strong, despite whatever is thrown at her. And now I know that she gets it from you and her grandmother, but I also know that she gets it from Anastasia, her mother. How old was Kelsey when Anastasia mother passed?" she asked gently.

"Four."

"I truly am so sorry Lucas," she said sincerely, reaching her hand up to touch his arm gently. She had always been a touchy-feely sort of person, so to her the gesture was innocent. The second she touched him, Luke felt the jolt of electricity rush through his body and he felt anything but innocent. Here they were, talking about his deceased wife, and he could feel his innards awakening to her simple touch. He wanted to step back, away from her touch but found he couldn't. She stood just inches away, so close that he could smell a flowery scent intermingled with a scent that reeked of pure seduction. He doubted that she wore perfume to school, let alone at a soccer game but was curious to know what the scent was. Without thinking, he heard the words escaping his lips.

"You really smell good. What is it you're wearing?" he asked innocently. Immediately seeing her blush, he quickly realized his mistake and would have done anything to be able to take it back. She really didn't know what to say or how to act, so she simply told him the truth.

"Thanks. I assume you're referring to my body lotion, and not my sweat, she kidded. "It's called Seduction, by Victoria's Secret. It's my favorite," she said, in a near whisper.

He looked at her, realizing that, at some point, she'd removed her hand from his arm; and was now subconsciously rubbing her crossed arms up and down as if to warm herself. He'd thought she was cute when he'd first met her. But standing her, in her leggings and school colors, hair pulled up and with barely a trace of makeup on; he really looked at her, as if for the first time. She was beautiful, in an all-natural sort of way. She wasn't the type of woman who needed to paint on an illusion with makeup. Her true beauty was in the simplicity of her look, and the way she carried herself. She reminded him of his Anastasia in many ways.

"No, I wasn't referring to your sweat," he laughed. Just as he was about to act on impulse, and ask her if she'd like to come to the Bistro for a cup of coffee, he heard his daughter's voice summoning him, breaking him out of the trance that he'd somehow slipped into. "

"I'll be right there, Kels," he shouted back. "The truck's unlocked. Let yourself in and I'll be there in just a minute."

Seeing his daughter wave, and take off towards their truck, he turned his attention back to his daughter's teacher.

"Alexa, Miss Greenwood I mean; again, thank you for taking the time to help my daughter. I sincerely appreciate it, and I really would like to compensate you for your time and effort."

Slightly indignant, she responded quickly and in her most authoritarian voice.

"First of all, it's Alexa, or Lexi to my friends; remember that. Secondly, there is nothing that I do if I don't want to so there is no need to think that you have to thank me or monetarily compensate me. I didn't go into teaching for the money. I went into it to help people, and that's just what I'm doing. I'm helping your daughter learn to work with the brain that God gave her and it is not only a pleasure spending time with her, but also something that I've been enjoying very much." Not one to be impulsive, but definitely one to speak her mind when she was fired up, she added one last statement before she turned to walk away.

"I don't need your money. But if you feel you need to compensate me somehow, why not take me out to dinner some night that you're not working at the Bistro?"

With that, she picked up her clipboard, water bottle and jacket, and left Luke standing there alone, and at a loss of words. He had no idea how he'd done it, but somehow his sincere gratitude had infuriated her, but also landed him a date. Standing frozen in place, he tried to absorb what had just transpired. Since the loss of his wife, he had reluctantly consented to a few dates over the last year or so; all of which had ended in disaster. As he stood there watching Alexa jog away, he knew that a date with Miss Greenwood probably spelled trouble in more ways than one. But for the first time in a long time, the prospect of female companionship actually held promise.

~Chapter 30~

"I know Mar, can you believe it? I have no idea what came over me?" Alexa laughed, as she spoke with her best friend. "One minute, he's thanking me for taking the time to tutor his daughter, and the next, I'm practically throwing myself on him!"

Maren had listened to the excitement in Alexa's voice as she'd told her about the game with such enthusiasm. She hadn't heard her best friend sound so happy in a long time, and she was ecstatic that she'd quite possibly found her niche. Since Alexa had moved back to their hometown, Maren had found that city life wasn't the same without her best friend. The things that had once excited her, she now found somewhat boring and quite frankly, irritating. The noises and fast pace of the city that had once been so intriguing to her, now was more of a nuisance than anything else. But she also knew that she'd never want to return to Old Forge. She remembered her hometown as boring, a place where everything moved at a snail's pace. Hearing the joy and contentment in Alexa's voice made her realize that maybe she'd misjudged her friend's decision to return home. Maybe there truly was something more to their little town; maybe she just hadn't realized it when she was growing up. Her mother would never leave Old Forge, nor would she want her to. In the same token, Maren found it hard trying to envision what life must be like for Alexa living back in the very place that they'd vowed to escape from for so long.

They talked for over an hour, much the same way they had when they'd both lived in the city. Maren told her of her latest dating disasters, while Alexa spoke affectionately about the girls on her soccer team and the drama associated with coaching teenagers. Both sipped on their respective glasses of wine as they caught up, with both wishing the other would move so that they could be in the same town again.

"So has he called you to go out with him?" Maren asked.

Laughing, Alexa smiled to herself. "Sort of."

"What the hell does sort of mean?" Maren demanded. "Either he asked you out or he didn't."

"He doesn't, or at least he didn't, have my phone number to ask me out. So he," she chuckled just thinking about it, "sent a note in with his daughter to school, giving me his cell and asked me to call him this weekend."

"So what did you do," Maren asked, suddenly very interested in her best friend's potential love life.

"I explained to Kelsey, his daughter, that I needed her to give her father a note back from me; to which she gladly agreed. In it, I told him that I was free all weekend, and that if he'd like to take me on a date, then it was up to him to call me. Oh, and I provided my number," she laughed. "It's so funny! I feel like I'm a school girl, trying to pass notes in class without the teacher catching me!"

"So are you going to go out with the hunky bartender this weekend?" her best friend teased. "You've never dated a man who had a child before. How does she factor into all of it?" Maren asked, suddenly very serious.

"Mar, we're going out to dinner, not walking down aisle. It's just a dinner date, nothing more."

"Bull shit Lexi! You wouldn't be going out with the man if you weren't interested in him. How many guys have you gone out to dinner with since Bradford? I could count the number on one hand. It's me you're talking to remember? Mr. Bistro owner must have something special or you wouldn't be going out with him. And all I'm saying, is if it works out and you two become a couple, there's a third party that you have to factor in, that's all. So tell me, what's his little girl like?"

Alexa knew that Maren was right and the point that she'd just stated was something that Alexa had thought about on several occasions since Lucas had finally gotten up the nerve and made the call, asking her out to dinner. Both he and Alexa knew that it was simply that, one person asking the other out for a few drinks and a meal together; not pledging their love and commitment to one another. But both also knew that it was a big step for both of them, for different reasons, and as the weekend grew near, Alexa found herself second guessing her decision to say yes.

"She's wonderful, Mar," she found herself saying, thinking about Kelsey. "She's smart, very articulate for her age, feisty as all get out and truly one of my favorite students in the class. She is outspoken, despite the fact that she's very sensitive about her reading disability. I think we're finally making a break through with her reading and even though I think she'll always be an auditory learner, she's becoming more comfortable reading aloud in class. She's really a great kid and when you come up to visit, you might quite possibly meet her since she has become quite the fan of the soccer team that I'm coaching."

Listening to her best friend talk, Maren responded in the only manner she knew how, which was honestly. "Sounds like you my friend, have a ready-made family; and you haven't even gone out with the man on a first date yet."

"Oh bite me, Mar," Alexa responded defensively. "I love all of my students, but I have a soft spot for a fighter. I always have, you know that. Kelsey reminds me of an underdog, and maybe that's why I'm drawn to her. You know the type; has been dealt some really horrific blows but keeps on fighting? That's Lucas's little girl. She's been through some pretty heavy stuff for someone so young, but still has a positive attitude and great outlook."

"Oh boy, Alexa. You're in deep. And I really hope that you and Luke hit it off because I would hate to see you or his daughter hurt."

Knowing that her best friend was right, Alexa responded from her heart.

"No matter what, if anything, comes from me dating her father; I would never hurt that little girl. Kelsey means the world to me and I would never do anything to hurt her."

They ended the call, but not without Alexa promising to provide her with all the details of her upcoming date. She just had to make it through work in the morning and then Saturday evening would be just around the corner. After hanging up with Maren, Alexa went to her closet to choose an outfit suitable for a first date. As she stared at the vast assortment of designer labels and fancy blouses and slacks that lined her closet from her previous life, she was in a quandary as to what she should wear. As the phone rang, she answered it not paying attention to the caller ID.

"Hello Alexa. You went so far as to change your phone number? Haven't you carried this little charade on long enough? You've proven your point, and it is time for you to come to your senses and return back where you belong. Mother and I were discussing you the other day, and she, like I, feel that you needed some time and space to get your priorities straightened out. I've given you long enough darling; it's time that you apologize for being so stubborn and come back to New York and leave the boonies behind. I've made arrangements for a moving van to be at your home next weekend and I've contacted your former employer telling them that you'd made a horrible mistake. It took some convincing, and a sizable donation toward the construction of their new library, but the superintendent pulled a few strings and was able to secure a position on their faculty for you. So pack your things, Alexa. I forgive you, and I will give you another chance. You'll be moving in with me, and I've even had Stella graciously clear out the third bedroom in my townhouse for your junk."

Alexa remained frozen in her bedroom, trying to absorb what Bradford had just told her. After changing her cell provider and phone number, she hadn't heard from him in over a month; and had thought that he'd finally gotten the hint and moved on with his life. That obviously wasn't the case from the pathetic barrage of instructions and orders that she'd just heard come out of his mouth. Could he be so arrogant to think that after all of these months, she'd just come crawling back to him, apologizing for ever leaving him? The thought would have made her laugh if his dissertation hadn't been so ridiculous, and something he obviously believed to be true. She took another moment before responding, forcing herself to take a deep breath and calm her temper. It was only then that she felt that she could answer the fool that had once been not only her lover, but a friend.

"Bradford, what a surprise. I thought that since we haven't spoken in weeks, that you'd finally gotten the hint and moved on. Obviously not, though I thought that I'd read something about you being engaged to your prep school sweetheart" she responded, trying her best to hold back the venom in her tone.

"Before you say anything else that could quite possibly upset me, and quite frankly, piss me off; let me let you in on a little secret. I love my new job and have no intention of leaving it. I do not miss the city, and have no intention of returning to its craziness, and lastly, I love living in the boonies as you put it. The people up here who have become my friends, aren't superficial leeches like so many of your friends in New York. They are genuine and come with no pretenses. What you see with them, is what you get, and everyone who lives here looks out for one another, but they also mind their own business and take care of their own. It's a great community, and for someone who never bothered to come visit, despite the numerous invitations that were extended to you back when we were dating, you have no right to judge me or the people who live here. So Bradford darling, crawl back under whatever rock you've been living under since I left you. I have no interest in returning to New York, to you, and I certainly have no interest in ever seeing that dreadful witch of a mother you have, ever again. Oh, and for the record, she's as much a bitch as you are a conceited, spoiled little man. Good-bye Bradford. And don't bother calling me again; your number will be blocked as soon as I hang up this phone, which is now."

With trembling hands, she hung up the line, and promptly blocked his cell number.

~Chapter 31~

The day flew by, with all of her students aware that it was the end of the school week. Alexa and her soccer team had a home game and, as with every other game, she saw not only Kelsey, and her grandmother, but also Lucas in the stands. He had become a staple, along with his daughter; and someone she looked forward to seeing. She smiled when they made eye contact, then quickly returned her focus to the game about to unfold in front of her.

The game had been touch and go, with Alexa's girls squeaking out a win, despite being the underdog against a previously undefeated team. She screamed in excitement, racing out to meet her team as the final whistle blew indicating a hard-fought victory. Lucas watched her interacting with her players, feeling something stir inside him. He dismissed it as pride and happiness for the home team, but deep down knew that it was something altogether different. Alexa did something to him that he couldn't explain, nor did he want to. He felt that he should be chastising himself for thinking about her so much, despite the fact that they hadn't even gone out on a date yet. "Well," he thought to himself, "we'll get the first date over with tomorrow and then go from there."

Alexa on the other hand, didn't fixate on the fact that she had a date with one of Old Forge's most eligible bachelors. She looked at Lucas as a savvy business owner, an attentive father, and an all-round nice person. She had absolutely no expectations for tomorrow night's date, and refused to allow the butterflies in her stomach to flutter when she saw him approaching her after the game. She noted that Samantha had kept Kelsey at bay, allowing Lucas to address her in private.

"Hey, great game," he greeted her enthusiastically. "I really didn't think that they could beat Remsen. You and the girls should be very proud of yourselves," he added. When he smiled, his dimples came out, just enough to make his boyish looks even more attractive than they already were. His blue eyes seemed to twinkle when he put his guard down and simply relaxed. He was attractive enough when he was bartending, or when she'd seen him at the grocery store, or at church, which she'd starting faithfully going to every Sunday. Not only did she enjoy the young priest's sermon, but also had realized when she'd moved back, that attending mass was also a social gathering. For a small town, whose population waxed and waned, depending on its seasonal tourists, Alexa realized quickly that Sunday mass was not only for cleansing the soul, but also for catching up with neighbors and friends. Every Sunday following mass, her little church offered coffee, tea and some sort of pastry. This gesture enticed its parishioners to stay just a little longer, mingle a little more with others in the congregation, and strengthen the unity of the people who called Old Forge home.

"Thanks! The girls played incredibly and have really come together as a team," she added. "Thanks for coming in support of the girls!"

"I come to see you." The words slipped out before he could stop them, surprising them both.

"Oh," was all Alexa could think to say, feeling herself blush.

Seeing what he thought was distress, Luke immediately tried to back paddle, knowing that he couldn't take the words back, but he could at least try to explain them.

"I mean, of course I like seeing you, and um, I bring Kelsey because she likes seeing you, but of course she sees you every day. And well, because she's really getting into soccer and excited about watching the team play, I figure why not bring her right? And yes, I watch the game, and yes I see you because you're like, right there on the field; but it's not like I come here just to see you. I don't want you think that I'm stalking you or anything. Does that make sense or am I just stammering and inserting my already big foot deeper into my mouth," he laughed, seeing the smile come across her face, replacing any look of distress that she'd had just a moment ago.

"You're fine," she replied, looking directly at him. "I've found myself looking up into the bleachers in search of you as well. I can't explain why, but seeing you and Kelsey in the stands provides me with a sense of security, despite what the scoreboard might be showing me at any given moment. Maybe it's because from what I know about you, you're solid and dependable and someone that anyone can count on, should they need help. So, I guess seeing you at the games supporting my girls is very reassuring for me." She blushed again. "Now am I the one stammering or inserting my foot into my mouth?" she asked, with a sly looking smile crossing her face.

Later he wouldn't be able to explain what came over him. But hearing the words leave her lips, and the sincerity in them; he acted on impulse, leaning in and giving her a very quick, not so innocent kiss on her lips. The connection was broken as quickly as their lips had touched, but not before the jolt of energy entered both their bodies.

As he separated himself from her, he said the only thing that he could formulate in his mind.

"I care about you Alexa, because you care about my daughter; and Kelsey is, and will always be the center of my universe. With that said, I'd really like to get to know you better, and am looking forward to our date tomorrow evening. One thing to remember about me Lexi, regardless of how our first date goes; we are friends and if you ever need anything, anything at all, you just need to call me and I'll be there for you."

Slightly taken back by the sincerity of his statement, and still reeling from their two second kiss, Alexa tried to formulate her words.

"Thank you, Lucas. That means a lot to me. And regardless how our date goes tomorrow, know that your daughter is very special to me and nothing between us will affect my feelings for her. So," she said, changing the subject, "where are we going tomorrow and what type of attire should I wear?"

Luke had been struggling trying to figure out who could stay with Kelsey while he was out on his date since his mother had already made plans with Jacqueline and Marsha that couldn't be changed. One of his young waitresses had offered to babysit her but Kelsey wasn't at all excited about the prospect of someone different spending the evening with her, and had made her opinion very clear. Luke had no idea how Alexa would react or respond, but he asked her anyway.

"About that," he started, trying to pick the right words. Feeling that he was about to dump her before they'd even had their first date, Alexa found herself tightening up, ready for rejection.

"I sort of lost my sitter for tomorrow night, and I know it's not traditional, but would you be totally opposed to us taking a rain check on the fancy dinner that I had wanted to take you on? And instead, would you possibly consider having a threesome?" As soon as he heard the words leave his lips, he blushed. "I mean, not a threesome threesome! I mean, do you think it would be okay if we went out on our date and brought Kelsey with us? She really likes you and she knows that we are going out tomorrow night, and wanted to come with us anyway. So, would you consider an unconventional dinner date with us?"

"Oh my God, of course she can come! Kelsey is always welcome to join us. Besides, it takes the stress out of it and alleviates any first date jitters don't you think," she joked. "So now that that's settled, where are we going to go and what attire should I wear?"

The idea hit him like a ton of bricks. "Um, since we're really going for unique, how about you wear something very casual, and warm? Maybe like layers since it's starting to get chilly in the evening. Do you bake?" he asked, changing the subject yet again.

"Yes, why?"

"Then how about you bake some brownies or some type of desert and let me take care of the rest. We'll pick you up, say around four?"

"Sure," she said, now intrigued, curious as to what he might be planning. "Does Kelsey have a favorite kind of cookie" she asked.

"Chocolate. Anything chocolate works for my girl."

"Good enough. I'll make something with chocolate," she said as she picked up her bag to finally head toward her truck. "Oh, and Lucas," she nearly purred. "Is there anything special you'd like?" she asked, knowing exactly how she was wording the phrase.

Looking at her standing there, tired, slightly muddy, but still very sexy looking, he found himself eyeing her up and down. "Yes there is…" He didn't need to say another word, his expression revealed everything she needed to know.

"Good night Lucas. See you tomorrow at four."

~Chapter 32~

He'd hardly slept the night before, yet he woke before sun up and had already mowed the lawn for probably the last time for the season, raked the leaves, harvested the last of the produce from their garden, paid the bills and started making stew before Kelsey had even woke. He should have felt exhausted, yet for some reason, he was full of energy and found himself whistling along to the tunes emitting from his radio. Samantha noticed her son's unbelievably chipper mood as soon as she walked in the house and saw him. Normally one who despised coffee, she wondered what the sudden metamorphosis was about; and then remembered that he had his date with Alexa coming up later that afternoon. She made herself at home, pouring a cup of coffee and sitting down at his table. Kelsey greeted her warmly, as she watched her morning cartoons and practically inhaled her cheerios. This was their habitual Saturday morning routine, and neither Samantha, nor Lucas would have it any other way.

"Well, isn't everybody up and in a festive mood this morning. Lucas, it smells absolutely fabulous in here, is that Grandma Parker's Irish stew recipe I'm smelling?"

"Yes mam! Right down to the caramelized onions, which by the way, are a pain in the ass to do. Oops, sorry, Kels."

Fixated on her cheerios and current TV show, she didn't look up. "What?"

"Nothing sweetie. Your father was just saying naughty words and looking to put himself in time out. Enjoy your show, pay no attention to us."

Turning toward her son, she encouraged him to join her on the porch, out of earshot of his daughter. As soon as he did, she turned to him and smiled.

"So what's the occasion? It isn't every Saturday morning that I find you chained to the stove, whipping up a scrumptious meal. Why today? And what time do we eat?" she teased, knowing full well that the meal must be for his dinner date later in the evening.

"Well, since you bailed on me and can't watch Kelsey, and she freaked about having Sarah come babysit her, I decided to take her with me on my date with Alexa."

"Oh? Does Alexa know that? Not necessarily the most romantic first date in history you know Lucas?"

"Mom, it's a dinner date, not a proposal. I did mention it and she's completely on board with Kelsey tagging along. I think it makes it less awkward you know?"

Taking a moment to sip on her coffee, and choose her words, his mother responded.

"Luke, it's been a long time. You know how much we all loved Anastasia, and no one will ever take her place. And yes, before you say it, I know that this isn't the first date you've had since she passed away. But what I do know, is that the other women whom you've gone out with since Ana died were insignificant, in the sense that they might have been great women, but they weren't for you. You know it, and as your mother, I know it. They were simply fillers so to speak. So that you could tell me, yourself and the world that you were still living and moving on with your life. They were never meant to help you fill the void, nor were they ever meant to become someone special in your life. With that said, I think that Alexa is different. I've seen the way that you look at her when you think I'm not aware. And don't you give me that look young man," she scolded when she knew he was about to argue with her. "Let me finish, Luke. I've seen the way you light up when she walks into the Bistro, and I've witnessed the smile spread across your face when the soccer game is over and you watch your little girl race towards her on the field. She's not only beautiful; but she's grounded, kind, and a genuinely good person. And Alexa gets it. She knows that you're a father first, and respects you for that. All I'm saying Luke, is give her a chance. Take it slow, and don't fight it if you find yourself becoming attracted to her. Ana wouldn't want you spending the rest of your life alone. That's all I'm going to say on the matter and I won't interfere, son. Well, at least not too much," she added, with a smile. "So Irish stew huh? Are you inviting her here or are you and Kelsey going there?" she asked inquisitively.

"Neither. Kelsey and I are taking her on a picnic."

"In this weather? Are you crazy?" she asked.

"Nope. It was Kelsey's idea. She said that she wanted to take Alexa hiking and show her the site of our future home. I figured that since it's not supposed to be overly cold out tonight, we'd take a drive up the mountain, have a bonfire and eat under the stars. Kelsey and I are heading up there this morning to set things up. WAna tag along?" he asked.

"I'd love to Luke, but Marsha, Jacqueline and I have our show at the Stanley this evening and we're heading to Utica mid-afternoon to grab a bite to eat and do a little shopping. Otherwise, I would have really enjoyed it. Make sure you bring extra blankets just in case it gets colder than you expect out. And take lots of pictures. I've always loved that spot."

"Will do."

Samantha got up to leave, but not before finding Kelsey who was currently glued to the TV. Kissing her only granddaughter on the head, she made her way toward the door.

"Remember Kelsey, help your dad get everything ready for your picnic tonight. And always remember just how much I love you."

Not looking up from the plasma screen and her favorite cartoon, Kelsey waved. "Bye grandma. Love you too. And look out for moose when you're driving," she added.

Always the little adult, Samantha smiled. "I will Kels. Thanks for the reminder."

Meeting her son at the doorway, she felt the need to hug him, and as she did so, was compelled to give him just one last word of advice.

"Go enjoy yourself tonight Lucas. No matter how the evening unfolds, remember that you deserve love and to be loved. And before you say a word, yes I know that it's only your first date with Alexa, and a unique one at that. I just want more than anything in this world for my two boys to be happy. It's been a very long time since either of you were and maybe after tonight, you'll be starting on the right path towards finding love and happiness once again."

"Love you too, mom. Like Kelsey said, make sure that you're looking out for deer and or moose tonight."

"No worries, she laughed. Marsha's driving; I'm just riding shotgun so I'll be on the lookout." With that, Samantha said her good-byes, leaving her son with a sense of foreboding, that he quickly dismissed, with his mind once again wandering back to Alexa.

~Chapter 33~

The day flew by for Alexa and as she changed her outfit for the third time, she realized that it was already 3:40 and Luke would be picking her up within the hour. She settled for the outfit that she'd just put on, quickly refreshed her makeup and packed up her picnic basket. Not quite sure what to make of their "date", and having absolutely no idea where they were going, she overpacked the basket with disposable plates, napkins, plastic utensils and other essentials. Just as she was applying another layer of lip balm, she saw the black truck approaching. Knowing it was Luke, she quickly checked herself in the mirror one last time, before opening the door to find Kelsey running towards her.

"Hi!"

"Hello Kelsey," she greeted the child warmly. "So are you going to tell me about where we're going? Or is it still a surprise?" Looking up at Lucas, she not only felt her heart warm, but also start to race.

He was dressed much like she was, in layers that included a cotton crew neck, flannel shirt, jeans, hiking boots and a down vest. And she couldn't help but think that he looked gorgeous; boyish grin and all.

"Dad told me that I can't tell you where our secret picnic spot is. But I can tell you that it's one of the prettiest places around here and you're gonna love it like we do. At least I think that you will. Right, dad?" she asked, looking toward her father for not only reassurance but support.

"How about we get going and once we're there, we can let Alexa decide for herself." He lifted the picnic basket from her arms, extended his hand to help her down the stairs, and then opened both the front and rear passenger doors for she and Kelsey. Climbing up into the front seat with him suddenly made it feel very much like a date. She would have gotten nervous except for the fact that Kelsey talked incessantly the entire drive out of town and up the mountain.

Alexa knew the general vicinity but once they started climbing in elevation on the unmarked dirt roads, she had no idea where they were. It wasn't until Luke pulled into a pseudo driveway, which if it weren't for the scattered crusher run that caught her eye, she would never have guessed it was a place to park. Lucas had no sooner put the truck in park when Kelsey was jumping out excitedly. Not quite sure what was going on, Alexa found herself turning toward Luke questioningly.

"Kelsey and I thought it might be fun to have a picnic and watch the sun set." He offered no more.

"Where are we?"

"We're on top of Blackman Hill, which connects to McCauley. I bought the land last year and someday plan on building a little log cabin up here for Kels and I. So far, all I've managed to complete after purchasing the lot and getting it somewhat cleared, was to put in the well, driveway and erect the garage. But it's a start, right?" he asked, smiling just enough to allow his dimples to pop.

He motioned for her to accompany him down the drive to where they could hear Kelsey shouting for them. When they turned the corner, it became very evident why he'd picked the spot. She nearly gasped when the entire Fulton Chain of Lakes appeared before her. Lucas had bought land high enough in elevation that it not only looked down on Old Forge, but also provided a panoramic vista of First through part of Fourth Lake. She turned toward him and smiled. He'd remained silent as she took in the view; studying her, as she was studying it.

"So, what do you think?" he asked sincerely.

"I think it's magnificent, Lucas. You and Kelsey couldn't have picked a better spot. Do you have your blue prints drawn up yet? I'd love to see what you're planning on building."

"Actually, I do. Why don't we set this stuff down in the garage, get some lights on, and start a fire before the temp drops too much. Then I'll pull them out and you can let me know what you think. Would you like a glass of wine before I start getting organized?"

"Sound like a plan. But the wine can wait until after I help you get everything going."

"Alrighty then," he laughed. "The wine can wait." And with that, their date officially started.

  The evening went off without a hitch. Alexa, Kelsey and Lucas spent the entire evening talking, eating, and laughing; with each genuinely having a good time. They absorbed the warmth of the fire, while gorging themselves on Smores, with Kelsey eating so many that she felt like she'd explode. Alexa talked about growing up in Old Forge, with Kelsey asking question after question about what school and the town was like when she'd lived there as a child. Lucas had to remind her on more than one occasion that Alexa was not a hundred years old and that she'd lived in their town less than a decade before. Looking at her for reassurance, Alexa confided that he was correct and that she was not quite twenty-nine years old, and had in fact, called Old Forge home up until she'd graduated from college and stayed in New York. He'd asked her about life in New York, her friends, school where she'd taught, and her family. She answered honestly and sincerely, asking him questions about himself as well. Over the course of the evening, they not only solidified their friendship, but really started to get to know one another. With Kelsey asleep in the back seat of the truck, they packed up the last of the food and prepared to start the trip down the mountain.

"Lucas," she said, breaking the silence. "I just want you to know that this was the nicest date that I can ever remember going on. Thank you," she added, sincerely.

"No, Alexa, thank you. I stopped living the day my Ana died. And of course I've gone on a few dates here and there over the years since she passed. But I can honestly say that this has been the first evening in a very long time, that I haven't wanted to end. Thank you for spending it with me."

With that simple proclamation, she knew that she had already fallen.

They made small talk on their way back down the mountain while his daughter slept soundly in the back seat. The sky was illuminated with the full moon and near cloudless night. Alexa commented on how many shooting stars they'd seen while sitting by the fire. It wasn't until they were nearly off the mountain, that his phone started chirping nonstop indicating that he had numerous missed calls and texts. He continued to drive, not checking his phone to see who had called him so many times. He didn't want business ruining the evening, and knew that whoever had called him could wait until he dropped Alexa off. When the phone rang again, and saw his brother's name appear on his console screen, he was inclined to ignore it. Seeing his hesitation, she smiled.

"You can answer it Lucas, I don't mind."

The second he answered, his brother nearly screamed into the truck.

"Where the hell have you been? Mom's been in an accident and you decide to ignore my calls? WTF!"

Taking a second to absorb what his twin had just told him, he nearly crashed his truck. Instead, he quickly pulled over, throwing it into park.

"What?" he practically screamed into the phone.

"Mom and her friends were heading north from Utica and some fuckhead was driving through the construction zone going the wrong way and hit their truck head on. All I know is that she was rushed to St. Elizabeth's hospital and it doesn't look good. The call I got was for family to come as quickly as possible and that they were taking her into surgery. I'm hauling ass to get there and I'm already on the thruway but Luke, but you need to get there now!" he pleaded.

Alexa gasped hearing the news. She watched the color drain from his face. He remained silent as if not able to process the information. And then it hit her. Maren's mother was one of the passengers. She forced the words out of her mouth.

"Logan, it's Alexa. Do you know anything about the other women in the truck?"

Surprised to hear a female's voice in his brother's vehicle, it took Logan a second to respond. And to Alexa, that second seemed like hours.

"The officer only told me that there was a fatality, but wouldn't elaborate more. He said that our mother was transported to St. Elizabeth's, and when I called there, the only thing I could get out of the nurse was that she was already in surgery. Get there, Luke. I'm already on my way, but have another three hours before I can get to her."

"I'll be there in under an hour," Lucas heard himself say, as he threw his truck into drive and raced toward town. He forced his mind to believe that it couldn't be happening for a second time in his life, with another woman that he loved. He hadn't even given his date or his daughter a second thought; the only thing he wanted to do was get to the hospital and his mother before it was too late.

"Lucas, leave Kelsey with me. You get to your mom and don't worry about Kelsey. A hospital is no place for a child." She didn't ask him if he wanted to entrust her with his child. He had just begun to really know her, but he already knew in his heart that he could trust Alexa with his daughter. Kelsey already adored her teacher, so the decision was already decided as soon as the words left her lips.

"I have to get to her, and I have no idea how long I'll be at the hospital," he said, starting to panic, remembering how his last trip to the hospital turned out. As if reading his mind, Alexa reacted without thinking, pulling him into a quick hug as soon as they exited his truck.

"She's going to make it Lucas. She's not Anastasia; and God would never do that to you again. She's going to be okay Luke. And please don't worry about your daughter. I promise I'll take care of your daughter as if she were my own. Now go, get to your mother."

He set his daughter gently down on the bed she'd indicated, turned to Alexa and spoke, though his throat felt like it was constricting on him.

"Thank you Lexi. Take care of my girl. I won't forget this," he added, in a near whisper.

"Go Lucas. Get to your mom. I'll take care of our Kels."

He raced out the door, into his truck and towards Utica without looking back. He willed himself to believe that his mother would not only live, but be okay. He called Jason, one of his best friends who happened to be a Town of Webb cop, explained what was going on, and told him to clear the path on 28 for him because he had no intention of driving the speed limit. It only took seven minutes for Lucas to see the patrol car pull out behind him, siren and lights ablaze. He never slowed up on the pedal and was damned if he was going to pull over. As he continued to drive as fast as he dared drive, the patrol car quickly pulled out and flew by him, but not before he made eye contact with its' driver. Realizing it was in fact his friend, their split second visual exchange was clearly communicated. As the patrol car pulled away and returned to the lane in front of him, he accelerated, now that he had a police escort, for at least part of the journey.

What should have taken 60 minutes, took 45, thanks in part to his friend. He raced into the Emergency Room entrance to locate his mother, only to find out that she was already in surgery, as his brother had thought. After pleading for answers, he was finally able to find someone willing to at least tell him about his mother's injuries. The young resident who met him was articulate in his speaking, but also straight and to the point. He didn't sugarcoat anything, explaining that his mother was lucky to be alive given the circumstances of the accident. He went on to elaborate that she was the least injured of the three women in the vehicle but still required surgery for the compound fracture of her leg, collapsed lung and fractured wrist. Lucas tried to absorb the information that he was being given. He heard the ER physician state that his mother was alive, and after that, the rest became a blur. After he processed what little information the physician had given him, he sat. As the physician offered his obligatory condolences, he turned to leave. As he started to walk away, Luke remembered that his mother's two best friends were also in the Marsha's truck.

"Excuse me, Doctor," he shouted to the physician.

"Yes?"

"What about my mom's two friends that were also in the vehicle?" he heard himself ask, not really ready for the answer.

"The driver is also in surgery. She's pretty banged up but should make it. The police are notifying her next of kin. The rear seat passenger wasn't wearing a seat belt, was ejected from the vehicle and died at the scene. I'm sorry," he offered, and nothing more, walking away, leaving Lucas alone in the room.

"Oh my God," he thought. He'd have to tell Alexa, knowing that she was best friends with Marsha's daughter Maren. He was about to dial her number, when his phone rang. Realizing it was his brother, he answered on the first ring, and quickly updated him on her condition.

Finishing their conversation as he paced in the surgical waiting room, his thoughts returned to Alexa. Knowing that she might very well be asleep, he called her, though he was prepared for her voice mail. She answered on the first ring.

Somehow hearing her voice calmed his frayed nerves. She grounded him; despite the horrible circumstances, somehow just hearing her voice soothed him and calmed him down. Before he could tell her about Maren's mother, she was asking about his mom. He gave her what he knew, and couldn't offer anything else, appreciative that she hadn't asked about the others yet.

Then she asked. Her voice didn't waver, but he could hear the hesitancy. His opinion of her only increased exponentially as he could tell she was battling an internal battle, yet she kept her composure as she spoke.

He refused to give her anything but the straightforward truth. He wouldn't sugarcoat the facts, knowing that she wouldn't want him to.

"Alexa, the driver of the other SUV was traveling at a high rate of speed, going the wrong direction on Route 12. He hit Marsha's truck head on, and there was a fatality." He heard her gasp. "Honey, Alexa, I'm sorry to tell you, but Jacqueline was in the rear seat and was ejected from Marsha's truck and died at the scene. The doctor told me that the trooper said that she didn't suffer and probably died instantly. I'm so sorry to have to tell you, I really am," he added.

"Oh my Gosh, that's horrible Lucas." Taking a deep breath, she continued, addressing what needed to be addressed, despite the devastating news.

"But it sounds like your mom is going to be okay, thank God. What do you want me to tell Kelsey, Lucas? Your little girl's very intelligent, and she's going to ask."

"I know," he responded reluctantly. "I've never withheld the truth from her and I've never lied to her. I hate putting you in this position and I wish I could be there to tell her myself Lexi, I really do. I guess just tell her the basics. Tell her grandma was in accident and that she has a few broken bones and won't be hiking any mountains anytime soon. But please stress that she's going to be okay and that I'll come home as soon as I can."

"Okay," she whispered, lost in thought. Then she spoke what was on her mind, like she always did. "Lucas," she asked softly. "Would it be easier for Kelsey if I brought her back to your home so that she's in familiar surroundings? Or do you want me to bring her down to the hospital to be with you? I'll do whatever you feel is the best for your daughter and for you? Please just tell me how I can help?"

"You're already helping more than you'll ever know, Alexa. But I don't think Kels should come down here until we know that mom is out of surgery and doing okay. Why don't you give Kels the option of staying with you or you guys heading back to our house and play it by ear? Oh, and Alexa," he said sincerely, "I won't ever forget this. Thank you."

"I care about you, Lucas. And this is what friends do; they help each other out in times of need," she responded, with just a hint of emotion in her carefully chosen words. "But before I let you get back to your mother, I have to ask. Do you know anything about Maren's mother? And do you have any idea if the police or the hospital have contacted next of kin yet? Maren needs to know about the accident and needs to come home."

"Oh God, Lexi; I totally forgot that Marsha's daughter is your best friend. I'm so sorry! I mean I remembered that she was when I got the call, but then I raced here, and everything has been coming at me at once and I quite honestly forgot to say anything to you about Marsha! I've been so fixated on my mom that everything else didn't register. Yes, I know that she's also in surgery and the doctor didn't offer much except to say that her injuries were more extensive than my mom's but that they expect her to pull through as well. God Lexi, I'm sorry to have been so insensitive."

"Lucas, stop. Your mom and your daughter are the two most important people in your life so I would expect you to be focused on only them. I'm going to let you go so that I can compose myself enough to call Maren and break the news if she doesn't already know. Give her a hug for me when she gets there. Lucas, she doesn't do well with stuff like this so please be supportive of her. And Luke," she added, with her voice going soft, "Don't worry about your daughter. I love your little girl, and I'll treat her like my own and take very good care of her. So stay with your mom as long as you need to. Just take care of yourself and be there for your mother."

She hung up, leaving him hanging on the other end, wishing there were words to thank her adequately for what she was doing for him. And in that moment, he realized that there was definitely something special about Alexa. Lucas took a deep breath, returned to the surgical waiting room, wishing that Alexa was by his side. He knew that his brother was probably breaking all speed limits to join him, but at that moment, he wanted a hand to hold and someone to reassure him that the matriarch of their family was going to pull through. He refused to think about Anastasia and compare the accidents. He refused to believe that the outcome could possibly turn out the same. And he refused to believe that God could be that cruel to one family, and one little girl. His daughter had already lost her mother, and he'd be damned if she was going to lose her grandmother in the same manner.

    Alexa tip-toed to her spare bedroom where Kelsey was sleeping soundly, curled up with an overstuffed pillow, and her down comforter pulled up nearly to her neck. She noticed that she'd moved the stuffed wolf that had been sitting in her grandmother's rocking chair. Now Niko the wolf was predominantly perched next to the child's head, as if to ward off any evil spirits. Lexi smiled as she gazed down at the sleeping child, noting how peaceful she appeared. As she lay sleeping, she could see how beautiful the little girl truly was, and quickly realized that she would be a stunning woman once puberty allowed her to grow into her features. Looking at the child, she could see she had Lucas' chin, and dimples, but also surmised that many of her features must have come from her mother. Alexa had never considered herself beautiful; wholesome and not ugly, but certainly not stunning the way Lucas's Anastasia must have been. She didn't feel jealous of a woman that she'd never met, just momentarily envious of one that could have produced a child with such great bone structure. She shut the door part way and returned to her kitchen in order to place the call that she knew had to be made, but she dreaded doing regardless. How was she going to tell her best friend that her mother had been critically injured? She took a deep breath and dialed Maren's number.

The call went much smoother than she'd anticipated. Maren had answered on the first ring and the second she had, Alexa realized that she was on speaker phone and that Maren was already in her truck, heading north. She quickly learned that one of the nurses had rummaged through Marsha's personal effects and found Maren's cell number as her mother's emergency contact. Maren had received the call and had a bag packed, her apartment locked up and was on the road within five minutes after she'd received the call. She sounded extremely composed as she relayed her current location, informing Alexa that she was already near Amsterdam and should be to the hospital within the hour. Alexa gave her words of encouragement, without giving her false hope, and promised to join her as soon as she could. She went on to explain that she couldn't be at her side and explained why. Maren thanked her for her support and promised to keep her posted on her mother's condition. And Maren being Maren, teased her for just a brief second about her first date with Lucas. They ended the call, with Maren focusing solely on reaching Utica and her mother. Alexa, always the organized, methodical one, paced, not knowing what to do next. She checked in on Kelsey again, who hadn't budged from the position that she was in when she'd checked in on her just moments before. She knew that she should sleep but was too wound, too upset, and too nervous. Instead of heading to her room, she made sure several night lights were on in case Kelsey woke during the night, then finally retreated to her overstuffed chair, with a large glass of wine. She didn't want the distraction of the television, nor was she interested in the latest posts on Facebook. She just wanted to absorb the silence and enjoy the solitude of the night. She finished her glass of wine, but not before she sent a quick text to Luke, letting him know that his daughter was sleeping soundly, and safe. She asked him to text or call nor matter what time if anything changed in his mother's condition, for the better or worse, and to simply call if he needed someone to talk to. She told Lucas that Maren should be arriving within the hour and might need someone to talk to and/or his support while they waited for their mothers to get out of surgery. He thanked her for her kind words and promised to keep her updated, and promised to be there for Maren as well. When they'd finished texting, she emptied her glass of the remaining drops, washed it, and made her way to the bathroom to wash up.

She had barely drifted off when her phone rang. It took her just a moment to orient and she answered her cell on the second ring. It was Lucas' voice that brought her to attention. Hearing the relief immediately as he spoke helped calm her racing heart. He was brief and to the point. He told her that both his mother and Marsha had made it out of surgery and that both surgeries had been successful from the respective surgeon's viewpoints. She was anxious to ask questions but let him finish, knowing that he needed to say the words in order to believe them himself.

"So, bottom line is, Maren's mom and my mom are two tough old birds as the doctors described them," he half laughed.

"And though they've both got a lot of healing to do, both surgeons expect that they will make full recoveries." She heard him sigh.

"Alexa, I wouldn't be able to go on if I'd lost her. I just wouldn't survive."

"Oh Lucas. You would survive. But again, Samantha isn't your Anastasia. And it wasn't Sam's time. Your mom is one of the strongest, and healthiest people I know, and believe in her, and what the surgeon just told you. She will get through this. It might take weeks or months to be back to 100%, but she will return to her old self before you know it. And Lucas, I'm here for you, and your daughter. Know that your little girl is a joy to be around and anything that I can do to help you through this, I will. Hey, that's what friends are for," she added, smiling.

Just hearing her voice calmed him and made him realize that he truly wasn't alone this time. He knew that his brother would be arriving any minute, and he'd spent the last half hour with Maren, laughing and crying when they'd heard the positive news about their respective mothers. He just wanted to see his mother and see with his own eyes that she was in fact, okay. And most of all, he wanted her to know that both he and Logan were there for her and would always be.

    As he returned to the waiting room, he returned to the loveseat that Maren was still sitting in, waiting anxiously until she could see her mother. She greeted him warmly and reassured him that not only were their moms going to be okay, but he needn't worry about his daughter while she was in Alexa's care. But she was telling him something that he already knew. He'd just shared his first date with her, but already felt as if he knew her so well. Thinking back to what had transpired over the last few hours, the amazing picnic date that he'd been on just hours earlier now seemed like light years ago. He continued making small talk with Maren, asking questions about Alexa, what she liked to do, what she hated, her past relationships and so on. He thought that he was being subtle but Maren saw through his charade the second the conversation circled back around to her best friend. She played right along with the questioning, dying to tease her best friend about the new man in her life. From what Maren remembered of her encounters with Lucas over the summer, and from her exposure to him now, she quickly realized that he couldn't be any more different from the snobbish Bradford Pendington, that had held her best friend's heart for so long. Where Bradford was arrogant, rude and had an ego the size of a tank; Lucas appeared to be genuine, kind and friendly. Though he owned a very successful business in a tourist town, her impression of Luke was wholesome and that he was just an all-round good person. He appeared to be just what he was, a business owner, devoted father, and concerned son. She was about to ask him a question, when his double came flying into the waiting room.

"Where is she? How's she doing? Is she out of surgery yet? Should we have her moved to a bigger hospital like Albany Med or Crouse? Christ, should we have her airlifted down to Manhattan? Several of my clients are docs so I could get her in with the best surgeons and therapists; that is if that's what she needs!" he nearly shouted, not realizing how wound he was, nor how far his voice carried. He then looked from his brother, around the room at the few other people in the waiting room, that were now staring at him, in disdain. He quickly apologized for the outburst and made his way across the room to his brother. They hugged briefly, with Logan taking a seat in the chair next to him. His eyes then locked onto Maren, who up until that point had sat silently watching the exchange.

"Hi. Maren right?"

"Hi. Yes, that's correct. Good memory," she added, with a smile.

"I never forget a pretty face, especially one with eyes like yours."

"Good to know. Excuse me for a minute gentlemen. That last cup of coffee is catching up with me." She stood, straighten her blouse and made her way towards the hallway. As soon as she was out of earshot, Logan leaned in towards his brother.

"What's she doing here? I thought you had a thing for the school teacher? What, did Maren decide to relocate to Old Forge along with Alexa?" he asked, having no idea why Maren was at his side in the middle of the night.

"First of all, I don't have a "thing" for anyone. Maren's here because mom had Jacqueline and Maren's mom Marsha in the truck with her. Logan, we're going to have to tell mom that Jacqueline is dead. The damn idiot that hit them head on was going the wrong way in a construction zone, and from the troopers said, was drunk off his ass and must have been flying. Jacqueline was thrown from the truck and dead at the scene. Mom and Marsha are going to have to be told and because the three of them were inseparable. I'm worried that they're going to have survivors' remorse," he added as an afterthought.

"We can't help Jacqueline, Luke. But we can help mom. Jesus," he stood as if on fire.

"How much longer do you think it's going to take before they'll let us see her?" he asked impatiently.

Just as Luke was about to answer, they saw not only Maren returning to the surgical waiting area where Logan was currently pacing, but also saw that she was in the company of two doctors. Maren quickly introduced both trauma surgeons to Logan and Lucas, explaining that the one had worked on her mother, and the other on theirs. The surgeons separated with the respective families and updated them on their mother's conditions. Logan processed all silently, and for once remained quiet as the surgeon spoke, occasionally glancing over at Maren to make sure that she was holding up okay, with whatever information the surgeon was providing her about her mom. When they finished, reassuring all three that they would be able to see their mothers once they were out of Recovery and moved to Intensive Care. They thanked the surgeons and made their way back the area where they'd been sitting. Maren had held her composure intact until she looked into Logan's eyes and felt the tears start to flow. Even though they'd only met briefly on two occasions, and couldn't even consider themselves friends, he was immediately at her side, to console her and reassure her that their moms would get the best medical care available to them. She held on tightly, and wept softly, leaving Logan unsure what to do next. Sometime during her temporary breakdown, he'd hugged her, subconsciously rubbing her back trying to do anything to calm and reassure her. He'd always been a lady's man and usually knew exactly what to say to a woman in any situation. But a woman's tears were his Achilles heel and he felt not only vulnerable but helpless as he held Maren in his arms.

She wept for only a minute, though to Logan, he would have sworn it was hours. When she was cried out, she discreetly wiped her eyes, blew her nose and straightened her shoulders.

"Thank you Logan. Thank you for allowing me to have my breakdown. I owe you one."

"You care about your mom, Maren; Lucas and I care about your mom. You don't owe me a damn thing," he smiled. He was about to say more, when they were silenced as two nurses made their way into the doorway. They didn't realize it at the moment, but all three held their breath waiting for them to speak. The taller of the two spoke on behalf of both of their moms. She explained that they had just been transferred to ICU and if they gave the ICU nurses a few minutes to get them settled, then they'd be able to see them shortly. All three nodded in agreement, and waited silently until they could be reunited with their respective moms.

~Chapter 34~

Kelsey woke early and made her way toward Alexa's room. She stood at the entrance to her bedroom not quite sure what to do, debating if she should wake her. Kelsey stood silently, holding the wolf that had been her sleeping companion, until she saw Alexa start to stir. As if she felt her presence, Alexa opened her eyes, and as soon as Kelsey came into focus, she smiled, waving the child to her side. Kelsey hesitantly made her way towards her teacher, suddenly very unsure of her surroundings and current situation. Seeing her panicked look, Alexa spoke.

"Good morning Kelsey. Did you sleep well?"

The child nodded but remained silent, as if waiting to hear the inevitable.

"I bet you're not only hungry, but also wondering what you're here at my house right now huh?" She didn't wait for the child to answer. "Your dad brought you to my house last night Kelsey after we had our picnic on the mountain. See, while you were sleeping, your dad got a call and had to go to Utica. Your grandma is fine Kelsey, but she and her girlfriends were in a car accident and your grandma Sam is in the hospital, and that's why you father went to Utica, okay?"

The child remained silent but nodded in understanding, breaking Alexa's heart as she stood there, trying to control her body from shaking.

"I bet you're a little worried about your grandma and your dad, but I promise you Kelsey, your grandma is going to be okay. Your dad told me so and I believe him. You know he wouldn't lie to you right?"

Again, the child nodded but remained silent.

She sat up and gently touched the child's hand. "Kelsey, I spoke with your dad late last night after you were asleep. He wanted me to tell you that your grandmother is going to be okay. She had surgery to fix her injuries and she'll be in the hospital for a while, but he promises, she'll be okay and back home before you know it."

Kelsey searched her eyes and knew that her father would never lie to her and believed that her teacher wouldn't either. So, if both would were saying that her grandmother would live, then it must be true. She willed her tears away but not before a few trickled down her cheek. Alexa saw her pain, and her relief and took the child into her arms.

"Oh honey, let it out. Let it all out and then we'll call your dad and check on your grandma okay?" Before Kelsey could respond, both jumped at the sound of her cell's ring tone. Alexa looked down at the caller ID and felt her heart start racing. Praying that he wasn't calling with bad news, she put on her best game face.

"Speak of the devil, Kels, it's your dad. Why don't you go wash up and I'll talk to your father for just a minute and then let you speak with him, okay?"

Even though she desperately wanted to talk to her father, Kelsey did as she was told, and exited the room. The moment she was gone, Alexa answered the still ringing phone.

"Hey," she answered breathlessly. Just hearing her voice somehow calmed him.

"Hey. How's my girl? I hope she didn't give you any trouble during the night. I forgot to warn you that she sometimes has night terrors. I'm sorry, but with the accident and everything, I totally forgot to tell you about that," he said, as if he'd done something wrong. Before he continued chastising himself, she cut him off.

"Lucas, Kelsey is fine. She slept the night and she and I were just getting up to have breakfast. I would have handled it if she'd experienced any night terrors. I told you before, I love your little girl and I'd never let anything bad happen to her. But more importantly, how is your mom and do you know how Marsha is doing as well?"

"They're both doing remarkably well, given the circumstances and the extent of their injuries. Both are in Intensive Care but both are stable and alert. Their rooms are actually right next to one another so it makes it easy to check in on Maren as well. Logan has sort of made it his mission to make sure that his fellow New Yorker is holding up okay."

Feeling immediate relief, she felt herself calm knowing that the two of them were not only there for their mother, but for her best friend as well since she couldn't be with her. She listened to Lucas describe, the best he could, their injuries and the physician's prognosis. She took it all in, knowing only slightly more about medicine than he did. As he finished, she felt confident that they were being taken very well care of, and barring any unforeseen complications, should both make complete recoveries. As she heard the water shut off in her hallway bathroom, she quickly asked Lucas if he felt that it would be okay for her to bring Kelsey in to see her grandmother, explaining that sometimes a child's imagination of a situation is far worse that what the actual scenario is. She heard the hesitancy in his voice, but trusting in the woman currently caring for his number one priority in life, he conceded and agreed. Smiling, Alexa handed the phone to Kelsey, who was back at her side.

"Hello," she greeted him nervously.

"Hey, Kels, it's dad. Grandma Sam wants to know if you'd come visit her today?"

Seeing the relief in her face, Alexa knew that she'd made the right decision in strongly urging him to allow his daughter to visit.

"Really? Grandma really is okay and you and Alexa aren't just saying that until you can be here to tell me she died like my mom?" she asked through quivering lips.

Knowing that her words must have stabbed Lucas through the heart, she longed to comfort not only the child standing beside her, but Lucas as well. Their family had suffered enough loss, and listening to the ten-year-old trying very hard to keep her composure intact broke her heart.

"Yes really, Kels. Your grandma has got some pretty nasty bumps and bruises, and a very big cast on her leg, and a small one on her wrist, but she will get better, I promise. So why don't you let me speak with Alexa again okay? After you ladies eat breakfast, I bet she'll bring you down here to the hospital to see your grandmother. You'll only be able to stay for a quick visit but I know that grandma Sam would love to see her favorite granddaughter."

"Dad!" she said exasperated, "I'm her only granddaughter."

"Yup! But you're still her favorite! Now go get ready for breakfast and your trip to the city. I'll see you soon, kiddo."

She handed the phone back to Alexa, and took off running toward the spare room where she'd spent the night. Before Alexa ended the call, she was dressed, hair combed and waiting in the kitchen.

They ate their cheerios in relative silence with Kelsey enjoying her hot chocolate and Alexa her steaming hot cup of Earl Grey tea. As much as she was anxious to get to the hospital for not only Lucas and Logan, but also for her best friend, Alexa insisted that they each eat a small serving of fruit in addition to their bowl of cereal. When Alexa put her fruit in the blender, along with yogurt, protein powder, granola and a little soy milk to make a smoothie, Kelsey took note, and decided that she wanted her mandatory bowl of fruit made into a smoothie as well. Having never tried one before, Kelsey hesitantly took the tall glass from Alexa's outstretched hand and tentatively took a sip. The expression on her face told Alexa everything she needed to know, as she smiled smugly. "There's more than one way to skin a cat," she said to herself as she watched the child practically chug the healthy concoction until the glass was empty.

"Alright, kiddo, go brush your teeth and we'll hit the road."

"Okay. Thanks, Alexa!" Giving her a quick hug, Kelsey ran off to brush her teeth, but not before putting her glass in the dishwasher. Alexa stood in awe, reminding herself that she'd have to compliment Lucas on doing such a fine job raising his daughter.

They sang along to most of the songs that played on her Sirius radio stations. To her surprise, not only did Kelsey enjoy country, but she also knew almost every classic rock song that came on. The child might have a country soul, but she definitely had the heart of a rocker, and that suited Alexa just fine. She kept the classic rock channel blaring as they pulled into the parking garage and found an open spot. Lucas had already given her directions on how to find the Intensive Care Unit waiting room, and had asked her to text him when they'd arrived. She and Kelsey were just rounding the last corner before finding the waiting room, when he spotted them, hand in hand, walking towards him. In that moment, he knew. He didn't know how or exactly what he knew; but he knew that from that moment on, his life would never be complete again if Alexa wasn't part of it. Watching his daughter, walking alongside someone who'd only gone from acquaintance to friend recently, tugged at him in a way that he'd never thought possible. They looked so cohesive, like a unit that belonged together, and that warmed his heart. It only took Kelsey a second to see him, and then bolt towards him as if she hadn't seen him in months, not hours. He crouched down, took her into his arms and held on tight. Looking up at the woman standing just a few feet away, he mouthed "Thank you" as he continued to hold his daughter. It was Kelsey who broke the embrace.

"Dad, Alexa likes REO Speedwagon, Boston and Styx too! And she sings their songs way better than you! I got to pick the stations, and we sang tons of songs the whole drive here! Can I see grandma now?"

Laughing, Logan, who'd joined them in the waiting room, chimed in.

"Kelsey, I'm sure that Alexa has a beautiful voice, to match her beautiful face; but if I recall, it doesn't take much to sing better than your father. We're twins but I'm the one who got the good looks and great singing voice. Your father sounds like a dying cow when he sings."

"Uncle Logan" Kelsey exclaimed as she left her father's side to hug her uncle, realizing that he'd entered the hallway behind her. He crouched down to take her into his arms and held her, watching the silent interaction between his brother and Alexa, who until that moment had remained in the background. They remained silent, but her subtle smile, and impermeable eye contact spoke volumes. Lucas walked to her and didn't take her into his arms, but instead reached for her hands, both of them and leaned in for a kiss. Though it was just a brief collision of lips, there was no mistaking the intensity of the contact. Their eye contact never broke and Alexa didn't realize how silent it was around them until Lucas finally spoke.

"I'm so glad you're here, Alexa. Thank you for taking care of my little girl and for bringing her here to me. I will never forget it."

"Lucas, that's what friends do. They take care of each other," she responded, suddenly uncomfortable being the center of attention.

Still holding her hands, he leaned in close.

"I'd like to think that we're heading down the road toward becoming more than just friends, Alexa. But keeping my daughter out of that equation, I meant what I said. You went above and beyond by not only immediately stepping in to take care of my daughter, but also by making sure that she wasn't scared or upset by the circumstances that landed her in your care. My mother has always spoken so highly of you, and truth be told, she's been hoping to get us together since you moved here in June. Remind me to thank her okay? Guess she knew a good thing even before I did."

Blushing, she smiled, not knowing how to respond to his proclamation. Logan coughed to get their attention, with both Alexa and Lucas jumping apart as if they were two kids caught necking under the bleachers.

"I believe I'm holding a kiddo who'd love to visit her grandma now. Would you like to bring her in to see mom and I'll walk Alexa over to Marsha's room so she can be with her best friend?" he suggested.

Alexa was the first to respond. Deliberately stepping towards him, she smiled. "Please. I'd really like to see them both now. Maren must be so upset about her mom."

"We're here for her, Alexa. I've told her the same, and I'm telling you. My brother and I will be here for her, no matter what she or her mother needs."

"That's very kind of you Logan, but don't offer something that you can't necessary deliver. Your home is in New York, and your mom and Marsha's is in Old Forge. I'm sure that Maren will appreciate any moral support you offer her while you're in town, but face it, once you leave, none of us will be able to count on you to help out."

Realizing how harsh her words must have sounded, she tried to backtrack immediately.

"Logan, I'm sorry. I just heard how that sounded and it certainly wasn't meant that way. All I'm saying is that your life is in New York, and I don't know you very well but I do know that you'd probably do anything to help your mother recuperate from her accident. But other than moral support and encouragement over the phone, it will be hard for you to do anything from five hours away. I will help Marsha once she's out of the hospital.

She's always been like my second mom anyway. And in regards to your mother, I will help Lucas with taking care of Kelsey in order for him to help your mother with whatever she needs to assist her in healing."

Before he responded, she saw dimples identical to Lucas' appear. His eyes seemed to illuminate even bluer than they'd been just moments before. He smiled, looking directly at his brother, and then at Alexa.

"No offense taken. My brother is right; you definitely are a keeper. And I guess it's a really good thing that I'm relocating back home so I can be around to do my fair share of helping our mom, and Marsha recuperate."

"What?" Lucas and Alexa both nearly shouted in unison, just as Maren walked into the now crowded waiting room. Before anyone could respond, she saw her best friend, and the little girl standing at her side, and shrieked.

"Alexa! I am so glad to see you," she burst into tears as she embraced her best friend. Not one to usually show outward displays of emotion, Alexa found herself getting choked up as well as she hugged her best friend tightly.

Both Logan and Lucas felt as if they were intruding on a very private moment, and silently excused themselves from the area in which they'd been standing. Once back in the hallway, it was Kelsey who spoke; who up until that point, had remained relatively silent, taking in the conversations going on around her.

"Uncle Logan, I'll share my room with you when you move here okay? I think it's a good idea because grandma says you're the smartest lawyer she knows and she misses you lots but doesn't want you to know it. Grandma Sam is always saying that she trusts only you for legal advice and she keeps telling me that she'd love it if you were living in Old Forge forever, instead of just visiting in the summer. I'd love it too and so would my dad. He says you're a pain in the ass, oops sorry dad, but I know he really misses you too. And you are my absolute favorite uncle," she kidded.

Eyeing his older twin brother, he winked, smiled, and crouched down to be eye level with his niece.

"Well it sounds like you've got it all figured out young lady. But how about I crash with you guys until grandma is out of the hospital and then I'll go stay with her okay? At least until she's feeling better and can be alone. Besides, I won't need to find a more permanent residence until we know that Grandma is back to normal and that might take a little while."

Suddenly very serious, Kelsey looked from her father to her uncle.

"Grandma Sam is going to get better right?" she asked, lip quivering.

Still crouched down at her level, Logan was the first to respond.

"Kels, has your dad ever lied to you? I don't mean little fibs to make you do your homework or things like that. Has grandma, your dad or I ever lied to you because we didn't want you to know the truth, no matter how good or bad the truth was?"

"No," she answered in a voice devoid of commitment.

Lucas took his daughter's hand as Logan held the other one.

"Kelsey, I give you my word, Grandma Samantha will get better. Your dad and I will make sure that doctors take very good care of her when she's here in the hospital and then it'll be up to the three of us to take care of her once she's out and recovering at home right?"

Kelsey thought about her uncle's words for just a moment and then smiled.

Uncle Logan, Dad, Grandma and I are always a team. Does this mean that you want to be part of our team too? Dad says that the three of us are unbeatable so I think that if there's four of us, we'd be unstoppable, right?"

The three pulled each other into a group hug, with her father and uncle saying "right" simultaneously. Standing upright, Lucas looked down at daughter.

"Now that that's settled, let's go see grandma, shall we?"

And with that, the three walked hand in hand into Samantha's room.

~Chapter 35~

The following week was nothing but a blur to everyone involved in Marsha and Samantha's lives. Alexa reluctantly returned to work the following Monday, and brought Kelsey home with her after school every day to allow Lucas to stay at the hospital until dark. Kelsey had been invited to stay with her best friend's home but adamantly refused, stating that she wanted to be with her teacher and friend. Lucas looked more and more exhausted every time he came to pick his daughter up after returning from the hospital, but declined staying for supper every evening. By the third night, Alexa had a care package waiting for him as he pulled into her drive to retrieve his daughter. As he had the previous nights before, he thanked her, and kissed her, before leaving with his daughter. She didn't say anything, simply took what was offered, and enjoyed that each night's kiss had grown slightly needier, and more intense. She knew that he was simply seeking comfort during a very emotionally draining ordeal and refused to read anything more into it. But that didn't mean that she wouldn't enjoy the kiss, however brief it was. He'd gotten into the habit of calling her once he had settled his daughter, eaten the meal that she'd sent home with him, and relaxed a bit as well. She now found herself making sure that her cell was close at hand as the evening wore on. They'd talk about his mother's progress and then would make small talk before saying good night and retiring for the evening. She'd come to look forward to the nightly ritual, even though it was born out of a sad event.

She'd also offered her home to Maren but was politely rejected. It had become evident from the beginning that Marsha's injuries were more extensive than Samantha's, and Maren refused to leave her mother's side for the first 72 hours. Even though it had only been a week since the time of the accident, Maren realized that her mother was going to need weeks of rehab and therapy, and that she'd probably need assistance at home when she was strong enough to get there. It only took Maren less than one minute of soul searching to make up her mind and once she was sure about her decision, chose to call her best friend to give her the news.

"Hey."

Slightly disappointed that it was her girlfriend and not Lucas calling, she immediately went on alert, afraid that something had changed in her mother's condition.

"Hi. What's going on? Everything okay at the hospital?" she asked tentatively.

"What? Oh yeah. The doctors and therapists said that she'd made a lot of progress and is getting ready to be transferred to an acute rehab setting. I'm not sure where that'll be, or how quickly it'll happen, but the case manager has given me some referrals and I was wondering if you knew anything about any of the places?"

"I don't personally but one of the teachers I work with, her husband is a physical therapist down in Utica at one of the hospitals. I can ask her tomorrow if her husband has any recommendations. What about the nurses and therapists caring for your mom? Don't they recommend any place in particular?"

"Yeah, they do but it doesn't hurt to get a second opinion."

"Well it's great news that Marsha's getting strong enough to get out of the hospital and on to rehab. That should ease your mind so you can get back to New York."

"Yeah about that. I'm not going."

Caught off guard, she sat upright in bed.

"What do you mean you're not going back? What about your job? I mean, it's great that you could take a leave of absence but they must expect you to return sometime soon, don't they?"

"What they expect and what they're getting are two different things. They told me that I could take up to three weeks of paid leave off as it falls under the category of emergency family leave. I explained to them that mom would need care for weeks, if not months afterward and they basically told me that it's not their problem and that after three weeks, they couldn't guarantee my job. So I told them that they'd have my letter of resignation in the morning. Mom needs me more than I need that job, so I quit. Guess you're stuck with me Lexi because I'm moving back home!" she exclaimed.

"The funny part about it is, I'm actually excited! I mean, shit, I wouldn't have wished the predicament we're in, on anyone. But when I thought about it, it just made sense for me to leave New York and return to my roots, just like you did. The simple fact that I have absolutely no regrets about my split-second decision, and it made me realize that it's the right decision for not only mom, but for me as well."

Alexa took a few seconds to digest what her best friend had just told her and although she was thrilled by the news, she hoped that Maren wouldn't come to regret her knee-jerk reaction. And then it hit her.

"Mar, I think that not only will your mother be thrilled, but I'm ecstatic as well! And I know that your mother will definitely appreciate that you're willing to relocate back north, but you and I both know that if she thinks you're giving up your life to help her out, she won't let you. So," Alexa stated calmly, but very convincingly, "I think before you mention anything to your mom, you might want to have your contingency plan in place. Because we both know that she's going to ask you a million questions and try and talk you out of it. Marsha is fiercely independent and if she thinks that your move is solely because of her accident, she will poo poo it and say she doesn't want the help, right?"

Maren thought about her friend's statement and had to agree. "So what exactly do you have in mind, Lexi?"

"Well, I know the circumstances are sad, but the fact is, with Jacqueline's passing, we now have an opening for a 4th grade teacher and even if they didn't hire you for a permanent position, you could at least tell them that you'd substitute and help out when you can, around your mother's schedule right? It's a win-win situation! The Town of Webb would immediately gain an experienced teacher, you'd have an income coming in, and you'd also have a reason to be here other than to take care of your mom. Think she'd buy it?" Alexa asked tentatively.

"Nope, not a chance in hell. She has always known I've loved the city life so she won't buy it. But you're right. I will eventually need some form of income, and the school will need a teacher so it sounds like a very logical solution to everyone's predicament. If you can find out for me who I need to speak with or to whom I should email a resume, I'd appreciate it. Thanks, Alexa. You, as always are the best!"

They ended their conversation, promising to get together in the next day or so. Maren hung up, and Alexa shut off her light for the second time of the evening. She'd just settled into her favorite position when her phone rang again. Fumbling in the dark to retrieve it, she answered it within two rings. Recognizing the caller ID, she smiled as she did so.

"Hello."

Hearing her voice made him smile. He didn't know what there was about the auburn-haired teacher, but she stirred something inside him that had been dormant for years.

"Hi. I hope that I'm not calling too late. I've got some news about mom and I really wanted to talk to you about, it if you have time."

Suddenly very awake, she sat up, worried that Samantha might have suffered some kind of setback.

"Sure, I have the time. What's up?" she asked, as her heart raced.

"Well, it's great news actually," he started out. "The doctors said that mom is doing so well that they're thinking about discharging her home instead of having her go to rehab. They said that she's made so much progress that she can attend physical therapy as an outpatient, and since her broken wrist isn't her dominant side, she doesn't need any occupational therapy other than what can be accomplished as an outpatient."

"Oh, honey, that's great news," she responded, not thinking about the term of endearment that she'd just verbalized; just the fact that his mother was doing well enough to come home. But her statement had not been lost on deaf ears. Lucas smiled on the other end of the line before responding.

"Yes, it's amazing how quickly she is recovering but she's not out of the woods yet. The orthopedist said that she'll need weeks if not months of therapy after she can bear weight on her leg again. And they're worried that the emotional scars might start to show once she's out of the hospital setting and away from its structure. So we'll have to be ready for that as well."

Alexa noticed how he had used the term "we" and wasn't sure if he meant we as in "he and Logan" or we as in "she and he." Either way she was thrilled to hear that Samantha was improving so quickly.

"Anything that I can do to help you out with your mom or with Kelsey, you know I'm here for you Lucas," she added when the silence seemed too prolonged on the other end.

"I know you are, and I really appreciate it very much. I'm not sure what we've got to do to get mom's house ready for her and how much planning is involved but I might be taking you up on your offer to continue to help out until Logan and I get mom settled in, and therapy in place."

"Logan?" she asked, slightly confused. "How much time is he taking off? I would think that attorneys keep pretty rigid schedules? I mean, I know he said that he was relocating up here but I assumed he meant just until Samantha was back on her feet so to speak. Samantha always said that he has the heart of a city boy."

"He sounds like he's actually serious about moving here," he replied, still finding it hard to believe that his brother was actually giving up his practice. They hadn't discussed all the details, and Logan didn't have a clear cut idea of what type of law he'd like to pursue in Old Forge, but he had sounded adamant about leaving New York in order to start a practice back in his home town. Earlier in the evening they'd talked about it briefly. Logan had reassured his brother that he'd not only be there to help their mother out at home, but also to help at the Bistro in whatever capacity he could be of assistance. While Lucas really appreciated the offer, he also knew that his brother was more of a suit and tie kind of guy than hands on, manual labor kind. But free help was free help and he was grateful for the extra set of hands.

"Well, it must be a day for surprises," Alexa commented, absorbing his news while she thought about her own.

"How so?" he asked, somewhat confused.

"Maren informed me today that she is giving her letter of resignation at the school where we used to teach together, and she too, is relocating to Old Forge. She said that she's been thinking about it ever since I left, and her mom's accident was the catalyst to finalize her decision. I'm still shocked, but I have to admit, I am so excited that we'll be together again. She's been my best friend for as long as I can remember and I'll love having her nearby. She told me the wildest thing, and I guess I was in such shock about her moving home, that I let it slide by me. She said that she's always wanted to own her own microbrewery and has been looking into starting one. She asked me if I'd like to go into business with her once she's settled up here and her mom is at home. I told her that I love a good beer as much as the next person, but I know nothing about running my own business," she laughed.

"That's wild! But I could see her pursuing her dream, and I could see her being very successful at it. Once the dust settles and we get our moms situated, tell her to meet with Logan and I to discuss her endeavor. We both might have some helpful hints from both a legal and business perspective. I'll be interested to hear about what type of business she's proposing."

"I will relay the message."

"Great. You sound tired, and I know I'm exhausted so I'll let you go. Thank you again, Alexa for being here for me, and for Kelsey. Good night. Sweet dreams."

"Good night, Luke. And, just so you know; I'm not going anywhere."

"That's what I banking on, and hoping for, honey."

The line went dead, but not before she very distinctly heard him call her "honey".

Alexa fell asleep smiling.

~Chapter 36~

Samantha was discharged home from the hospital Sunday afternoon, while Maren's mother had been discharged to acute Rehab the day before. The two women were allowed time together prior to Marsha's departure, to talk about the accident and to mourn their friend. Neither had been able to attend Jacqueline's funeral, and even though their three children had gone in their places, it wasn't the same. Logan had followed up with the police and learned that Daniel Brewer, the bastard who'd caused the accident, had not only been driving drunk, but was also full of painkillers at the time of the accident. It was surmised that he'd driven from his home in Rome in search of his partner who'd walked out on him, or at least that's what he kept wailing about at the scene of the accident. He'd been so drunk that he hadn't even realized that he had been going the wrong direction on the arterial when he'd hit the women head on. Logan had dug a little deeper and learned that he wasn't the respected business owner that he appeared to be; but in fact, was nearly bankrupt, and had been convicted of drunk driving in California, Montana and Ohio, where he'd lived previously; yet somehow had been able to obtain a New York state driver's license. After concluding that his mother's accident could have been easily prevented, Logan had silently vowed to make sure that the scumbag was prosecuted to the fullest extent of the law and never able to harm another person because of his reckless behavior. Logan knew that when he was through with him, Mr. Brewer's ex-lover would be the least of his concerns.

Alexa had brought Marsha a huge basket of essentials when she'd been transferred to rehab. She filled it with colored washcloths, towels, hair care products, toiletries, books, magazines, hard candy, and anything else that she thought might make her transition a little easier. Maren remained with her all day, every day but had finally started spending the nights alternating between her mother's and Alexa's home. When Samantha was finally discharged the following day, Alexa had informed both Logan and Lucas that she and Kelsey would be taking care of dinner that evening, and that she would see them upon their arrival home. She and her helper had spent majority of the afternoon cooking and baking as they awaited Samantha's arrival. While Lucas had offered her full range of his mother's home, Alexa had insisted that she preferred to do all the prep work in the comfort of her own home. When she and Kelsey arrived at Samantha's home, she was shocked to see that somehow between visiting her daily, caring for his daughter, and running their business, Logan and Lucas had built a wooden ramp from her driveway to her front door. When she arrived home, Samantha was shocked to see not only Kelsey and Alexa, but also Maren exiting her front door to greet her. Logan jumped out of his seat in the rear of Lucas' truck to open the door for his mother and hand her the crutches she'd need for the next six weeks or so. She'd refused to be dependent upon using a wheelchair, and had told her boys in no uncertain terms that she was going to walk into her own home, despite however long it took her to hobble up the stairs. Now staring at the recently installed ramp, she felt her eyes welling with tears as she watched her granddaughter wave excitedly and race toward her.

Maren and Alexa waved as well, as they watched her make the arduous journey up the ramp and into her home. Her sons greeted the women and it didn't take a rocket scientist to realize that the four of them had become a cohesive foursome over the course of her hospitalization. She accepted the woman's hugs and warm welcome as she eased herself down into her favorite chair. Alexa knew that she was probably supposed to keep her injured leg elevated and helped her recline the chair as soon as she was settled. The aroma emanating from the kitchen smelled heavenly and soon everyone was thinking about their empty stomachs.

"I hope it's okay that I came over to welcome you home, Samantha. Alexa cooked enough for an army and didn't think you'd mind. But you are probably exhausted from the trip up and I should probably go," she offered, suddenly feeling very self-conscious at the way that Logan was looking at her.

"Don't you dare think about leaving us," Samantha snapped, even before Logan could object. "We're all in this together and you're practically family, so sit your boney ass down and let's enjoy this fabulous smelling meal that my granddaughter and Alexa have prepared."

She smiled, just enough to catch Logan's attention, as she sat down on the couch. Logan promptly joined her, leaning in close enough to whisper.

"Your ass is not skinny nor boney, but perfect just the way it is."

Samantha didn't know what her youngest son had said to her best friend's daughter, but from her immediate blushing that could be seen on her face, she could only surmise that it was sexual.

After his mother was seated and comfortable, Lucas walked over to his daughter, patting her on the head.

"So, what did you and Alexa make us for dinner young lady?" he asked, while his eyes darted between his daughter and the woman standing beside her. Kelsey smiled and excitedly answered her father.

"Alexa asked what Grandma Sam's favorite meal was and I told her I didn't know but that you loved meatloaf and mashed potatoes with those little green things cut up in them. Lexi told me that they're called chives so guess what daddy? We went to the store and got everything to make a fantastic home cooked meal for everybody. We've got meatloaf, mashed potatoes with gravy, carrots, a green bean casserole thing with funny looking onions on top, fresh bread that Alexa taught me how to make, and a surprise for dessert!"

"Wow, you ladies have been very busy today and I'm sure everything will be wonderful," he responded, with his gaze locked on his daughter's teacher. His look was not lost on Alexa. Maren, and Samantha watched intently, with both finding their unspoken interaction speaking volumes. It warmed Samantha's heart to think that maybe, finally, her son was ready to move past the loss that fate had handed him so many years ago. And maybe, just maybe, Alexa would be the one to help him start to live again. As Maren watched their exchange, she knew that Alexa was falling, and falling hard.

The dinner was better than either Luke or Logan had anticipated. After eating mostly hospital food for the last week, the spread that Kelsey and Alexa had prepared was beyond belief and not only was it tasty, but it was very filling. After everyone ate until they felt that they'd burst, the brothers immediately got up to assist their mother to her Barco lounger in order to elevate her leg, with Alexa, Maren and Kelsey clearing the table.

"You really outdid yourself, Lexi. That was fantastic!"

"Thanks, but I had an excellent helper," she said, looking over at Kelsey.

Kelsey smiled and exited the kitchen to grab the last of the dishes still on the table. Maren took the opportunity to not only quiz but tease her best friend.

"I think it's wonderful how much you're helping out, and I'm sure Lucas is very appreciative," she said sarcastically, winking at her.

"I'm glad I could help out. But it's not a big deal," she responded, fluffing off her friend's statement.

"Uh huh."

"What do you mean, uh huh? We're friends, and his daughter is in my class. Anyone would have done the same," she said, trying to convince not only her friend, but herself as well.

"Uh huh. Yeah, that's it. Anyone would have spent the entire day making the man's favorite meal. And you haven't even shown him the piece de resistance that I saw hiding in the pantry. You made him your famous seven-layer red velvet cake. Yes, I saw it, and yes, you're hooked on the bartender, and don't you dare deny it!"

Knowing it was true, Alexa turned and looked directly at her best friend.

"Is it that noticeable? I mean, we were really just getting to know one another when the accident happened. And I don't want him misconstruing gratitude for genuine feelings for me. I think that we might be at the start of a great relationship, but obviously, his main focus right now is his mom and her recovery."

"Trust me, Lexi, the way that man looks at you, it's not gratitude that he's exhibiting. He wants you. Period."

Blushing again, Alexa looked at Lucas's daughter as she entered the kitchen, arms full of dishes. Alexa rushed over to take some from her as they rested precariously on her arms. Kelsey quickly brushed her off, explaining that her grandma and the waitresses at the Bistro had taught her how to carry stacks of dishes. Alexa stepped back and let her proceed to the sink with the load. Maren quietly whispered into her ear that not only was she hooked on the bartender but his daughter as well.

    They finished scraping and loading the dishes into the dishwasher, put the coffee on, and filled the kettle with water for tea, and then joined the men and their mother in the living room. Everyone made themselves at home, making small talk for the first few minutes. It was Samantha herself who broke the ice.

"Maren, your mother must be so happy that you're moving back home!"

Maren looked at her dumbfounded that she knew about her relocation. Logan also was whipped into attention with that one sentence. Samantha could have heard a pin drop in the room as she continued.

"Alexa told Lucas the good news, and he shared it with me. I hope that it wasn't supposed to be a secret. I'm not sure how long you're planning on staying, but for the interim, why don't you talk to the school board about substituting when you can. With Jacqueline's death, God rest her soul; there is a classroom full of wonderful children who will need a compassionate teacher to take her spot, and I know that you'd be perfect for the position. Also, while we're on the subject of surprises, were you and Alexa aware that my Logan has decided to come back home as well?"

Seeing the look of shock on Maren's face, she realized that she had not been privy to that piece of information. So she continued talking as her two sons sat quietly.

"It came as a shock when my Logan told me that he is sick of the hustle and bustle of the city and wants to open a law practice here in Old Forge. Isn't that wonderful news?"

Maren was the first to answer.

"Yes, it's not only wonderful, but also very unexpected news. Say Logan, I'd like to set up a time speak with you, on a professional level, sometime when it's convenient for both of us."

"Okay, sure. But if you've got a husband you want to get rid of, I don't do divorce law."

Nearly choking on the water she was drinking, she laughed. "Nope. No husband, no kids, not even a pet. I had told Alexa that I'm thinking about starting a microbrewery once I'm settled and my mom is on the mend. It's always been a dream of mine to run a business, and we used to make homemade wine when I was a kid, so I thought I'd try my hand at making beer."

"Very cool," Logan responded, sincerely. "I would love to be your legal representation, and since I happen to love drinking beer, have you ever considered having a business partner for your venture? Or even just a silent partner who assists in the financing and startup costs?"

"I haven't actually thought it out that far, but would consider going into business with a partner. Why, do you know someone who might be interested?"

"Yes, as a matter of fact I do. Me!"

He smiled, making her nearly spill her water for the second time in less than a minute.

Everyone looked back and forth between Logan and Maren. It was Samantha who broke the silence.

"I think that's a great idea! Logan has an excellent business sense, and if you're business partners, you'd have built-in legal representation. Our area doesn't have many options for home grown beers and you could capitalize on that fact. Lucas and I would offer it as a house special at the Bistro. Yes," she exclaimed excitedly, "You kids might very well be on to something that's not only a very cool idea, but one that's extremely marketable!"

"Wow, mom, slow down. Don't freak Maren out! She sounds like she's just in the preliminary discussion stages of her concept," Lucas offered.

"While it definitely sounds like her idea has merit, I'm going to assume that Maren will need to relocate, find housing, get her mom settled at home and find a source of income before she considers such a big undertaking."

Not one to easily be shot down, Maren squared her shoulders and responded.

"Lucas is correct, to a degree. My mother is the reason I'm relocating home, and therefore the most important part of the equation. But," she added confidently, "I will be living in my mom's house until she comes home, and is doing well enough to be left alone for short periods of time. That answers the question about my housing. And as far as a source of income, I intend to speak with the school board this week about taking over, at least as a temporary replacement in Jacqueline's classroom. Besides, I'm about as frugal as they come so I have a very sizable nest egg to not only tide me over, but also to use toward securing a building in which to house my microbrewery. I'm one who likes to jump on an idea and run with it, full steam ahead," she smiled. "I intend to check out the local real estate listings this week as well, and if you'd like to join me Logan, you're more than welcome."

He pondered on her invite for just a moment before responding.

"Then let's come up with a rough outline for what you'd like to accomplish right away. Does 7pm work for you tomorrow evening? We can discuss your ideas over dinner" Logan asked confidently.

She looked him directly in the eye and smiled the sexist yet coy smile that she could muster.

"Make it 7:30 and you've got yourself a date," she responded.

He felt something suddenly come to life as she accepted his offer, innuendos and all. He'd dated dozens of women over the years, some more seriously than others. But to date, none had stirred his interest and libido the way Alexa's friend had. "Yes, this was going to make for an interesting adventure," he thought to himself as he surprised her by taking her hand in his and gently bringing it to his lips.

"7:30 it is. And I am already looking forward to our first date."

"Be assured Logan, it's a business date; and I never mix business with pleasure."

"But that's where we might have an issue, Maren. It will definitely be a business date, but spending the evening with you will be nothing but pleasure for me," he added smoothly.

"Oh Christ," Lucas interjected. "Before it gets too deep in here, do you think we can have whatever dessert Alexa and Kelsey made? I think I just heard my stomach growl," he winked at Kelsey, and smiled.

"Wait until you see what it is, Dad!" Kelsey exclaimed, excitedly. "Alexa is a really good cook and it's gonna totally blow you away!"

"From the way he looks at her when she's not looking, I think it's safe to say that it's not just her cooking that's blown him away," Samantha whispered to Logan as he helped her out of the chair to stand.

"I know, and the funny part about it is that he doesn't even have a clue that he's already hooked," he whispered back, laughing as he reached for her crutches.

They made their way back to the dining room table as Alexa and Maren scrambled to bring coffee, tea and more ice water to the table. It was Kelsey who was given the honors of bringing out the dessert. Both brothers went silent as she skillfully carried out a huge serving platter with a cake housed on it that was nearly as tall as she was. The tiered cake was layered in strawberries, raspberries, with a few dollops of frosting placed in various spots shaped in the form of flowers. If his daughter hadn't already confessed to assisting in the baking of the cake, Lucas would have sworn that it had come from one of the gourmet Italian pastry shops back in Utica. All eyes remained on Kelsey as she carefully set the towering cake down in front of them, and smiled.

"Guess what kind it is Dad? Hint: it's your favorite, and I didn't even tell Lexi. She made it all on her own as if she knew! Isn't it awesome?"

"Yes baby, she's awesome alright," he responded, not realizing his slip. The comment went over his daughter's head but was not lost on the five adults in the room. Alexa suddenly felt very uncomfortable, being the center of everyone's attention. She quickly picked up the server and walked over to where Samantha had sat down.

"Since this is your home, and you are our honored guest, why don't you be in charge of cutting the cake. If you haven't guessed, it's a Red Velvet cake, and hopefully it tastes as good as it looks," she added shyly.

"Alexa," Samantha spoke softly, wiping tears of gratitude from her eyes. "You, my boys, my beautiful granddaughter and Maren, have done more for me than you'll ever know and I don't know how I'll ever thank you all."

Maren and Alexa, gently put their hands on Samantha's shoulders as they stood on each side of her, as if in unity. They both answered simultaneously with the same response. "We just want you to get better Sam."

Kelsey remained oblivious to the dynamics playing out in the room as she waited for her slice of cake. And the cake wasn't as good as it had looked; it was even better. After everyone had inhaled their dessert, and the last of the dishes were loaded, Maren and Alexa took it as their clue to excuse themselves and head home. Neither brother wanted them to leave but both also realized that their mother must be exhausted and ready to retire for the evening. Kelsey said her good byes while sitting next to her grandmother, with both Logan and Lucas insisting on walking them to their truck. Lucas allowed his brother to take the lead, escorting Maren out first. He gently touched Alexa's hand, holding her back so he could have a moment alone with her. The second his brother was out of earshot, he took her hand in his, drawing her nearer. His heart raced as he searched her eyes for any sign of approval. He couldn't think rationally whenever she was this close. He could smell her body lotion, shampoo and a hint of the cake that she'd baked for them. She smelled like heaven, pure seduction, and innocence all rolled into one. When their eyes locked, he fell. In that instant he knew that he'd been wrong so many years ago when he'd vowed that no one would ever make him feel the things that his Anastasia had. And in that moment, he was so thankful that he'd been wrong. Instead of acting impulsively, this time he looked Alexa in the eyes and held her gaze as he slowly brought his mouth to hers. Her heart was beating nearly as fast as his as she offered herself to him. Her lips parted as he neared, welcoming him in. He willed himself to go slow, and savor the moment; but when she leaned in to meet his lips, his need outweighed his restraint. Their lips met and every rational thought left their minds. In that moment, they were one unit, one entity; not two people desperately seeking something that they didn't even realize was missing. Unlike the others, this kiss wasn't rushed, nor hesitant; both took what they needed, nothing more. She held him as their tongues danced, a slow waltz with no leader nor follower. Both were in control, yet neither was. She felt his hands as they subconsciously caressed her back. She found herself melting into the kiss as her body molded against his, a fact that he was very aware of. It took only moments for every part of his body to awaken as their kiss progressed into want and need. Realizing that humping her on his mother's porch would probably be frowned upon, he reluctantly pulled away, breaking the trance that both of them had fallen under.

Now, looking at her standing just inches away, he wasn't sure what to say or how she felt about the kiss, so he spoke directly from his heart.

"Thank you Lexi. Thank you for more things than I can mention. Thank you for taking care of my daughter, thank you for caring about my mother and making such an amazing meal to welcome her home. Thank you for knowing what to say when I stumble and the correct responses escape me, and thank you for not saying anything when I totally blunder what I mean to say. I'm not very good at saying what I feel, and for that I'm sorry. But I know what I feel Alexa, and for that," he whispered, again, drawing her in, "I sincerely thank you."

He smiled, allowing his dimples to pop just a bit. "I'm not sure what this is or where it's going, but I sure would like to find out. That is, if you're feeling it too," he added.

"I don't know what this is either Lucas, but nothing would make me happier than enjoying this dance, however long or short it is, with you."

He heard her response, and once it registered, he leaned in for one more kiss. When it ended, he smiled again, taking her hand and leading her outside. "Deal."

Maren wasn't sure what had transpired in the few moments since she'd left Samantha's home, but from the look on her best friend's face, and the smirk on Lucas's, she knew that it must have been monumental. Though it was nearly dark out, she watched both Alexa and Lucas blush as they approached the truck. Logan knew the look and had only seen his twin look at a woman that way once before. He couldn't wait to get his brother alone to not only tease him but also drill him about what had transpired inside.

"We'd better get going," Alexa offered.

"Um yeah, you're right Lexi. Thanks again guys for allowing us to be part of your mom's homecoming," Maren shouted at she started to climb into her truck. "Oh, and Logan, I'm looking forward to tomorrow evening. See you at 7:30."

She climbed into her truck next to Alexa, who was already inside, and buckled up. The second they'd backed out of the drive and she'd put her truck into gear, she turned to her best friend and spoke.

"Spill it Lexi. What happened in there? And don't you dare tell me nothing because it most certainly was something from the look on your face."

Alexa was still reeling from the effects of the kiss. She waited nearly a minute before responding, still trying to wrap her head around what had just happened.

"He thanked me for everything, and said that he'd like to see where things could go with us."

Staring ahead as she drove, Maren responded nonchalantly. "Okay, that's good. I mean, he seems very nice and you like him right? I mean, you haven't been taking care of his kid just out of the kindness of your heart right? You attracted to him correct?"

"I don't know Maren. I mean, yes, naturally I'm attracted to him. He's good looking, gorgeous actually. He's a great person, awesome father, attentive son, and savvy businessman."

"Cut your sales pitch Alexa," she cut her off quickly. "Do you like him or not? I know that's he's definitely hooked on you. The way he looks at you makes it very evident that he's quite attracted to you."

She remained silent as Maren rambled on, offering what she believed to be Lucas' best attributes. They pulled into Alexa's drive, when she finally let it slip.

"He kissed me. And I didn't see shooting stars, fireworks or any of the clichés that everyone speaks of."

"Oh Lexi, I'm sorry," Maren offered. "I thought for sure that you guys had something special going on."

As Alexa slid out of her best friends' truck, she smiled. "We do Mar. I have no intention of trying to replace his Anastasia but think that we have a shot at creating something really special. And I think I'm in love with him already. Oh, and they weren't shooting stars, I saw the sun and the moon collide when our lips met!" she added, shutting the door before Maren could say another word.

~Chapter 37~

The next three weeks flew by in the blink of an eye. Logan and Lucas watched with amazement as their mother worked diligently with her therapists, growing stronger every day. In the evening, Logan worked alongside his brother bartending and managing the day to day operations of the bar. He would never admit to his twin, that he was learning a lot about how to run not only a bar, but a successful establishment, and quickly discovered that there was a lot more to it than he'd ever imagined. He'd met with Maren as planned, and had been pleased to find that not only did she have a very solid vision of what she wanted to create with her microbrewery; but she also had a very clear, realistic approach for how she was going to achieve her plan. Their business dinner had led to coffee and desert at her mother's place, with Logan reluctantly saying good night at the sun started to rise. They hadn't had sex, though the thought had been on both of their mind's throughout the evening. Aside from a few intense kisses, the evening had been about business, with only a few sprinkles of fun intermingled. Before he'd left for his brother's home, he'd secured another date with her for the following weekend.

Lucas and Alexa had crossed paths on numerous occasions, and although their schedules were both very hectic, they'd still managed to get together for a dinner date at Alexa's home. He'd brought her flowers, red roses to be exact, which should have impressed her, but he got the distinct impression that they weren't her style. Unbeknownst to him, red roses were a constant reminder of Bradford, and a life she didn't ever want to revisit.

Lucas felt that the more he tried to do things to impress her, the more he fumbled. To say that he was out of practice was a mild understatement. After listening to him apologize repeatedly for his perception of mediocre ideas for their dates, Alexa decided to take the reins and told Lucas that she'd pick him up Saturday at 1pm. She offered no information, except to say that Maren would be available to babysit Kelsey should Samantha get tired during the afternoon. She informed him that their date would end in time enough for him to be back at the Bistro for the dinner hour, to which he was quickly relieved.

He tried to pry more information out of her regarding their upcoming date, but she avoided the topic every time they spoke. Her only instruction had been to wear layers and hiking boots, to which he quickly agreed.

They spoke nightly and he had grown accustomed to hearing her voice just before drifting off to sleep. As the days had turned into weeks, he found himself opening up to her more than he ever thought he would, and couldn't help but feel the bond they'd formed was something stronger than friendship. She'd included his daughter in so many elements of their friendship, a fact that spoke volumes about her character. The few times he'd dated in the past, none of the women had any interest in hearing anything about, let alone, learning about his daughter. Alexa on the other hand, hadn't just accepted that they came as a package; she'd actually embraced the fact that his daughter was his world and the reason for his existence. Alexa continued to tutor Kelsey after school and during recess, and had insisted on bringing her home on the nights that he had to be at the Bistro early. Numerous occasions when he'd stop by his mothers to check in on her before work, he'd found her refrigerator filled with homemade meals that either Alexa or Maren had prepared. Even his mother had informed both he and his twin, that both Alexa and her best friend, were keepers and that they shouldn't let them get away. Despite his downplaying to his mother, for prosperity sake; he too, was beginning to feel that there was definitely something very special about her, and found that he was beginning to think of her more and more each day. He was in love with his daughter's teacher, even if he wasn't ready to admit it.

Friday night rolled around and the restaurant was packed. Both Logan and Lucas were behind the bar, and barely able to keep up with not only the patrons seated in front of them, but also the waitresses' orders. They had developed a rhythm and it was now very apparent that they were comfortable working side by side. They still dressed very differently, and their mannerisms were almost polar opposites of one another; but anyone could tell within a matter of minutes that they were twins. Where Lucas remained friendly but reserved, Logan continued to turn on sensuality and charm to every new female patron that entered the room. Both had received more propositions than they could count and both had politely turned all of them down, though Logan eluded to the possibility of hooking up with several of them in the future. Logan was in the middle of a deep conversation with a very voluptuous redhead when he spotted not only Alexa but Maren making their way to the bar. Having no idea how long they'd been there, he smiled, quickly concluding his discussion with one Colleen O'Malley, politely telling her that he'd definitely keep her offer in mind. Maren had no clue what the young woman had said to Logan, but from the way she'd been leaning over the bar, she was sure that her point, all 38D of them, had come across loud and clear. Not one for jealousy in any way, shape or form, she sauntered up to bar like she hadn't a care in the world. When she and Alexa were greeted by Lucas, they ordered, with Maren asking Lucas to send Logan over ASAP. Not sure what was up, he got their drinks, and quickly made his way to his twin. Logan looked over their way and upon making eye contact with her, made his way toward them, with the red head never letting him out of her sight, a fact that Maren was very aware of.

"Hi. What's up? Everything okay Maren? Nothing's happened to Marsha right?" he asked sincerely. "Luke said you needed me?"

"Actually yes," she purred, her every move was calculated and deliberate. "I do need you for something."

"Sure honey. What?" he asked innocently, having no clue what she was talking about.

"This," she said, grabbing his designer shirt and pulling him towards her. She brought his mouth to hers, and took. Her tongue entered his mouth just enough to awaken everything within his system. The kiss was short, but spoke volumes, without words ever being exchanged. For anyone in attendance and paying attention to that particular corner of the bar, the kiss made it abundantly clear that he wasn't nearly as available as he might have led some to believe. When she pulled away from him, she smiled.

"That's what I needed Logan," she whispered. "And come tomorrow, I'm sure I'll need several more of them; for starters. We can figure out the rest from there."

She shifted her eyes down the bar to where the redhead had been seated, and found nothing but an empty bar stool.

"Mission accomplished," she thought to herself, as she picked up her chocolate martini and took a sip.

Logan didn't know what to say at first, and even if he had, there was no way that his brain would have allowed him to form an intelligent sentence. He could feel the tingling from his nose to his toes, and also in another very specific location. No one had ever gotten to him as quickly as Maren, and for that, he didn't know if he should be grateful or scared. When he found the ability to speak again, he looked directly at her and said only one thing, "I'll pick you up at six. Tell Alexa not to wait up."

"Good, I was planning on that." And with that, she let him get back to the business of tending bar, knowing full well that she'd be on his mind for the remainder of the evening.

~Chapter 38~

Alexa baked all morning, trying to keep herself busy. She didn't know why she was nervous about going out with Lucas, but something told her that their date would be another milestone in their developing relationship. She found herself making so many decisions based on what she thought Lucas would like, or Kelsey would enjoy. It surprised her how much they'd become part of her day to day life. She never read anything into their friendship, only took what was offered, despite sometimes wishing for a little more. As she placed the last of the chocolate chip cookies on the cooling rack, she looked at the time and panicked. In the midst of all the baking she'd done, she'd allowed the entire morning to slip by her and realized that she was supposed to pick Lucas up in less than an hour.

Whipping off the apron that she'd been wearing all morning, she raced toward the shower to wash up. She had no clue how she accomplished it, but found herself not only showered and ready, but also loaded up with the necessary props for their date, and out the door with five minutes to spare. She pulled into his drive exactly on time and found him sitting on the front stoop.

"He looked so young, so scared and so darn cute," she thought to herself, watching the smile come over his face, as he stood, greeting her. She wasn't sure how, why or when it had happened, but she had to finally admit to herself that she was definitely falling for Lucas, and falling hard.

She watched him stand, and walk toward her truck. When he opened the door, and slid in, he offered her a bouquet of Shasta daisies, and a quick kiss on her cheek. She knew that she was blushing but the warmth spreading through her body wasn't isolated solely in her face.

"Hi."

"Hi yourself."

"Gotta tell you," he smiled. "I love a gal who's on time. And who drives a truck. I think it's sexy," he offered.

"Huh, you don't say. Here I thought it might be my cotton flannel that turned you on," she kidded, as she put the truck in reverse and backed out of his drive.

"Actually, that works for me as well," he added and he gazed over her body; almost immediately chastising himself for the immediate physical response that he felt. Knowing that he was, in fact, still human, and Alexa was a very attractive woman, he quickly dismissed his response as being only natural when placed in the close proximity to a beautiful woman.

"Yes, he was attracted to her, but mainly because she was a good friend and a great person" he tried to convince himself. He decided that the response that he felt whenever he was around her was simply a spike in testosterone and not a big deal; it meant nothing. "Yeah right," he replied to himself; knowing full well that he wasn't fooling anyone, himself included.

"So where are you taking me?" he asked as he noted they were heading through town. She remained silent for just a second, and then turned toward him before responding.

"Your daughter and I were talking the other day, and she mentioned that we never finished our date up on the mountain. I hope it's okay, that I've packed a picnic basket, and thought we'd try it again. That is if that's okay with you? There are many places and adventures that I'd love to go on with you Lucas, but I thought that you'd probably be more comfortable if we stayed close to town, in case Kelsey or your mom need anything."

"So you thought we could just head up the mountain, and start again, where we left off?" he asked, more hesitant than challengingly.

"No. A lot has transpired since that night on the mountain Lucas. And I don't think neither one of us wants to relive the memories of that evening. I was thinking," she said, now feeling very insecure in her decision, "that maybe we should go back to your land, and finish the picnic that we started; you know, have the evening end on a happier note than it did the first time," she offered, almost in a whisper.

"I think you are amazing Lexi. And I think that your idea is as perfect as you are."

Now it was Lexi's turn to blush as she continued heading up the side of the mountain. Lucas watched in astonishment, as she navigated the unmarked roads and pulled into his drive without requiring his assistance with directions.

"Wow, I'm impressed Alexa. How did you remember how to get up here? I mean, it's been weeks and I only brought you here that one time."

"It was our first date Lucas, and since I wasn't sure if you were a stalker or possibly a nutcase, I paid attention to the roads that you drove on, in case I needed to plan my escape!" she kidded. "No seriously, I've always had a great sense of direction, especially in the woods. You should see Maren," she laughed. "She can't find her way out of the woods, even if there was a neon sign pointing to the parking lot. She picks most of our hikes, but I'm always the navigator and leader up and down the mountain."

They exited her truck. Lucas grabbed the picnic basket and small cooler and came around to her side of the truck. He opened her door with his empty hand and as she started to get out, leaned in for a kiss. And his aim wasn't for her cheek. Their lips locked, with Alexa slowly opening her mouth, inviting him in. Time seemed to stand still as their tongues slowly explored each other. When they separated, neither said a word, just smiled.

The sun was high in the cloudless sky, and while the air had a nip to it the temperature remained mild for late fall in the Adirondacks. Still unsteady from his kiss, Alex grabbed the two collapsible chairs that she'd packed, and also the small bag of newspapers and kindling that she'd collected in her yard. He followed her lead, and headed towards the fire pit that he and Kelsey had erected the year before. His legs remained wobbly from the exchange at the truck, but he managed to set their lunch down, excusing himself to go into the garage to grab the folding table. When he returned, he was impressed to see that not only had Alexa started a fire, but had it roaring to life in a matter of seconds. She'd unfolded the chairs, and standing there, watching her, he couldn't get over how comfortable she appeared. Her hair was in a sloppy ponytail, with multiple strands trying to make their escape from her under her baseball cap. He said nothing, just stood silently watching her; finding it hard to move and almost as hard to breathe. She was so different in appearance from his Anastasia, yet so many of her movements and mannerisms mirrored his first wife. He knew enough to never compare the two, but he still couldn't help but think that Alexa possessed every one of Anastasia's best qualities.

She saw him out of the corner of her eye as he exited his garage, the only structure on his property. He was carrying an old wooden table, and presently had it perched precariously on top of his head.

"Need help?" she shouted over the wind.

"Nope. I've got it. Glad to see you're a pyro," he kidded, setting the table down next to the chairs and roaring fire.

"Hey," she smiled, as she pulled out a bottle of wine, "If you're going to do something, I say go big or go home," she laughed. Not necessarily a connoisseur of wine, he smiled as she pulled out a six pack of his favorite beer. She handed him the wine bottle opener and wine, as she opened a long neck for him. It took him less than a minute to open the bottle, let it breathe, and hand her back her glass, half full with a sparkling Pinot Noir that she'd chosen. They clanked bottle to glass and made themselves comfortable in the chairs that she'd unfolded. Something inside her warmed when she noted that he'd pushed the two chairs closer together before sitting down. They sipped on their respective drinks, both enjoying the scenery, warmth of the fire and serenity of the woods. It was Alexa that finally broke the silence.

"Tell me about the home you'd like to build on this lot Lucas. I would love to hear what style and ideas you, Anastasia and Kelsey have come up with."

Taken back hearing his wife's name mentioned so nonchalantly, as if it was a natural part of their conversation, Lucas remained silent for a brief second. In that simple statement, Lucas realized that his first wife would always be a part of his life, a fact that Alexa had already accepted, and welcomed. She wasn't intimidated nor threatened by the memory of her; and was comfortable enough to incorporate his past with what hopefully would be his future. If he wasn't already falling in love with the woman sitting next to him sipping on her wine, he would have voluntarily taken the plunge at that very moment.

"My daughter and I designed the house, and bought the land after relocating to Old Forge. I let Kels have a large input into the design of our home. My only request was that I really wanted it to be a log cabin because Ana had always wanted one. Luckily Kelsey was on the same page, even though she wasn't aware that it was her mom's favorite style home. We have the blueprints, and a builder picked out. We just haven't gotten around to doing much more than putting in the driveway and erecting the garage. Something has always held me back from moving forward on the construction. I can't honestly pinpoint what it was, but until recently, I think I had sort of put my dream of building on hold."

"If it hurts to talk about Ana's dream home, it's okay Lucas. You don't have to tell me about it," she offered.

"No, it's not that. Kelsey and I know that we'll someday live on this mountain, in a home that we designed and built together. Ana wanted a log cabin, and the home that we want to build will be constructed out of logs, but nothing like what Ana and I used to dream about when we were first married. God," he said, remembering back to his life with her, that now seemed so long ago.

"We were so young, so poor and scared half to death most of the time. Sure we loved each other, at least as much as any two teenagers knew how to love. And we were fortunate enough to have very supportive parents, at least they were after they got over the initial shock that is," he laughed.

"Now having a child of my own, I can't imagine what went through our parent's heads when we sat them down and told them we were having a baby. But they never questioned our decision to have our child. Abortion was never even mentioned, even though we know it would have been an easy solution to the predicament we'd gotten ourselves in. From the moment that Ana found out she was pregnant and we told our respective parents, they've been here for us. Kelsey still sees Ana's parents often and they will probably always remain an important part of her life."

"As they should," Alexa responded. "Kelsey is an extension of their daughter and it would be cruel if she weren't part of their lives. They've already lost their daughter so I'm sure Kelsey holds a very special place in their hearts."

"You're incredible Alexa. You really get it and mean that don't you?" he asked sincerely.

She turned to Lucas and smiled.

"Of course I do. Family is the most important thing in the world Lucas. Kelsey's grandparents play a vital part in her life and should always be active participants in her upbringing. As a teacher, I've seen how detrimental it can be to a child, to have absent or poor parenting.

Grandparents are just as influential and important to a child, as parents are."

She stood and took a step toward the table. "Let's eat before everything gets cold," she said, handing him a plate.

He took the plate from her outstretched hand, and set it back down on the table. Food was the farthest thing from his mind as he pulled her into his arms and kissed her. She didn't resist, and melted into his embrace. When they finally separated, both knew what they wanted; but for now, they'd both settle for a hot meal.

~Chapter 39~

He drove through town slowly, occasionally glancing at his dash. His navigational system said that he was less than three minutes from her house, and he found himself alternating between anger and excitement thinking about seeing her again. As he looked at the homes lining Main Street, he felt nothing but disdain.

"How could she have left everything I had given her, to live in such a place," he thought to himself. "Maybe she's lower class, and nothing but a low life after all. Maybe she enjoys slumming it," he said under his voice. With no one to hear him or argue with him, he kept on muttering and swearing to himself as he turned onto Alexa's road.

He was still so pissed that Katherine had broken off their engagement.

"No one breaks up with a Peddington, and Katherine should have known better. So what if he'd slapped her around a bit," he thought to himself.

She should have known better than to disagree with him in public. A man of his stature was not to be argued with, let alone embarrassed in front of his peers. She'd needed to be taught that valuable lesson and if she hadn't fought back, it would have been over quicker and with far less bruises.

"Then the bitch had the nerve to break up with him and get a restraining order?" he shouted to himself, as he pulled into Alexa's driveway, looking for any signs of life.

"She'd learned the hard way not to cross a Peddington, and her body will never be found," he laughed, as he thought about it. Now it was time to claim what was rightfully his, and he had no intention of heading back to the city without her.

Nearing sprinting up to the door, he clenched a bouquet of red roses in one hand, and pounded on her door with the other. He noticed that her truck wasn't in the driveway but as he approached the house, he knew that she must be home. He could hear music playing and noted that numerous lights illuminated the interior; so he pounded again, and again. When she didn't answer, he found himself getting more and more infuriated by her lack of respect. Finally, he heard her, or at least what he thought was her.

"Give me second, I'm coming!" she yelled from the kitchen, trying to balance the roast as she pulled it out of the oven. It only took her a few seconds to set the roast down, pull off the oven mitts and walk to the door, opening it without looking through the peep hole. But in those precious seconds, Bradford had worked himself into a rage.

Maren opened the door, and gasped. Standing in front of her was Bradford, Alexa's ex-boyfriend. Or at least she thought it was him. The man glaring at her, holding a half dead bouquet of roses certainly resembled the man she'd known, and had despised for years, but his eyes weren't the same. His appearance certainly wasn't either. This man, Bradford's twin, was disheveled, unshaven, and in clothes that Bradford wouldn't have been caught dead in. Then he opened his mouth and she knew.

"What the fuck are you doing here? Where is she?" he asked, pushing Maren out of the way, and entering Alexa's home.

"Bradford, what a pleasant surprise," she responded, forcing a smile. "What are you doing in my neck of the woods? I can't imagine you ventured this far north without a good reason," she spewed, her tone full of venom.

"Maren, you're a bitch and I've always thought of you as nothing but a two-bit slut; but that's irrelevant at the moment. This has nothing to do with you."

He turned and faced her dead on.

"I've come to take what is rightfully mine, and I'm not going to ask you again. Where is Alexa?"

She almost laughed in his face, and would have if not for the look in his eyes. She knew that the man standing just inches from her was in fact, Alexa's old boyfriend. But something had changed in him, and in looking into his eyes, she saw nothing but evil.

"I don't know where she is Bradford."

His move was swift and unexpected. Before Maren had time to react, Bradford had her in a chokehold and pinned against the wall. And in that instant Maren knew that she was in imminent danger. She struggled to slow her breathing and didn't fight. His hand only partially restricted her airway, a fact that she was sure he wasn't aware of. She forced the words out as if she couldn't breathe, silently thanking her drama coach for being such a good teacher. Maren gasped as she answered him, all the while trying to figure out how she was going to save herself.

"She's at the school for soccer practice. She's a soccer coach and her girls have a tournament next week.

They're on the north field." As she finished the words, she started to slump as if passing out.

Bradford loosened his grip and allowed her to fall to the floor. Even though she was very uncomfortable with him looming over her, Maren remained frozen in place, still pretending she was unconscious.

He kicked her because he could.

"You're still a bitch," he spewed as he left her lying on the floor, and headed toward the door.

"I'm coming Alexa; and this time you're not getting away," he said under his breath as he made his way out toward his SUV, slamming the door behind him.

Maren remained frozen in place until she heard the sound of his engine and then the squeal of his tires as he gunned it, backing out of Alexa's drive. She forced herself to wait another ten seconds, then sat up, raced to the front door, flipping the dead bolt as she dialed her best friend's number.

~Chapter 40~

Their meal had been not only filling, but fantastic. Lucas was amazed what a great cook Alexa was, and she was shocked at how much the man could eat. They'd made small talk, asked candid questions about one another, and found that not only did they have more in common than they'd ever realized, they also shared the same core values and beliefs.

They'd finished the bottle of wine that Alexa had packed, and were working on finishing the six pack in between kisses. Sometime between dinner and dessert, Lucas had decided that he'd eaten too much and informed Alexa that he needed to burn off a few calories. Having no clue what he was thinking, she reluctantly agreed. He said nothing, just stood up, extending his hand to help her stand as well. With a quick adjustment of his phone, he turned on Pandora and a slow ballad started playing. Pulling her to him, he held her, moving slowly to the music.

Alexa, one who prided herself on always being in charge, submitted to him freely. For once, she thought to herself, it felt so good to have someone else take control and do things for her. He controlled the rhythm, pace and mood and she couldn't have been happier. Who would have thought six months ago, that she'd be here, on a mountain, dancing with a man that she hadn't known existed back then? Yet here she was, living life the way she always knew she should have been, in love with a man and his daughter, and making the most of everything that God had given her recently. She truly felt blessed, and had never been happier in her life. She didn't know where their journey would take them, but for now, she was very content simply being held by strong arms.

~Chapter 41~

Maren frantically dialed, and redialed Alexa's number, and when she didn't answer, resorted to texting her. She didn't want to totally freak her best friend out, but knew that it was imperative that she warn her about Bradford, and his threat. She'd always thought of Alexa's ex as nothing but a spoiled rich kid who couldn't fight his way out of a paper bag, unless of course, someone else opened the bag for him. But, the man who'd burst into Alexa's home, was a very different, very terrorizing version of the wimp she'd known. As she hit redial for the fifth time, she felt a growing pit in her stomach, and feared for her best friend's safety.

Alexa and Lucas continued swaying, holding each other, long after the song ended. As their kisses grew longer, and more intense; both realized that if they didn't move to a warmer, more comfortable area, they'd probably wind up making love right where they stood, despite the frigid temperature.

"Um, maybe we should pack up, and start heading down the mountain?" she asked innocently. I know that Maren has a date with your brother this afternoon, so my house will be empty," she continued, with just enough edge in her voice for Lucas to understand exactly what she was implying.

"You've read my mind," he responded, already starting to pick up the remnants of what had been a fabulous meal.

She saw the flicker of not only understanding but desire in his eyes, and while she felt her heart start to race in anticipation, she knew that it was time to take their relationship to the next level, and knew that she wanted to do so, as much as he did. It wasn't until they had everything loaded up, and climbed into the cab of her truck, and had made it halfway down the mountain that she picked up her phone and saw the missed calls and texts from her best friend. She felt herself starting to shake as she viewed the text from Maren. Her message had been short but direct. "Bradford is here, crazy, looking for you!"

Lucas felt his blood pressure surge, and fought to control his temper. He knew virtually nothing about her ex, but knew that no one or nothing was going to come between he and Alexa, not this early in their relationship. He rubbed her arm reassuringly.

"Get in, I'll drive so you can call Maren and see what the hell she's talking about."

She didn't argue, and climbed into the passenger seat of her truck. With shaking hands, she dialed her friend's number. Maren answered before the second ring.

"Oh my God Lexi! He's here, that fucker is here and looking for you! He's nuts Alexa, absolutely nuts!" she said, all in one breath. Alexa could tell from her tone, not so much the words, that not only was her friend upset, but also scared.

"Calm down Mar, what are you talking about? Bradford is here looking for me?" she asked, having absolutely no idea what her best friend was talking about.

"Did you not listen to my messages?" she nearly screamed. "Bradford is here, in Old Forge, looking for you. He says that he's taking you back where you belong, with him to New York. He's crazy Lexi. It's him but it's not him, he barged into your house demanding to see you and went nuts when I said that you weren't here. He started choking me Alexa," she said in a near whisper, "so I had to tell him something. I told him you were down at the soccer field with the girls at practice. Please hurry up and get here Alexa, I'm scared."

As Lucas listened to their exchange, he found his blood starting to boil with hatred over a man that he'd never met, but knew he'd maim if their paths were to ever cross. He had his phone out and was hitting speed dial for his brother. It took a few rings but eventually he heard his brother answer. Before he could ask about his date, Lucas cut Logan off with rapid fire questions and directives.

"You need to get to Alexa's house now. Seems we have little problem, and that problem went there and roughed Maren up some." Before he could ask where he was and how long it would take him to get to her bungalow, Logan had registered what his brother was saying, and was ready for a fight.

"What do you mean someone roughed up Maren? Who the fuck needs to die Luke?" In that very moment, he knew that Alexa's blue eyed friend meant more to him than he'd realized she had, and he wanted nothing more than to get to her, to comfort her and to make sure that she was safe.

"What is going on Luke? I thought you and Alexa were on a date?" he asked, trying to control his temper. "Who hurt Maren and is she still at Alexa's house? I'm at the soccer field with Kelsey and a few of her friends kicking balls around. I'll need to round them up and drop them off at mom's before I can get to Maren. I wasn't supposed to pick her up for another hour and a half and told mom I'd bring Kelsey here to let her burn off some energy."

Calmly, Lucas responded. "Logan, listen to me carefully. Alexa's ex-boyfriend is in town, and from what Maren said, he's snapped and crazy. He's here thinking that he's taking her with him back to New York. Maren's okay, a little banged up, but okay. She got rid of him by telling him that Alexa was at soccer practice at the school. I need you to get my daughter, and her friends and get the hell away from that field right now!" he shouted. "He's got no agenda that involves you, but I don't want my daughter anywhere near some lunatic. Get her and get out of there!" he nearly screamed, as he gunned the truck and sped down the mountain as fast as he dared drive.

"No one is gonna touch your daughter and our women Lucas. You have my word on that." He hung up, calling out to the girls as he did so.

Bradford made his way through town, searching both sides of the street for her truck. He made sure that he kept his car well below the town's speed limit. The last thing he wanted was to have any type of confrontation with the local yokels that called themselves police in the one horse town that Alexa called home. While Bradford was thinking about the cops, Lucas was calling them.

Lucas didn't bother calling the Town of Webb Police Department, he called his closest friend on the evening shift directly. When Jimmy answered his personal phone and listened to what Lucas was saying, he explained that he was on the other side of Inlet but would be there post haste. Before he hung up, the seasoned cop warned his friend to not only avoid any confrontation with the city slicker, but also made Luke promise to not take the law into his own hands if he were to find the jerk first. Lucas grumbled just enough for Jimmy to realize that he better be the first one on scene.

Alexa had remained silent as Lucas spoke. He continued racing down the mountain, staring straight ahead, but reached over, and took her hand in his; both to reassure her that everything would be alright, and to calm himself. The thought of some nut job making his way toward the soccer field where his daughter was playing, made him sick to his stomach, but he had faith in his twin, and knew that he'd never let anyone harm his only child.

It was Alexa who finally spoke. "Why is this happening Lucas? I haven't heard from Bradford since I blocked his number."

Calmly, Luke responded. "What do you mean, he hasn't contacted you in a while? Are you saying that your ex has been in contact with you since you moved up here?" he asked, trying to keep the venom in his tone contained. He'd never been in a situation where he had felt jealousy before, and quickly deduced that he not only didn't like it, but wasn't going to tolerate it.

Hesitantly, she answered. "I was with him for five years Lucas. So yes, he has called me a few times since I moved back home. At first it was more of a taunt, telling me that I was foolish to leave everything he had to offer behind. Then, once he realized that I wasn't returning to the city, he called me a few times, begging me to reconsider. I had heard that he got engaged to his old girlfriend, so I assumed he'd finally given up on me. I never said anything because it wasn't relevant to us. Besides, we all have past relationships, and he was part of my past, certainly not my present or future."

"If he's here, in this town presently making his way to the very same soccer field that my daughter is playing on, then I'd say he's pretty relevant to us," he nearly growled.

The harshness of his words sunk in, and for the first time, she saw not just anger, but real fear in his eyes. She, though indirectly, had caused that fear. She squeezed the hand that was still holding hers.

"His issue is with me Lucas. He doesn't know anything about you or Kelsey so I can't imagine that she's in any type of danger. Besides, Logan will get her away from there," she replied, reassuringly.

"We're going there Alexa. I need to know my daughter is alright. If this Bradford fool starts with you, he'll have to go through me. Nobody will ever hurt you again, I promise you Alexa."

"I know Lucas. That's part of why I love you."

The words slipped out, without her meaning for them too. What she'd actually meant was that was one of the redeeming qualities that she'd come to love about him; but in the heat of the moment, her true feelings presented themselves instead. Blushing when she'd realized her error, she was afraid to make eye contact with the man sitting beside her. Luckily, it only took a nanosecond for him to alleviate any insecurity that she was feeling.

"I know it's sort of early on, in what we're building Alexa, but I've been in love with you from nearly the moment I met you. You had me at hello, but my heart became yours the second you fell for my daughter, and took her in when momma had her accident." He gave her a moment to let what he was saying sink in, as he continued driving toward town.

"I will never forget what you did for us, and even then, I knew you were the one. I love you Alexa. That simple. No one is going to hurt you, emotionally or physically. And he sure as hell isn't bringing you back to New York with him."

He turned to her and smiled, letting his dimples show. "So how about you, Jimmy and I show Bradford the way out of town. Then we can get on with our lives, and the life I hope that we can build together. Sound like a plan?"

Feeling her heart burst, and tears coming to her eyes, she smiled.

"Sounds like a wonderful plan Lucas."

~Chapter 42~

He pulled into the parking lot and immediately started searching the vehicles in the parking lot for her truck. Realizing that she could have traded in her truck for something more suitable for the rural area that she now chose to call home, he stared going car to car peering into the windows of the parked cars and trucks. He found his rage once again rising as he searched for her. It wasn't until he looked across the lot onto the field, that he saw a familiar face. There, standing literally yards from him, was the bastard who'd stolen his Alexa. He was rounding up a bunch of noisy bratty girls, and obviously had no control over them. As the girls whined about leaving the field prematurely, he let them piss and moan, showing no authority whatsoever.

"So, this was the weakling that she was currently spreading her legs for?" he thought to himself. Disgusted that his Alexa would settle for someone with no backbone or leadership skills like his, he snorted in disdain.

"She certainly seemed to have lowered her standards since leaving New York," he thought to himself. But staring down at the picture that the P.I. had provided him, he knew that the fool in his designer shirt and cowboy boots leaving the field was Alexa's new love interest. And he thought to himself, "what better way to find her, than through him."

Logan had already spotted his vehicle as soon as he had parked. Fancy cars with designer plates had a tendency to stand out in small towns, especially during the off season when the tourist trade waned. It'd only taken two seconds of watching the him peering into the windows of parked cars to realize that he must be searching for something or someone. It didn't take a rock scientist to deduce that the slick looking asshole must be Alexa's ex. From the way he was currently storming towards him, Logan quickly realized that he was either crazy or in a rage. Before he could close the distance, Logan snapped an order, and the girls froze in their tracks. It was only then that Logan matched the strangers gait and closed the gap, extending out his hand, like he was greeting a long lost friend. Putting on his best bull shit tone, he smiled and spoke first.

"Oh my golly, would ya look here! If it isn't Snyder, Snyder McGilligan! Lord help me, you haven't aged a bit, you damn critter!"

Reaching out to grab the stranger's hand, even though it wasn't extended, Logan wanted to ensure that he had control of the situation, and more importantly, control of the potential problem. As quickly as his hand had been grabbed, Bradford pulled it away and shook his hand fervently, as if trying to shake off any germs. His eyes bore into the man standing within striking distance, and even though he wanted to drop him where he stood, he reframed from doing so, knowing that he was his means to finding out where Alexa was.

Playing along, he squared his shoulders and addressed the man he thought was Lucas.

"Well how've you been yourself? I just got back into town and already heard that you've got yourself a hot little thing since I've been gone. So much for swearing off women," he chuckled, as if talking to his long lost friend.

Realizing that he must have mistaken him for his twin, Logan played along with the charade. He glanced toward his car quickly and saw that Kelsey and her friends had done exactly as instructed. When he heard the doors shut, he knew that they were out of harm's way and relaxed.

"Women? Hell, can't live with em; can't live without em. Nobody special in my life. Can't afford one, even if I had time for one," he kidded. Even though he'd told Lucas that he'd get Kelsey away from the field, he searched the road, knowing that his brother would head straight there anyways. And he'd been right. Before he could get another word in, he heard the truck make the turn, tires squealing as he turned the corner too fast. Lucas pulled the truck into the parking lot, threw it into park, and was out of it before the dust settled.

Bradford did nothing but stare as he saw another one, identical to the one standing in front of him, approach. Lucas was the first to speak.

"If you're Peddington, you've got no business being here so I suggest you leave the same way you came; alone. Alexa is not interested in whatever you're selling."

"Interesting, Alexa never needed anybody to speak her mind for her before," he responded, in a tone that didn't sound human.

"While I appreciate your opinion, I'd like to hear it directly from her. Why don't you ask her to join us," he said, spying her sitting in the passenger side of her truck.

She felt his eyes lock in on her and could feel the heat, and the hatred almost instantly. Wanting to sink down in the truck, she had just started to crouch when she heard her name being called. Looking out, she quickly realized the source as she saw Kelsey exiting Logan's passenger side door and running towards her truck. She willed her away, but to no avail. Both Logan and Lucas watched as Alexa exited the sanctity of her truck to greet the little girl. It took a second for both to realize that Bradford had already started moving toward her. Before either Logan or Lucas could react, Bradford was at her side, grabbing her arm, pulling her toward him. She launched her own counterattack, grabbing Kelsey and pushing her protectively behind her before shifting closer to her attacker to ease the excruciating pain that he was creating by twisting her arm behind her back.

She refused to call out; she wouldn't give him that satisfaction. She kept her arm firmly in place, squared her shoulders, and looked directly into the face of evil. In the one second of silence that they shared, she searched his face for the man that she'd thought she'd once loved, the man whom she'd spent five years with, and had briefly considered spending her life with. Staring into his eyes, she saw nothing but a cold, menacing man who appeared to be filled with not just contempt but hatred for her. She didn't understand why he was here, searching for her. They'd broken up months before and she assumed that he'd moved on, as evidenced by the fact that she had heard he was engaged. The reality was, she didn't really care if he was engaged, had moved on, forgotten about her, loathed or still loved her. He was her past and there would never be any future between them, and she intended to make that fact very clear to him once and for all.

"Bradford, you need to let go of my arm right now."

"Shut up," he nearly screamed, twisting it tighter." Before Lucas or Logan could take another step closer, Bradford pulled out a gun from behind his back, brandishing it in the air, making sure all were aware that he was carrying. Logan froze in his tracks, while Lucas glanced between his daughter who remained frozen by Alexa's side, and Alexa, and continued to make his way toward them. Bradford was the first to speak.

"Take another step closer and the kid is toast. Ask Alexa if I'm bluffing? She'll attest that I'm an excellent marksman and at this range, I certainly won't miss," he said, laughing.

Alexa, suddenly very concerned with Kelsey's welfare, nearly screamed at Lucas. "Luke, stay there. He means it; he's an excellent shot. Don't come any closer."

She didn't know how this was going to end, but one thing she knew was that she'd die first before she'd ever let anyone hurt the two people that she loved. She didn't know what Bradford intended to do to her, but she knew that she needed to get him away from the man and child who'd become her world.

"Lucas, I want you, Logan and Kelsey to go on home. My Bradford's here, and I don't need you anymore," she shouted.

"Coming up here was all a ploy to make him jealous and swoon for me, and now that he's come for me, I just want to go back to my old life and be done with commoners such as yourself."

Bradford listened to what sounded like music to his ears. Alexa then spoke directly to him, in a hushed tone that only he, and Kelsey could hear.

"Bradford, I have made so many mistakes, and I pray that you can forgive me and will consider taking me back. I'm so sorry to have hurt you honey. Will you ever be able to forgive me?"

Before he could answer, Kelsey spoke up. Nearly screaming, she let them both know what her opinion was. "No! You can't leave Lexi. I love you! Dad loves you; and everyone in our class loves you! You can't just leave with him," she said disgustingly. She purposely stepped out from behind Alexa's protective stance and addressed Bradford directly. It was then that she saw the gun, but continued anyways.

"You are a mean man, and you're hurting her arm!" she shouted. "She doesn't love you anymore, she loves us and I want her to marry my dad! So you need to just climb back in that fancy car of yours and go away. We don't want you here!" she nearly screamed. Her lip quivered as she tried to stare down the man towering over her. The gun he held terrified her, but she refused to be bullied by the man trying to take her friend away. She'd lost her mom so many years ago, and Alexa was the closest thing she'd ever had to a mother and she wasn't about to let her walk out of her life.

Bradford laughed. The nerve of some snot nosed kid. Sure he gave her kudos for having guts but no one spoke to a Peddington that way. He was about to address the little brat when Alexa spoke up.

"Bradford, darling, let me handle this, please," she nearly begged. She tugged on her restrained arm.

"Let me have a word with the child and then we can be on our way back home. Give me a second to say good bye to her and then I'll tell you all the things that I'd like to do to make up with you," she nearly purred, even though it repulsed her to allow the words to escape her lips.

Instantly feeling something come alive inside his designer khaki's, he loosened his grasp.

"Make it quick Alexa, and don't try anything stupid. This time the gun is on your lover, or should I say former lover," he chuckled. He let her arm go so that she could squat down eye level with Kelsey, who now had tears steadily flowing from both eyes. From where she was crouching, she could see that he did in fact have his 380 pointed directly at Kelsey's father and Uncle, and she knew the scenario could escalate at any time. She wanted nothing more than to get the three of them out of harm's way.

"Kelsey, I need you to listen to me honey. I'm going to be leaving with Bradford and I need you to go home with your father now okay? Remember everything that I taught you in class, and most importantly, on the soccer field okay? Remember everything that I taught you and my girls during soccer practice when we were about to play Remsen," she asked, quickly flashing her fingers in front of her in a "2, 1" gesture.

Becoming impatient, Bradford spoke up. "Wrap this up Alexa. I want to get out of this one horse town before dark."

She didn't respond to him, but kept her eyes on Kelsey. She could tell by the change in the child's eyes, that her message had not only been conveyed, but understood. She wrapped her arms around her and held her tightly, but for just a brief second. "I love you Kelsey Rose, never forget that."

"I love you too Alexa, and I'll never forget you." Kelsey drew away from Alexa and looked directly up at Bradford.

"Can I go to my dad now. You and Alexa can leave and I want to go home with my father now," she announced boldly.

"Get out of here you little snot. Take your father, and uncle and get the hell out of here before I change my mind. Little brat," he said, dismissing her, turning his attention back to Alexa.

They'd all been so focused on the scenario playing out in front of them, that no one had noticed the unmarked patrol car. Jimmy exited the car silently, and quickly evaluating the situation, started making his way toward the parking lot. Lucas whose eyes never wandered from his daughter, his love, and the madman holding them at bay didn't see his approach; but Logan had noticed the flash of movement out of the corner of his eye and felt a momentary sigh of relief that they now had backup.

Lucas, Logan and Alexa nearly held their breath as Kelsey started walking toward her father and uncle. She didn't run but walked slowly, in a very straight line, and then as she approached them, took three large strides to her left. Embracing her father, she whispered in his ear when he grabbed her and held on for dear life."

"Daddy, she didn't mean it. Alexa loves us, and we've got a plan," she said confidently.

He was trembling so hard, that Lucas never allowed what his daughter was saying to registar. His only focus at that very moment was that she was safe and in his arms. He forced the tears at bay, but couldn't control the shaking. It was his daughter who snapped him back to reality.

"Dad, we need to go home," she said. Alexa said that we need to go. She's got it covered. We need to get in Uncle Logan's car NOW," she shouted.

Logan wasn't sure what was transpiring but had seen Alexa's finger gestures to his niece and knew that they had something cooking. He quickly glanced to his left and could see that Jimmy had aligned himself behind a Black Tahoe and had Bradford and Alexa in his sights. Not knowing what Alexa was planning on doing, he prayed that his hunch was right.

"Lucas, she's right. We really need to get out of here. If Alexa wants to be with that jerk, then the hell with her. You've got your daughter, so let's just leave those two lovebirds alone so they can go back to New York and be out of our lives once and for all."

Shocked that his own brother could be so cold, he turned to him and swore under his breath. "I'm not leaving without her."

It was Bradford's turn to speak up. "Listen to your brother or you might eat some lead my friend. Take your bratty kid and leave while you still can."

Lucas watched in disbelief as Alexa leaned her body into Bradford, kissing him on the cheek and smiling. It repulsed him to see her not only close to her ex-lover but actually kissing him, when she'd been making love to him with her tongue just an hour earlier. Maybe he didn't know her as well as he thought he had after all. Watching the asshole with the gun put his hand on Alexa's backside, purposely grabbing her ass for all to see, he felt his blood start to boil. Knowing it was just a matter of seconds before he reacted, Alexa spoke up before Lucas could. She snuggled in closer to Bradford, placing her arm on his chest as if embracing him.

"You heard the man Lucas. Take Kelsey and go home. Sure we had some laughs but my place is with Bradford and I'm going with him now. I just need my purse out of my truck and we're out of here. We're through and I need you to leave me alone."

It broke her heart seeing the look that came over her face.

"Come one Lucas, let's go," Logan encouraged him. It's time for us to leave. Alexa's made her choice." Logan, grabbed Kelsey's hand and started walking towards his car. Lucas looked at her one last time, before turning and then walking away.

She purposely allowed her hand to wander down his chest, stopping to rest on the zipper of his slacks. It completely repulsed her to be touching him this way, but she also knew how there'd been a time that this very same gesture could turn him to putty. She only prayed that it still had the same effect on him. It took just a second for her to realize that it still did. Capitalizing on his sudden testosterone rush, she whispered into his ear.

"Baby, I don't need anything that I brought here to Old Forge, except my purse and driver's license. Give me just one second to get it out of my truck and then we'll be on our way out of this one horse town, okay?" she asked, nearly purring.

He didn't say a word, but pulled her to him assaulting her mouth. She kept up her charade, allowing his tongue to tangle freely with hers, all the while forcing herself not to gag. She allowed him to lead, and played the willing participant. She wrapped her arms around his waist and playfully grabbed his backside as he continued to kiss her. She could feel the cold barrel of the gun against her back; a very real reminder of how quickly everything could go wrong. When he ended the kiss, he pulled away, but not before grabbing her breast and twisting it. Shocked and in immediate pain, she gasped.

"Go get your purse Alexa. But remember," he said, once again, brandishing the gun. "One stupid move, and I'll make that child an orphan right in front of your eyes. You've got thirty seconds to get what you want out of your shit box truck and be back here to me, or he's history," he sneered. "Got it?"

"Don't worry baby, it won't take me twenty seconds and then I'm all yours love," she responded in her most convincing voice.

Logan, and Lucas watched as she separated herself from him. The second she did, Kelsey shouted loudly. "Uncle Logan get ready!"

Before he had time to ask his niece what the hell she was talking about, everything happened. Lucas, who was in the passenger seat of his brother's car watched the scenario playing out in front of him as if it were in slow motion. One second Alexa was sucking face with the psycho with the gun, and the next she was running in a mad dash away from him. He felt his heart stop as he saw her ex raising the gun toward her back as she raced towards her truck. He started reaching towards his door handle in an attempt to stop what was about to happen, when his daughter grabbed his shirt.

"Trust us dad! Alexa knows what's she's doing. Uncle Logan be ready to drive really really fast towards her truck. Listen to me Uncle Logan, you've gotta drive fast and go towards to passenger's side of her truck when she turns. Got it?"

Everything played out too fast for her uncle to respond. Alexa ran as fast as she could to her truck, reached in, grabbed her purse, made direct eye contact with Logan not Lucas, and started racing back toward Bradford. She took four strides in his direction, and then in an instant, raced to her left. She'd tried to turn to her left at such a sharp angle, that she tripped. Her momentum carried her another two steps before she hit the ground, falling in front of her truck.

Kelsey screamed "Now," and Logan didn't think, just reacted, pushing the pedal to the floor. He sped across the small parking lot, stopping his truck between Bradford and the spot where Alexa lay. Screaming for his niece to get down on the ground in the back seat, he watched as the gunman turned his aim towards his car. Lucas was already out of the passenger's door and at Alexa's side.

He tried to help her stand. Before either could move from their spots, they heard her name being yelled. In a split second, Bradford had redirected his aim from Logan's car to the two of them.

"This is all on you Alexa," he screamed, and fired.

~Chapter 43~

Crouching in the back seat as her uncle had ordered her two, Kelsey heard one, then two shots, and screamed. She didn't care what her uncle had said; she knew that her dad and Alexa were out there and might be hurt. Logan was out of the car door almost as quickly as she was, with both racing toward Alexa and Lucas. The wail of sirens could be heard in the distance and Logan wasn't sure what had happened, but he saw Alexa's ex was lying prone on the blacktop, with a pool of crimson red blood already forming around what had been his head. As he ran towards where his brother lay, he saw Jimmy running towards them.

A million thoughts rushed through his mind as he thought about potentially losing his brother. He reached his twin just before Kelsey did, instantly trying to shield her when he saw the blood where Alexa and Lucas were lying on the ground. Immediately he searched his brother for evidence of a wound and it was then that he saw the source of the blood. Lucas was already taking off his vest and rolling it tightly into a wad and pushing it into Alexa's side. His face said what his words couldn't. Logan quickly knelt down beside Alexa, grabbing her hand.

"Stay with us honey. Help is on the way. Alexa, listen to me," he demanded. "You need to stay awake. My brother and my niece love you and need you in their lives, so you need to stay with us honey. You hear me? Don't you dare fall asleep on us!" He looked into his brother's eyes, and had only seen that look of pure despair one other time. Jimmy raced to their sides, evaluating the situation, calling for an ambulance as he did.

"Alexa Rose, what the hell did you go and get yourself shot for? Jesus Christ woman, how many times do I have to save your life?" he asked, trying to put some levity into the situation. "What the hell did you go and put yourself directly in that asshole's line of fire for?"

Still semi-conscious, Alexa smiled. "James Eugene, I've seen you shoot before and I know you can't hit the broad side of a barn," she teased, attempting to laugh. As she did so, she grabbed her side, gasping for air. "He was going to shoot Lucas Jimmy, and I had to do something. Bradford wouldn't have missed. I had to do something, I love him more than anything in this world," she said, starting to drift off. "And I love Kelsey like my own. We take care of our own."

Listening to the words being exchanged, Kelsey pulled away from her uncle and raced to her father's side.

[317]

"Tell her dad. You said that you were waiting for the right time. Tell her now dad, now before it's too late!" she pleaded. "Please dad!"

He looked into the eyes of his only child. Knowing that this was about as opposite a setting that he could have ever planned, he did as she requested. Alexa drifted in and out of consciousness and though he doubted she could hear his voice, he started speaking anyways.

"Alexa. Lexi, stay with me. If you can hear me, please stay with us. You are my world, my everything and I love you, we love you. Kelsey and I both love you and since you've entered our lives, you have filled in the parts that were missing, and we can not imagine our lives without you in them. We both love you and if you're willing, we'd love for you to join our family. Alexa Rose, you are already part of our family, but we want something more permanent. If you'll have us, Alexa, will you marry me, marry us?"

After pouring his heart out, he looked down into her eyes and saw nothing but eyelids. He watched her color turn from pale to ashen grey in front of him, and heard her gurgle, cough, and take her last breath.

Kelsey's scream would have been heard throughout most of Old Forge if not for the wailing of the ambulance as it pulled into the parking lot. The volunteer paramedics rushed toward the group, to find one of their own administering CPR to the young woman. Immediately recognizing her as her daughter's soccer coach, the 1st responder asked Jimmy what he knew as she knelt down next to him and placed an ambo bag over Alexa's now blue lips. She fell into rhythm bagging Alexa while her partner placed an IV and started administering fluids as rapidly as they would infuse. Visibly shaken, the seasoned cop rattled off what he knew, including her down time and immediate start of CPR as they loaded her onto their gurney and into the rear of the ambulance. Before anyone could say any different, Lucas was jumping into the rear of the ambulance along with the EMT and Alexa. He simply looked at her.

"Jimmy's on duty and can't accompany you and you can't do CPR for an hour straight. I can help. Let's go!"

And thirty seconds later, they were on their way racing against time towards Utica.

~Chapter 44~

She was afraid to open her eyes. Everything hurt and she felt as if she'd just run a marathon, and lost miserably. She felt something or actually someone grasping her hand and squeezing it every once in a while. There were so many unfamiliar smells and sounds surrounding her and she felt so confused. Her head was spinning with an assortment of memories all jumbled together with none of them making a lot of sense. Then she heard her name and instantly knew the source of the voice. It was Lucas, her Lucas speaking softly to her. She willed herself to open her eyes. Try as she might, she didn't have the strength to squeeze his hand back, but knowing that he was there holding her, comforted her more than she'd ever imagined.

He spoke to her as if she were participating in the conversation. He rambled on about Sunday mass and the congregation all saying a prayer for her speedy recovery, and about Logan stepping up to help Maren coach her girls' practice in her absence. He told her that his mother, crutches and all, insisted on cooking all day for him and that he'd saved all of it for her, for when she got better and came home. She listened, trying to formulate what was going on, and where she was. She had fragments of memories, almost like a slideshow flashing in and out of her brain, but nothing was detailed enough to allow her to make any sense of them. She wanted desperately to wake up, talk to Lucas and figure out what was going on around her. She felt herself fading, drifting back into the black abyss that had held her captive for what felt like eternity. She fought it, for each time she felt herself slipping back under, she found it harder and harder to wake. She was so tired, and the pain was indescribable. She never gave up at anything she tried, but this time, the calmness and serenity of the abyss was a welcome sight. She used every ounce of her strength to squeeze Lucas's hand, just enough for him to feel one last time. And then she was gone…

~Chapter 45~

It took two days, three hours and twenty-six minutes for Alexa to return to him. He refused to leave her side, except to relieve himself. He ate, drank, and slept in the chair beside her bed. In the time that Alexa remained asleep, he had gotten to know her parents, all of her brothers, and felt that he and Maren had become best friends. The tiny room in ICU was a steady stream of family and friends, all coming to not only show their love and support for their school teacher, but also one of their own. Over the course of those two days, it appeared that everyone in town had heard how Alexa had not only saved his daughter's life, but his as well, and practically the entire town had made the pilgrimage to St. Elizabeth's to pay their respect and show their support. Her room was overflowing with get well cards, flowers, and enough candy to fill a candy shop.

Samantha insisted on bringing enough food from the Bistro to not only feed the entire staff of the Intensive Care Unit, but majority of the visitors in the waiting room as well. Logan left Maren's side only long enough to shuffle his niece back and forth to the hospital. Even with their strict visiting policies, the staff was kind and supportive when it came to allowing Kelsey in to visit Alexa. Lucas had primed his daughter and tried to prepare her as best as he could before she entered Alexa's room. He held her hand as they entered the room together. To Kelsey, she looked like her teacher, only in ugly attire, and sleeping. To a ten-year-old, the IV's, monitors and beeping of the machines was irrelevant.

Taking in the surroundings, Kelsey left her father's side and immediately walked toward the head of Alexa's bed. She leaned in and gave her a kiss on her cheek, then stood upright, and started dictating orders.

"Lexi, we need to talk."

Everyone was slightly caught off guard by her blunt statement. But before anyone could interrupt, she continued talking. She looked back at her captive audience and they remained silent as she spoke.

"You've been sleeping long enough and it's time to come back to us. I know your side really burns and your legs feel like they weight a ton, but mom said that we need you and you need us and it's time to wake up so we can bring you home. Besides, the substitute teacher sucks compared to you; and I don't want my grades to drop, so hurry up and wake up!" she all but demanded.

Lucas who'd been standing closest to his daughter, gently put his hand on her shoulder. Leaning in, he whispered to her.

"Honey, what did you say?"

Kelsey answered him as if it were an everyday conversation.

"Remember how I was afraid that I was starting to forget mom? Well, after Lexi's accident, mom's been visiting me every night. She sometimes comes to me in dreams, and sometimes I can feel her in my room, and know that she's there with me. She said that she's been here with Alexa and they've become good friends. Mom said that Lexi wanted to go back with her to heaven but mom told her no, and that she had to stay here with us so we can take care of her and she can be part of our family. Mom said that she will always be my mom, but that it is okay that I love Alexa just as much as I love her."

There wasn't a dry eye in the room as Kelsey spoke matter of factly about her conversations with her deceased mother.

"Mom said that someday you'll get around to marrying Alexa, and that she wants you to know that you couldn't have picked a better person to be with and that she knows that you'll always love her. Mom also said something weird dad."

He discreetly wiped his eyes before addressing his daughter.

"Yeah, what'd she say kiddo?"

"She said that I need to remind you not to overwater her lilac bushes. She said you're practically drowning them!"

Everyone in the room laughed, as Lucas took his daughter into his arms. "Is your momma here with us now Kels?" he asked, as his eyes swept the room.

"Nope. She said that she needed to go back up to heaven. Dad, she promised me that Alexa is going to wake up and be okay. Mom wouldn't lie right?"

"No honey. Your mom wouldn't ever fib to you about anything. If she said it, then we have to believe it's true."

"Good," she smiled, with a very mischievous look on her face.

"Kelsey," he said, smiling. "What else did your mom say to you? Or don't I want to know?" he laughed.

"I'm not supposed to tell. But she said that you and Alexa are gonna get married, and have twin boys. She said they'll be even wilder than you and Uncle Logan were," she chuckled. "And that it serves you right for all the trouble that you and Uncle Logan got into when you were kids," she added, laughing.

The room burst into laughter and then went immediately silent when Alexa coughed slightly. In an instant, he was at her side, and as her eyes started to flutter and then open slowly, her mother burst into tears.

"Get the nurse, she's waking up!" she all but screamed.

Everyone was ushered out of the tiny room, with the exception of Lucas, Kelsey and her parents as Alexa rejoined the world. The bright light burned her eyes, and Lucas quickly closed the blinds. She forced them open and though still a little foggy, scanned the room for familiar faces. What she was greeted with, was pure love, the love of family.

She squeezed both of her hands. Her mother was holding one and Lucas was holding the other as if his life depended on it. She focused in on Kelsey and smiled.

Coughing again, she tried to speak. Her voice sounded froggy but she spoke anyways.

"Hi honey. Sounds like you and your momma have been talking an awful lot about me," she kidded. She looked at Lucas for reassurance before continuing. What she saw in his eyes reaffirmed what she'd always known, and now believed with all of her heart.

"Kelsey, while I've been asleep, you mom came to visit me a lot too. She's a wonderful person and I'm so glad that she's your mom. You need to know that you are the love of her life, you along with your dad; and that no one could ever be more proud of you than she is. She told me that even if you don't know she's around, she is always with you and she always will be and that she loves you very much."

She then turned her attention to Luke. "Lucas, your Ana is an amazing woman, and she is not only beautiful to look at, but is even more beautiful on the inside. I wanted to go. I'm sorry momma," she said, looking up at her parents standing beside her. "I wanted to give up and rest because the pain was so horrible. It was Ana who made me fight and made me want to come back. I owe my life to her Lucas. I don't know how she did it, but somehow she absorbed the pain, or made the pain go away. If she hadn't, I wouldn't be here today."

He digested what she had said and then looked out the window, as if expecting to see her there. He didn't know how he felt about his wife taking someone else's pain but he was grateful that she had. As he looked into the eyes of the woman in front of him, the woman he'd grown to love, despite only going on a handful of dates with her, he suddenly felt his wife's presence and very distinctly heard her whisper a direct order into his ear. He didn't search the room for her, just knew that she was there, and smiled.

"Alexa Rose, I've been given a very direct order by Ana, and even though this certainly isn't how or when I'd expected to ask you, I've been told there's no time like the present. So," he took a deep breath and continued.

"You mean the world to Kelsey and I. When you pushed me out of the way and took a bullet intended for me, I thought that I would die seeing you lying there bleeding. Lexi, you scared the hell out of me, and everyone else. The thought of losing you, another woman that I love, was too much to bare. Kelsey and I love you Alexa, and we want to spend the rest of our lives showing you how much we love and need you. What I'm trying to say, or actually ask, is" he took another deep breath. "If I have your father's permission," turning his attention to Alexa's father, "which I had all intentions of officially asking you beforehand."

Alexa's father felt tears welling up, simply nodded yes.

"Alexa, you've had me from the moment we met, and I would be honored if you would simply say Yes. Alexa, will you marry me?"

Before Alexa could say a word, Kelsey grabbed her hand and added what she thought of her father's proposal.

"Lexi, say yes. Become part of our family. I love you Lexi."

Alexa remained silent for a brief moment, not because she didn't already know her answer, but because she couldn't believe that she could be so lucky. She looked into Lucas' eyes and smiled. As she was about to respond, she felt Anastasia's present and felt her hands touching hers. Kelsey felt it too and nearly jumped.

"Momma's here, I felt her daddy! My mom is here with Alexa and all of us."

"Say yes Alexa. He loves you and you love not only Lucas but my little girl. Say yes and continue to love them the way I know you will; the way I would have if things were different. Please say yes..."

[327]

Alexa felt Ana's hands lift off her own, and could feel the air change.

"Don't go," she pleaded to the one person that she couldn't see in the room. She immediately turned her attention to Lucas. "Yes! I love you Lucas, and yes, yes I will marry you but I have a few conditions," she laughed.

"Yes?" he repeated, completely stunned. "She said yes," he exclaimed, looking around the room at her family, his family and their best friends. Returning his attention to his fiancée, he answered her quickly and without reservation. "Anything. Any condition you have Lexi, we'll work with. You name them and consider them done."

"There quite simple actually. I want your brother and Maren to stand up for us. Also, I'd really like get married at night, under the stars by the lake when it's a full moon. There's something magical about a full moon and I would really like us to make our first memories as husband and wife under the canopy of moonlight."

"If that's all, then I agree," he said excitedly, raising her hand that he was still holding. "Moonlight memories it is."

She, and everyone in the room, saw for just a brief moment, Anastasia materialize in front of them. The room went silent, with all eyes on the apparition.

"It's about time you asked her Lucas, and you couldn't have made a better choice. Be happy my love. It's time for me to leave you for a second time. But remember my sweet Kelsey, I'm never far away. I love you…"

And with her last words barely a whisper, Ana dissolved into thin air and was gone.

~Epilog~

Fall slowly turned into winter with the first flakes of snow appearing before Thanksgiving. The emotional and physical scars of being shot healed quicker than she'd expected. Alexa returned back to her classroom quicker than Lucas had wanted, and was once again teaching in a classroom next to her best friend, who'd accepted Jacqueline's old position. Kelsey had insisted that Alexa couldn't be alone after she left the hospital and had all but packed her clothes in order for her to move in with she and her father. It hadn't taken but a few days for everyone to get into an easy routine together, and Lucas couldn't be happier.

Their wedding was scheduled for the third Friday night in June, with planning already underway. Maren and Kelsey, along with her future mother-in-law and Maren's mother helped with the organization and planning on weekends, and everything was falling into place.

Moonlight Memories: An Adirondack Love Story

Despite a few emotional and monetary setbacks, Maren and Logan's dream of opening a microbrewery was quickly becoming a reality and was the talk of the town. Their business arrangement had slowly blossomed into a romance, and no one could be happier than Alexa.

Sitting in Lucas's overstuffed chair, Kelsey's puppy snoring beside her, Alexa looked outside as the first flakes of snow made their descent from the sky. She looked over at Lucas, sleeping on the couch just a few feet away and knew that her life had not only come full circle, but was more complete than she'd ever thought it could be. As she watched the full moon make its' way from behind the clouds, she knew that she was already on her way to making Moonlight Memories, and couldn't wait to see what the future had in store for her.

Author's Note: I hope that you have enjoyed Moonlight Memories and these new characters. There is something incredibly special about twin siblings and I have enjoyed introducing Lucas and Logan and their story. My sister Beth has twin daughters and it was their idea to incorporate identical twins into this storyline. We spent an entire day kayaking between Rollins Pond and Fish Creek, and during the course of those eight or nine hours on the water, Moonlight Memories was created. I have really enjoyed telling their story and I'm sure that someday they'll be back. The relationship between Maren and Logan remind me of "fire & ice" and I'm sure that they have a lot of turbulence, turmoil, bickering and romance to deal with, before their microbrewery can become a success!

See you around town...

~Erin Maine~

Made in the USA
Middletown, DE
19 June 2019